The Blunt End of the Known Universe
Road Trips and Modern Fables
Dave Roberts

Quantum Dot Press

All rights reserved

Copyright © 2024 by Dave Roberts

The right of Dave Roberts to be identified as the author of this work has been asserted in accordance with section 77 of the Copyright, Designs and Patents Act 1988.

All rights reserved without limits under copyright reserved above, no parts of this publication may be reproduced, stored in or introduced into a retrieval system, or transmitted in any form, or by any means (electronic, mechanical, photocopying, recording or otherwise) without the prior permission of the copyright owner.

The names of all persons appearing in the stories have been changed to protect their identities.

Published by

Quantum Dot Press (quantumdotpress.com)

Contents

Acknowledgements	VI
Twenty Four Hours to Tulsa, or Vegas	1
Driving to Marriages	15
Sorributamentit	30
Bittern	40
Spaceship Brian	51
A Brush with Religion	56
Peak of My Powers	65
Considering Gayness in the Tropics	76
Sid	83
Gordon	93
Fucked by Vulcans at the Skill Centre	98
Life of Crime	111

The Prophet	114
Benefit Fraud when Innocent	117
Catch 22	122
Ergonomics Explained	132
Mechanical Frontiers	136
Shaving	146
Removal Man	152
Small World	156
The Information Superhighway	168
From Master to Pupil, featuring Glamorous Women	175
Back on the Road	187
Incoming Missile	198
Passion	214
Tribal	220
Olympian	226
Peace and Love and Fighting	230
Spiritual Quest	238
Horses versus Fishes	243

Evolution	251
The History of Exploration	256
An Economist Speaks	262
The Ragged Yellow-Jacketed Philanthropist	268
Journey to the End of the World	285
Bibliography	295
Music	297
Filmic	298
About the author	300

Acknowledgements

With thanks to

Janet
Purveyor of domestic bliss.

Bob
Provider of political perspicacity.

Edwin
Proprietor of Quantum Dot Press.

Twenty Four Hours to Tulsa, or Vegas

I'd been on the bus for over a week. It felt like more than whatever it was.

'Anybody going west, who can drive?'

The guy looked about forty-one, or maybe a well-worn thirty-nine. Tall, blond. White shirt. White trousers. Expensive.

The waiting area in the bus station contained the usual sample of slightly down at heel humanity. Nobody who could drive seemed to be going west. Or if they were, they weren't saying anything. After a few seconds I got up. Walked across to where he stood in the middle of the hall.

'What's the deal then?'

He wanted somebody to drive a U-Haul van for him, to Las Vegas. Save them the bus fare. He asked where I was going.

'Detroit, maybe, but it doesn't matter. I'm just travelling.'

I told him I'd been a truck driver in the UK, which seemed to help.

'Are you paying anything?'

'Wasn't going to. What were you thinking of?'

I looked at his furrowed brow and estimated what figure would provoke him to simply turn around and try again tomorrow. It must have been about ten p.m. by now. A few extra dollars would provide the odd luxury for the rest of my trip. Maybe even a motel room one night.

'Thirty dollars.'
'Twenty-five.'
'OK.'

I'd started out from Mexico City about eight days earlier. My allocated seat turned out to be next to the Mexican version of Sydney Greenstreet, circa 1978. After perching politely on the edge of the double seat for about a minute, I moved and went to the wide seat at the back, which had nobody on it. This was good until the reserve driver needed it to sleep on, about a hundred miles later. I found another seat to myself, which was good also, until a wide woman got on at the next town. I smiled and turned to watch the Mexican night, like a cornered moth.

Laredo. Changed money in a store. Greyhound to San Antonio. Rebecca sat next to me. The Jewish daughter of a Columbian diplomat and a Mexican mother, she said. Studying to be a diplomat too, she said.

Houston to Port Arthur. A retired sea Captain. He'd been to Liverpool, he'd been all over the South Seas.

'That's where I've spent my life, that's where I want to spend my last days.'

He got off at Port Arthur. A very dignified man.

The bus moved along through Orange, through Lake Charles. I don't really remember why I'd chosen to go that way.

The guy in white was called Bill. We were in Norfolk, Virginia. His car was a Cadillac coupe, which would have qualified for the role of the great white whale in Hunter S. Thompson's *Fear and Loathing in Las Vegas* (Thompson, 1971).

His apartment was in Newport News, a suburb a few miles from the bus station. As the long white prow of the Caddy swung in to the courtyard, I saw the U-Haul van parked there. It was a big truck of a thing, with a boxy load container attached to the chassis, separate from the cab.

We climbed the stairs, only one floor up. There was probably a sea view from the flat in the daytime, but all we saw now were dark windows in empty rooms, empty except for several wardrobes of clothing, the contents of which we proceeded to stuff into his car. The vehicle was built for style rather than space efficiency, but somehow the clothes were crammed into the boot and the small back seat area.

We took down a large painting which he had forgotten to load. After some shuffling, it was accommodated in the already crammed van. He seemed to judge its value by the amount of oil paint which had been lavished, rather than by the quality of the composition. Regarding the depiction, I remember now, forty-four years later, the same as what I remembered five seconds after loading it into the van. Nothing.

There was little more to do. I reminded him about the six pairs of expensive leather shoes still on the floor of the wardrobe.

'Oh, I don't want them. Take some if you want.'

A good offer if I'd had room in my rucksack, and if they hadn't been five sizes too big.

There remained one last item. A passenger.

The bus from Lake Charles reached New Orleans at four a.m.

I went for a coffee. Fell into conversation with a girl who turned out to be French. Monique. She said she had been sleeping on the 'coches'. I wasn't quite sure whether she meant the benches in the bus station, or the seats in the Greyhound coaches. It was the same thing either way. Something that was not a bed, under milky lights on your way to somewhere else. She dozed off on one of the chairs. I didn't. Maybe thirty-four hours out of Mexico City and the body clock was already shambolic.

At eight a.m. we had coffee and a bun and then walked into New Orleans. Went past a bar somebody on the bus had mentioned. There was a Tourist Centre with a free café.

Monique said she was going to look for a job. We said our goodbyes and I wandered around town.

Later I bumped into her again. No job, it seemed. We ate in Frank's Deli.

She wanted to see the cemetery which featured in *Easy Rider*. We went there and hung out for a while. Hung out in the hippy sense of lying on the grass wondering where we belonged in the world whilst time passed by.

We caught a bus to Canal Street.

'You wanna ride this bus it's thirty cents.'

We wandered. Monique looked at jewellery and looked at cameras. She started to cross the narrow street. There was a big police cruiser powering through. I shouted and pulled her back. Probably saved her life.

We laughed about some old women in floral dresses. We walked to Preservation Hall, where ancient men of teak blew saxophone. We walked along Bourbon Street. Pretty much all I remember of it now is pulling her out of that cruiser's path.

I used some French to show I was trying, but said *piscine* instead of *poisson*. Swimming pool, when I meant fish. She looked at me like I was the world's all-time loser.

Back at the Greyhound station, she said she wanted to go to Panama City. We said our goodbyes.

She came back. There were no connections for Panama City that day.

We took a bus out, and I woke up at Chattahoochee, Florida, early the next morning.

Bill's passenger was called Pete. He was Bill's parrot. He travelled on a big square wooden board, which had raised edges to retain the shavings, litter pellets, or whatever the normal carpeting is, for bird accommodation. It had two sturdy wooden struts which supported a round wooden bar a foot or so above the base. This would be Pete's perch for his transcontinental journey.

There was no cage over it. Pete seemed pretty chilled though. There was no question that he preferred the front passenger seat of the Cadillac, to an uncertain future in the open air of Newport News at midnight.

I familiarised myself with the controls of the van, nodded to Bill, and followed the two of them out of town. We drove west for about three hours, then pulled in at a rest stop, where Bill and I slept in our respective vehicles. I guess Pete slept too.

It was six a.m. the next morning when we set off again. We stopped from time to time at truck stops, where the waitresses would refill your coffee three or four times for free. Bill got tetchy once when we had to queue for more than five minutes for food.

'It doesn't bother me. This is normal in England,' I told him.

By and large, he wasn't too hard to get along with. I got to know that he worked as some sort of salesman involved in land development deals. He had a job to go to in Vegas, but also had some relatives in Oklahoma, where he said he might stop on the way through, and leave some of the stuff in the van with them.

We drove for twenty-four hours. They still had a nominal fifty-five miles per hour speed limit in force after the early seventies fuel crisis, so it was just a steady glide of a journey. I was glad the truck had a radio. Bruce Springsteen would periodically undergo a bout of existential angst in the *Darkness at the Edge of Town*, *Love* was *Like Oxygen* for The Sweet, and, from time to hallowed time, the cab was filled with the soaring saxophone solo from Gerry Rafferty's *Baker Street*.

At six a.m. we pulled in to a service station on the outskirts of Memphis. There was a large parking area behind it, where Bill positioned his car next to a fence. Here there was a payphone on a pole with a little hood over it, no kiosk. He sat in his car with the window down, receiver extended into the car from the payphone, and began to make some calls. I made myself as comfortable as I could in the cab, and dozed off.

It was ten a.m. when he woke me up. He seemed in brighter mood. I followed him for a few blocks until we pulled in to the large yard of a trucking company.

He spent some time in the office, after which I had to back the van up to the warehouse. We opened the back and started unloading. Boxes and boxes, marked Debbie Harper. A Las Vegas address. They were all at the back of the van.

The next stop after Chattahoochee was Tallahassee, Florida, where we changed buses. The new bus had a friendly driver. I had to stop him setting off without Monique, when she zapped off to the restroom just before we were due to leave.

We moved south, through Inverness, Tampa, and then across a bridge to St. Petersburg. Had a walk round. There was a replica of The Bounty ship in the harbour. 'Ze Bunty', she called it. Say it again, Monique. I'll be your very own cliché of an Englishman.

We looked around for somewhere to crash. One hotel would not admit couples.

'*Canard*!' She spat the word out. In France they must think ducks are nasty, worthless creatures.

A kind woman at a motel left us alone to decide if we were happy with the price, then showed us the room.

We settled down. Monique told me she 'liked women'. It might not have been completely true but the message was clear enough.

The next day we wandered round, had a meal. She left her purse in a shop; luckily it only had small change in it. When we went back the shop had shut. Later she came out of another shop and showed me the purse she had 'ripped off' to replace the other one.

'Maybe put it away, Monique, and maybe let's walk so we're not so near the shop you've just stolen from.'

Walked out to the lagoon, got caught in rain, sheltered, black guy gave us a smoke, she examined her new purse, stoned. Lagoon. Pelicans and 'lie-lees'. Torrents of rain. Edge of a tropical storm. Sheltered near a house. Lush overgrowth. Soul music blasting on a radio. Guy from house gives us a lift to the bus station in his pick-up truck. Rainbow as we sit near Bounty. Walk round town. Sky, purple, orange, turquoise, red. Incredible colours all around.

We stopped at a KFC on the way out of Memphis. Bill came back to the van with a huge bag of fried chicken and tins of lemonade. Getting on the move straightaway, we stopped for a hitchhiker on the outskirts of town. He was a young guy of about nineteen, checked shirt, fairly straight looking. He squeezed in next to the fried chicken.

We stopped at the first rest stop and tucked into the food. The hitcher wasn't too hungry. There was far too much to eat, but it was fuel. I don't think I've ever ordered food from a KFC since that day. Back then you hardly saw a McDonalds or a KFC in the UK, but you knew that was all going to change. Now we're all semi-lobotomised clones queuing to cope with the logistics of gnawing around bones and undoing minuscule sauce containers and finding somewhere to dispose of cartons. Members of a doomed herd on a deforested planet at the edge of the universe.

Bill had surprised me the night before during one of our stops, suggesting that if we saw a couple of hitchhikers at some point, we could pick them up and get them to drive, while we slept. He hadn't seemed the type to involve himself with hitchhikers as a species, but when you thought about it, perhaps it wasn't too far removed from walking into a bus station in Norfolk, Virginia and asking if anyone wanted to drive more than halfway across the USA for him.

The young guy could drive, although he told me he was a bit out of practice. We swapped things around. Our rucksacks went into the back of the van, and Pete was transferred to the passenger seat of the U-Haul, whilst I ran through its controls with our hitcher.

'OK?'

'Er. I guess so.'

'You'll be OK, mate. This is Pete. He's OK.' Pete had no comment to add.

I settled into the soft white leather of the Caddy's driving seat. Bill operated the passenger seat buttons and reclined fully. He hadn't slept since six a.m. the previous morning. It was early afternoon now.

I nosed out of the rest area, checking the mirror. Our guest driver had got moving all right. Looked good so far. Destination Tulsa.

I lasted less than a hundred miles in the Cadillac before having to stop at a service area. The car, with its air conditioning and climate control, was like a pillowed cocoon after the U-Haul truck. I couldn't pull a window down to create a refreshing breeze, and was getting perilously close to the tempting coma which might be enjoyed for a precious few seconds before the sixty miles per hour accident.

Bill wasn't overjoyed, insisting I left the engine on, since he would 'fry' without the air con. I got out and the young guy and I went for a coffee. Pete was happy where he was.

I gave the lad a pep talk, and we agreed that I'd follow him: less stressful for both of us. He was trying to get to Houston and needed to be dropped at a junction near Little Rock.

When I pulled alongside him as we neared the junction, he was making frantic gestures, conveying his fear that I might have forgotten the plan. I signalled that I understood, accelerated past, and further along pulled over on the hard shoulder. When I checked the mirrors, the van was nowhere to be seen.

The carriageway split into two ahead of us. On the left was a very wide area forming the central reservation. Fortunately.

I turned as I got out of the car, and saw the van marooned there. Bill woke up at this moment.

'You're going too fast for him, he's not used to driving a truck...' He rambled on, still half asleep.

'Don't worry, he's in the middle, I'll run across and drive the van over.'

I didn't have to, as it happened. The kid had found a quiet moment in the traffic and brought the van over to our side. He wasn't in the most relaxed state.

'I got stuck in the wrong lane. I hate that. I hate that.'

We got his rucksack out of the back. He walked off to find a good spot to wait for his next lift, and a more relaxed future life. Pete didn't even say goodbye.

We arrive in Miami. Crazy girl in the bus station. There was often a crazy person in an American bus station, it seemed to be part of the health care system. This girl doesn't look like a resident though. She's going to Key West like us. Ends up sitting next to me. Monique comes over.

'What's your *probleme*?'

Here we go. The crazy girl has an expression on her face, something between incredulity and complete catatonic indifference. Monique sits with a German guy, his T-shirt says Nuclear Nein Danke. Then she says, 'He is wearing me out,' and changes seats. A stupid delay when the bus in front bumps a car, then finally the passengers from that bus get onto ours and we move.

In Key West we walk round. Sit on a blue water quayside. Monique goes for a job. I walk round. Dave from New York buys me a beer in his bar. Shows me his new shoes. Shows me his scars from stab wounds on his torso, inflicted by a guy that he killed. Says there might be a job for me clearing up in the bar. I say I'll come back tomorrow then. He wants me to start right then. Tomorrow's no good.

I find Monique at the bus station. She has a job lined up. We decide to stay on, get bus to official camp site. A rip off at six dollars. Eat tuna on a table by the tent.

Next day. Catch bus into Key West town. Say goodbye again. Some guys are outside a supermarket, buying buns. They look like The Eagles rock band in a parallel universe where they hadn't washed or changed their clothes for weeks. That tough hippy look, beards and 'taches and desperate eyes.

They're waiting for one of their number to come back, he's trying to sort out a dope deal. They need the money to repair their car. One of them tells me he's from Washington State, tells me his girlfriend was shot in the face. I walk around.

I see one of them, he's collecting empty bottles. Tells me how he lives on milk, bread and peanut butter. Tells me about a big rig he used to drive illegally.

I watch the waves at the far end of the peninsula. Tiny rocky beaches, a lot of the land belongs to a US Navy base, fenced off.

It rains. I'm standing at a quay. A girl dives in with her clothes on. She climbs out, tells me she's Canadian. She was arrested up north somewhere, now she's suing them for false arrest.

She drinks lime juice and water. Lime juice is a feature of Key West, it's as though you've got to drink it. Be a hippy, swim in your clothes, drink lime juice. Try to sell the dope you brought with you, to get enough money to fix the car and get out of the place. One road in and the same road out. It was like the end of the world at the end of time.

I find my way to the bus station. There's a crazy guy there, talking non-stop. A girl tells me he's in a world of his own. I could see that.

Monique shows up. She's cutting out too. We get on the crowded bus. Driver gets a ticket for being over the axle weight. We stop at a Dairy Queen, which is just another hamburger joint. Somebody there says 'Hello Jack' to the non-stop-talking guy. We arrive in Miami.

I get a peaceful bus towards Jacksonville. I get off at Daytona Beach and walk along the hot, hot sands. Cars everywhere along the beach. I think Monique stayed in Miami. I don't think we said goodbye. The surf is refreshing.

I ride north to Savannah, Georgia. Twilight here. I leave the bus station for a walk. There's a policeman keeping people out who don't have tickets. Another end of the line type of place. I'm stuck here until the next bus to anywhere comes in.

I see a bit of the town. Wander back to the outskirts where the bus station should be. I've cut the corner and find myself in a housing area. The buildings look like cheap council flats would look like in the UK.

A black youth asks me for a light. He gives me a cigarette and we talk. I walk on. An upstairs window opens and a black kid, about twelve years old, shouts.

'Hey man, what 'you doin' in the black area?' I shrug and spread my arms, smile.

'I didn't know it was the black area.'

At the bus station the policeman guarding the door seems just as incredulous as the black kid, to hear that I came that way.

Midnight bus to Richmond. Black guy on the bus next to me says, 'You smoka de 'erb?' He reckons the driver is OK about it.

'Why not?'

We stop at an outrageous souvenir shop. He buys me a beer.

From Richmond I ride to Jamestown. Carry on to Virginia Beach. Swim. Night has become day has become evening.

I get to Norfolk. I'll go north via the night bus, spend a day in New York, then towards Detroit. My old boss asked me to check an address there for him. It's as good as anywhere, and I've still got a few days left.

And that's when Bill Harper walks in.

We stopped somewhere in the Ozarks. This time Bill bought a civilised meal and, as we sat in the diner, he told me more of the story. He'd rung his first wife, who was in Tulsa, that morning, and she'd said, 'why don't you come back?'

Clearly, Debbie in Vegas was the second wife. It was interesting to me that all her possessions were at the rear of the van, yet the earlier version had been that he was going to drop stuff in Oklahoma on the way to Vegas. Maybe he'd been all that time on the phone fixing up work in Tulsa instead of Vegas. I wondered how Debbie had taken it. Or if she even knew yet.

He confessed that it had been 'a big decision' for him. You don't say...

We motored a relatively short distance, to Broken Arrow on the outskirts of Tulsa. A suburb surrounded by a plain. From a respectful distance I watched the joyful family reunion.

She seemed to hold some reservation in her eyes. They had three daughters. Debbie had one baby.

After a quick coffee he gave me a lift to the highway, where I would have to hitch the ten miles into Tulsa, since there was no bus station in Broken Arrow. No matter. I was twenty-five dollars better off and Tulsa wasn't as far away from the east coast as Vegas was.

I still had my two-week unlimited travel Greyhound pass. My mobile hotel. I could go north towards Kansas City and spend the trip surmising about Debbie.

Maybe he had been Twenty Four Hours from Tulsa somewhere, when he first met her. Maybe he was only one day away from his wife's arms when he "lost control" as he "held her charms." So that's what they were called. I never knew until I was sorting out my mother's sheet music collection many years later, and checked the lyrics.

Powerful enough to wreck a marriage in a small motel, anyway. Hal David and Burt Bacharach, who knew?

Now the first Mrs Harper had managed to reverse the tides of time, and she and Bill would be sitting in a suburb in the Midwest, surrounded by a plain, with no bus service. He would go out and sell some building plots on the plain, and she would sit at home with slight mistrust.

And Debbie would be in Vegas looking for childcare, wondering what good her charms had done her.

And Bill would still be the kind of guy who might drive halfway across the States without being quite sure which wife he would prefer.

DRIVING TO MARRIAGES

I think it was a Friday. I know it was 1980. Probably.

Get back in time for the night shift. The Granada was a fast car in its day. Like a police cruiser, except that this particular one was a little closer to the borderline of legality. If it had been mine, I probably would have maintained the screenwash mechanism.

I accelerated gently, nosed up nearer the truck in front, and eased out into its slipstream. The spray from its wheels on the damp patch of road covered the windscreen with mud-tinted water. I worked the wiper stalk, cleared the screen, pulled all the way out and accelerated past, carefully at first so as not to spin the wheels. The straight stretch was enough for a safe overtake before the bends began again.

One of the all-time great overtaking manoeuvres, I thought. The road stayed clear until the T-junction north of Ashbourne, where I turned right onto the A515. Then the long open stretch to Buxton, Roman straights punctuated by flowing fast bends, up and down bare hills, a white quarry in the distance. There was a little-remembered proposal back in the fifties to use this stretch as part of a triangular road-race circuit, along the lines of Le Mans. Of course it never happened, the British straight-faced in tooth and claw, preferring their carnage best taken on foreign fields.

I loved the freedom of the speed, the change in the routine. There was enough time when I got back, for a snack and a cuppa, before the grind of delivering the residents of south Manchester to their familiar watering holes.

I knew Nottingham quite well, from when I was at Trent Poly in the early seventies. And I remembered that Tina, my friend Tony's ex-wife, now had a job in that self-same Poly. The School of Art and Design. Things may come and things may go, but the art school dance goes on forever. I can't remember who said that now. Hang on, I do. It was the title of an album by Pete Brown and Piblokto! This was after Pete Brown was sacked from Pete Brown and the Battered Ornaments, shortly before they were due to support the Rolling Stones at the famous concert in Hyde Park. And Pete Brown formed Piblokto!, who had their own exclamation mark and weren't surprising just because I suddenly remembered them just now. He probably included the exclamation mark because he was an enthusiast for art schools, and they did things differently there.

I'd gone for an interview at the Polytechnic, bored with working in a quantity surveyor's office adding up figures, and carrying documents around Manchester on the more interesting days. The chief art school personage, a Mr Conn, asked if I had a portfolio.

'Er, no. We never did art at my school.'

'Well, you look artistic.'

I was wearing dark red corduroy jeans, with a yellow suede belt, and my favourite shirt with green, blue and purple vertical stripes. A vital career move, as it turned out.

Mr Conn's list of qualifications far exceeded the length of his name, on the letterhead, when I was offered a place. Who was I to argue?

I stayed nearly a couple of terms before dropping out to pursue a life of drink, drugs and not enough debauchery, stating my clear aim to 'become a writer.' I did achieve this in 2019, about forty-seven years later. So there was a bit of a gap.

We had set off from the clinic near the taxi office quite early, so I had been able to have a little tour around some old haunts after dropping the girl off at the Nottingham clinic. The fact that the daytime drivers, who normally did the job, called it the 'Abortion Run' tells you all you need to know about why the girls generally weren't too chatty. The clinic near the office was owned by a surgeon who had his initials on the number plate of his Rolls Royce motor car. I concentrated on the driving.

I drove past Wildman Street, where we used to live. Apt. The houses there are all new little boxes now, and the short street is unrecognisable. My past history erased like an incriminating dossier.

I parked near the Poly and wandered into the Art Department building to ask after Tina. She was out, but should be back soon. I hung around, went for a walk, came back. She still hadn't returned.

'I think she was going to a wedding. She must have gone straight there. It's only just down the road at the registry office. Do you know it?'

I knew where the receptionist meant.

'Have a walk down. You'll see her there. It won't have started yet.'

I had a stroll. It was, indeed, not much more than a hundred yards away.

A small group stood outside. There were two young men in freshly laundered blue boiler suits, with red carnations on the collars, and three young women, smart casual. Emphasis towards casual. The smartest of the three was wearing white jeans and a white blouse with a bit of frilliness. I think she even had a wide brimmed hat on. And a bunch of flowers in her hand. They all looked like students, early twenties.

I asked about Tina. They were expecting her, but she hadn't turned up. It was nearly time to go in.

'I'll just wait outside.'

'No, no, come in with us.'

'Are you sure?'

'We insist.'

The registrar seemed mildly amused by the compactness of the wedding party. The best man turned and pointed towards me.

'And he only came to deliver a parcel.'

The formalities were completed, and we all moved, jovially, to the pavement outside. There were only a few steps between the entrance and the street. Snaps were taken. They insisted I joined the tableaux. The man with no name, to be recalled in some distant future, in a dusty, and very small, album.

Caught up in the mood and the chat, I moseyed to the corner with the happy young people.

'We're off to the Newcastle Arms. Come along, you're really welcome.'

'Thanks, it's really nice of you. But I've got to drive to Manchester. All the best to you.'

I retraced my steps. There, standing near the registry office, was Tina.

'You've missed it.'

'No, I watched it from the window of the library across the street.'

'Oh.' I performed a slightly furrowed brow, the degree of furrowment intended to indicate mere puzzlement, rather than an out-and-out vibe of 'why on earth would you do that?'

She explained why on earth she would do that by embarking on a long story, which began with somebody who knew both her and the bride saying something to somebody who Tina knew from elsewhere, being involved, and not somebody you could trust who might talk behind your back, and one of them had said something about her, so she had decided to come but just watch, not to come in. And that was fine. She was going to come but what with what the person from that family had said, who she knew from before, then clearly it was too much of a slight to actually turn up. But she was happy she'd seen it. And how was I?

We chatted until we reached the college. Caught up. In one hundred yards plus five minutes. Then it was time to go.

I thought there was something about Nottingham people. That they were quite complicated.

I remembered the Newcastle Arms as being the scene of an altercation involving Tony, Tina's ex-husband. I wasn't present, he had told me about it one time when I visited.

Periodically I would have a weekend away, staying at wherever Tony was living in the East Midlands. In those days he would buy a house, do it up nicely, buy another, and so on. One time, I helped him by assembling a rather finicky curtain rail. When he held it up, the fancy cord was at the wrong side.

'Don't worry.'

'No, I'll do it again. Give it a try anyway.'

I managed it, although it was a close-run thing, my cognitive processes being somewhat hard to marshal after the amount of dope we had smoked. Actually a superhuman feat, I thought, taking it all apart and putting it all back together as a sort of mirror image.

A scientific documentary was on the TV.

"The human brain loses about nine thousand brain cells every day..."

'Wanna bet?' said Tony, taking a long draw on the joint.

Tony seemed to get into altercations more than most people, although I never saw any of it. Unless you count the two of us hiding in long grass from a gang of Greeks near a bar in Corfu. Which was my fault for mocking them by dancing with a chair held in my teeth. And it was hiding rather than altercating, so to speak.

The altercation in the Newcastle Arms involved Tony, another man, and a woman to whom Tony was speaking. I think the other man probably wanted to speak to her as well. I think she was called Nicola, or Karen, or something like that. I only met her once or twice.

Some time after the altercation, Tony married, let's call her, Nicola. Coincidentally, she was the main prosecution witness in the case against him about the harm done to the other man during the altercation. It was useful for him that a wife can't testify against her husband.

There was another wife in the late eighties, whose name I don't even half remember, even though I was best man for him. I only remember the meal being in, I think, an Indian restaurant. I don't remember the registry office bit at all, even though I must have been there. It was difficult to give a speech at the meal, as I knew nobody there, apart from Tony, his wife, and his dad.

By the nineties, I'd got a house in Hull, and Tony used to visit me sometimes when he felt like a break from his house renovations. He helped me once to get an old TV aerial off my chimney stack. He climbed up, took it down, and handed it to me from the roof as I stood very near the top of the ladder. It was a two-storey house, but old and quite high.

'Oh, I forgot. You don't like ladders do you?'

'I'll be all right, Tony. I'll just take my time.'

I wouldn't go more than six feet up nowadays. It just shows what two men and some willpower can do.

I had supplied him with a couple of second-hand cars over the years.

'What happened to that Vauxhall you had last time I saw you? It seemed all right.'

'Oh. It's, er... in the canal.'

'Oh. So you want something else then?'

This time it was a van. Seemed logical for a builder. My friend Bob and I found a Nissan "Urvan" in the salvage yard. Got the front straightened and got it MOT'd.

Tony was happy with it. He took a girlfriend to Morocco and asked if they could leave the van on my parents' drive whilst they were away. My mum and dad lived only a few miles away from Manchester Airport. No problem. The third wife was no longer on the scene at this point, of course.

My mother was on the phone later.

'A man left a note on Tony's van which said he will pay fifty pounds for the van as scrap value. Shall I show it to him when he gets back?'

'No. No. Throw it away. Definitely don't show it to him.'

He came back with the van a few months later. I was going to smarten it up for him. Together with Mike, a friend who lived nearby, I had persuaded the landladies of a property behind my house to renew the broken roof of a large but semi-derelict garage at the back of the house they owned. We put some money into the deal to run power, after which Mike used it for making cat scratching posts, and I installed some paint spraying equipment. Woodworking and paint spraying don't constitute ideal bedfellows, but beggars can't be choosers.

I had the van outside the garage, all rubbed down and masked up. There was little room to manoeuvre inside the garage, with my stuff on one side and Mike's woodwork bench and power saw on the other. I had a type of paint that would give the gloss finish with the final coat, not like the cellulose type which required lots of flatting between coats, and polishing for the final flourish. Lots of labour on the acreage of a panel van.

I planned to spray it, then carefully reverse it into the garage, lock up, and leave it to dry overnight. The downside was that this 'coach paint' took longer than cellulose to dry. Random dust on the breeze of the outside world versus wood shaving dust, and no room to work properly, in the garage. Clinical. The average Aston Martin restorer probably doesn't have to make these tricky sorts of technical choice.

The girlfriend from the Moroccan trip was no longer part of Tony's equation by now, although I had personally benefitted from the trip to North Africa, being the recipient of a thoughtful gift, a bottle of a local spirit based on figs. I never did open it, considering at one point using it to prevent the screenwash mixture freezing in the winter. But it would have probably have been too sticky.

Tony had a new companion with him, though, in the shape of a dog, a Spaniel-looking brown thing. I'm not particularly keen on dogs, but it was well behaved. Of some pedigree, apparently; some hundreds of pounds were spoken of. Also a useful ally in meeting attractive women in the park, who were walking their dog or dogs.

Bob had called by on this particular day. He had a car he was working on for a customer. Tony sat with him in the car, smoking a joint, opposite the garage, as I started the compressor.

I'd done nearly three quarters of the van when I noticed a small raindrop on the paintwork. Then another.

'Damn and bloody blast the f*cking blasted bloody goddam son of a bloody blasted son of a bloody f*cking bitch. F*ck!'

Continuing to rail at the sky, my pace speeded up considerably. I downed tools after coating the final area, and dashed round to the front of the van, carefully opening the door and climbing in behind the wheel. In the dark of the masked-up cabin I started the engine. If I didn't steer, it would go back into the space I had cleared for it. I began to reverse.

A week or two before, I had cleverly improved my tool storage, by knocking some large nails into a rafter that ran across the garage near the doors. Here I hung several hammers, each snug on two nails, the wooden shafts hanging down between them.

The Nissan Urvan was larger than a car or small van, high enough to catch all the hammers I had forgotten about.

Fer dunk ker dunk ker DUGGA DUGGA PER DOMF per takka takka ting.

I swore, in the same manner as I had earlier, but for twice as long.

Then got out of the van, shut the door, looked at the various hammers on the floor as I shut each of the two large wooden doors of the garage, and locked the padlock. Then made my way to the back door of my house.

I think when people use the rather strange verb, to storm, as in 'he stormed out of the room,' that this walk to the house might have fitted that sort of description. I would myself have called it, 'a determined aggressive plod, seething with inner rage and characterised by an unwillingness to be deflected.' Storming always sounds silly to me.

I settled down on a chair in the living room, there to indulge in a session of depression and trembling fury.

Tony and Bob were still sitting in the car, smoking.

'Should we go and see how he is?' said Tony eventually.

'Nah. He gets like that.'

Tony took a deep toke on the joint.

'My dog's in that van.'

Time moved on and Tony worked his way up the property ladder to a large house in Mablethorpe. He was within sight of achieving his ambition to run a guest house. He found one or two neighbours and small-time dope dealers to argue with, and settled down.

Later he told me that he had made the acquaintance of a woman whom he liked. The only thing was, she was quite a devout Christian.

Hmm.

I try not to be too judgemental in life, but maybe that's a failing sometimes. The use of a sardonic smile to suggest that such a liaison might be fraught with pitfalls, during one of his visits, might not have been quite the forceful message I should have offered.

'No, Tony. No.' might have been better.

I thought about this as I looked at the invitation that had come in the post. I held it in my hand as I reached for the phone. Denise, my lady friend, answered.

'Hello?'

'Hi. Do you want to come to a wedding?'

Mike invited himself along on the trip. He'd got to know Tony during his visits to Hull. Mike was a little bit older than me, a would-be builder, actual market trader in posters and trinketry, manufacturer and entrepreneur in the field of cat scratching posts, and sometime hippy minstrel wandering the cities and couches of Europe. His long hair was tied back in the defiant pony tail of the alternative lifestyle adherent, undeterred by the wispy thinness on the gleaming crown. Despite various business setbacks and a house which lingered in a state of stalled renovation for several years, he maintained the admirable, if wearing, demeanour of an eager and bouncing puppy, for most of the time. Unless his back was playing up.

On the day we were to set off for the wedding, we'd planned quite an early start. He was late. And his back was playing up. And his innards.

Could he ride in the front?

I had an old Toyota coupe. It was a four-seater, but the back was rather cramped for a large adult. I looked at Denise. I knew the answer she was going to give, but her eyebrows forming a 'V' just backed it up.

'No, Mike. If you want to come, you've got to go in the back.'

He folded himself in, groaning, and we set off. Along the way he was peckish, despite his stomach feeling queasy, and asked if we could stop at a shop. We found one, really in the middle of nowhere, a house standing on its own with a small shop window at the front.

Maybe it was a would-be shop and, as such, didn't carry much stock. I don't even recall any houses near it. A mystical shop that we would never find again no matter how many times we plied that lonely road.

He returned to the car, hobbling, with a haul of vittles. A plea to be allowed in the front fell on deaf ears and he reinserted himself into the back seat, huffing and puffing. The vittles turned out to be mostly chocolate. Did we want any?

'No thanks, Mike. It's still a bit early in the day.'

Munch munch. Rustle rustle. Munch munch.

Denise and I discussed Tony's wedding as we drove along. I hadn't been told much about Kate, other than that she had devoutness. A faint suspicion of devoutness that patched a degree of insecurity, but maybe that was just my prejudices coming through. One wished them well.

The wedding was due to take place in the meeting hall owned by the Christian sect. Tony had told me that he had been mending some doors and windows for them, in the back room of the building, which action had found great favour from the... what were they, the elders? The committee?

'So they like him, do they?' said Denise. 'It's a funny set-up though.'

'Perhaps they went, "Bless him, for he hath carpentry skills",' I said.

We found the hall and parked the car without difficulty. I have revisited Mablethorpe in recent years, and become acquainted with its charms, but on that out of season day, it felt bleak and windswept. And above all, empty. We had a walk through a gap between the shuttered premises near the sea. Sand was piled up at the walls. We looked at the sea for a few seconds, succumbed to the withering wind, and made for the building.

People were starting to gather. No sign of Tony. No sign of Kate. A middle-aged man welcomed us warmly. When he had a moment between meeting and greeting congregation members, he came back over and told us the story.

Kate was upset. Very upset. They had heard from Sean, the best man. I knew Sean vaguely, having met him once many years ago. He was very straight compared to Tony. Like a normal citizen. Tony was always convinced I remembered him well.

'You remember Sean, don't you? Sean and Jenny?"

'Er, yeah.'

'You know, from Heanor?'

Oh yes. The days of drug-induced hazes in Heanor.

The man in the tie and blazer carried on talking.

'We've heard from Sean. He's with Tony in a pub in Lincoln.'

Oh.

'It doesn't sound like he'll make it.'

'Sadly, no. But you must enjoy the buffet. You're very welcome.'

The buffet was very welcome. Unassuming but wholesome. We were quite hungry by now. There were plenty of sandwiches and savouries.

Mike didn't bother with the sandwiches and savouries. His eye alighted on some Black Forest gateau and he apportioned himself a gigantic slice. After that he had a helping of some sort of trifle, and some more rich, rich, creamy cake.

After a while, the man in the blazer informed me that they would be doing some singing soon, despite the absence of both Tony and Kate. I could see an acoustic guitar being made ready near the stage.

I rounded up Denise and Mike.

'If you nip to the loo, we're going to get going soon.'

There was time to inform the kind man that we would 'have to get back,' and leave in a civilised manner, before the first strum heralded something uplifting.

Mike's groans increased in volume as we drove. On the outskirts of Grimsby is a roundabout, where back then there was a Little Chef, now long derelict.

We pulled up. Mike crawled out of the car and set off towards the toilets. Like a giant in some grim fairy tale he thumped slowly, very slowly, across the tarmac, one foot raised and thumped down, then the other foot raised and then thumped down. In a slow motion bow-legged sailor's gait. Like Batman 'climbing' up the side of a building in that old TV series, but without the rope to pull himself along.

As I waited in the car for Mike and Denise to return, I remembered Julie, an ex-girlfriend. I knew her from uni., but she'd had a boyfriend then. Meeting her later by chance, we'd had a bit of a fling. In the interval since I first knew her, she'd had a mild breakdown of sorts. A bit disconnected from the world.

I think it had left her feeling vulnerable. She had listened with a tad too much interest to the theories of some religious zealots. Armageddon was coming, and all that. We used to joke about it. Jehovah's Witnesses. Bhagwan Rajneesh with his followers all dressed in red and orange and his commune in Oregon. The Moonies.

We set off again. Mike lasted out until we dropped him off, and he groaned to his door. We chuckled as we drove to Denise's house.

I remembered Julie asking me what I thought about Armageddon.

'Well, if it's coming, I think we need to pack in as much sin as possible before it happens.'

Sometimes things are just fated not to work out.

I turned to Denise.
'Pub?'
'Pub.'

Sorributamentit

Growing up in the fifties, then. Perfect. The streets were grey, our Austin Cambridge was black, and there were some red and some white roses in the garden. The sun shone all day long in the summer, and I sat carrying out mass murder by killing wasps with a stick. My mother left a jam jar, containing some orange juice, between the back door and the roses.

The stick was a plank, to be precise, but two inches wide to give the wasps a chance. 'Sport.' One day I swatted nearly thirty to death. Whatever the numbers, they were too great for it to ever seem possible to counterbalance the carnage with later good deeds.

'Remember those seventy-four wasps you swatted to death in Sutton Coldfield in the nineteen-fifties?'

'Yeah, I suppose.'

'Well, you were never going to get that back, were you? You had quite a blameless life since then, mostly. I say mostly but... well anyway. No more mass murder, at least.'

I give a barely perceptible shrug, staring at the detail of the metalwork on the pearly gates behind him.

'You're not very contrite, are you? It's a disappointment to us really...'

And on, and on. Yada yada yada. Just say I'm never going to get in, and get it over with.

One day, I had a bit of an epiphany. I remember I was standing by the French windows at the time, looking out at the rose beds. I wonder if anybody else has had this? It went:

Here I am. I am three years old. I am Me and I will always be Me. There are no different choices and everything that happens to me will be my experience alone. I wonder what will happen.

The birth of an ego I suppose. The dim realisation that I would not remain forever like a cat, reacting to stimuli as they happened, running, eating or sleeping as the mood dictated, living entirely in the moment.

I don't know what I did immediately after this mind-blowing revelation. Probably went outside and pretended I was the Lone Ranger. Tonto, at this stage, was a faithful friend rather than a racial stereotype.

The other big moment in my infancy came during the family celebration after my brother's christening. The adults sat at a large table, and I was with some cousins at a smaller table, as we began a midday meal. All at once, suddenly, inexplicably and out of the blue, and also without warning and from nowhere, a slice of egg took off into the air and flew up, in an arc which took it six feet towards the adults' table.

There was no rational explanation. We hadn't seen anybody flick it. Some of the cousins were convinced it was telekinesis. I had never liked egg. There was a lot of chatter and amazement. I suppose somebody, probably my mother, must have got up and picked the slice of egg off the floor.

I wondered about telekinesis for a while. Maybe I could develop it into a superpower. But it never happened and I lost interest. It would only ever be a bit of egg from a salad flying a few feet. Superman, in the comics, was pushing huge asteroids through space if the situation demanded it. And all I had ever managed, maybe in some subconscious plot to demand attention in the context of my brother's arrival, was to mentally catapult a bit of egg across a room. Fuck.

The first time I heard the word fuck, whilst we're on the subject, was in connection with a tortoise. There was a kid a little bit older than me, who lived a few doors away. I knew by now, after my epiphany, that he would always be a little bit older than me, and that I would never catch up or overtake. Actually I asked my mother about this, to back up the epiphany, if I'm being strictly honest.

He was called Robert. Sometimes we would find some game or other to play at, if his mother visited mine for coffee. There were fewer working mums in those days, the child care was more thoroughly on sexist lines than it is today.

On one occasion, I was encouraged to go and play with Robert at his house for a change. He owned a tortoise, which roamed on the lawn. You can tell this was a middle class neighbourhood without extensive alleyways. We even had fields at the back of the house.

The tortoise, for reasons, presumably, of good animal husbandry and security, was attached to an extremely long piece of string, anchored somewhere near its hutch. This provided a lengthy arc of travel for the tortoise, in particular when I tripped over the string whilst running about. I sprawled on the lawn, watching the tortoise as it barrel-rolled several feet, over and over and over again. It was a good shape for barrel-rolling.

Robert was able to loom over me, considering that I had sprawled. As he loomed, he shouted.

'Look what you've done to my FUCKING TORTOISE.'

At this, his mother appeared from the back door.

'Robert, do NOT use words like that.'

Whereupon he was led into the house, I think by hold of his ear, though I would not swear to this in a court of law.

I hung around on the lawn for a while. It became clear that he wasn't coming out in the near future. My mother was surprised to see me back so early.

'Robert used a bad word.'

It didn't really seem that bad to me, in isolation. The worst my father would say was 'Damn and bloody blast,' if he was really cross. You didn't get angry or annoyed in those days, you got cross. That's what the Ladybird book would say. Cross.

I had 'bloody' down, as the worst thing you could say. Although damning things wasn't ideal. Damning things made it sound as if you were saving the Devil a job by doing that, which was obviously a negative in the eyes of God. Not good for the balance sheet at the final reckoning.

It wasn't until secondary school that I got my proper hierarchy of swear words sorted out, with various pupils competing to fit the 'f' word in whenever possible in order to prove they were rufty tufty men of the world instead of spotty twelve-year-olds. Really, it was better cherished as the last resort blunderbuss of swear words, to be brought out only when the pistols, revolvers and rifles of the damn and bloody blasted brigade had failed to bring the audience to a gaping-mouthed standstill. It needed creativity in order not to weaken its impact through over use, as for example in the sentence 'Fuck the fucking fucker,' which is nevertheless admirable in demonstrating the word's versatility as verb, adjective and noun in 75% of the entire declaration.

We're getting ahead. All that was some way off when I was dropped off for the first time at primary school. Transport consisted of a pram for my brother, with mother and myself on foot. Nowadays it seems to be de rigueur to deliver the toddler in a fat arsed Audi or Mercedes SUV, safe from hoodlums and marauding paedophile zombies. What happened?

I was introduced to the teacher and herded into a building. I didn't think much of it. At playtime, we were cast adrift like small wide-eyed turtles upon an asphalt sea. From time to time, a larger and older child would emerge from the teeming shoals of inexperienced humanity, and march up to you. They would stare at you for a moment or two, sizing you up, and then punch you in the chest. As they punched, they would recite the litany.

'Sorry but I meant it.'

The way they said it was more like 'Sorributamentit,' so that it was no longer a real sentence but a chant, a hypnotic drone invoking a superior power, a mystic overseer that had given them, its acolytes, permission to thump someone. Most of the thumping was not seriously damaging, more a declaration of intent that the perpetrator was interested in a career involving bullying if things panned out for him.

So I stood there, watching as they scampered off to sorributamentit on someone else. This was going on all over the playground.

'Sorributamentit, sorributamentit.'

'Sorributamentit, sorributamentit.'

I divined that, probably, a parent somewhere had given its child a clip, the child had repeated the behaviour with the wording but without the prior history, and the whole thing had become a craze, like marbles, card collecting, or, in adult life, rioting.

I didn't, at that time in life, have an appreciation of how the actions of an exasperated parent could have serious repercussions in child psychology, even though I was dimly aware that the misguided parent had probably not intended to indirectly unleash such a tsunami of thuggery at Mere Green Primary School that particular term. No, I just thought that these children were really, really stupid.

I think it was not that day, but the following one, when I finally decided that the whole set up was simply too unreasonable for words, and that I should go home.

I stood near the gate, meticulously calculating my plan for the trip. I had never gone anywhere without my mother before. I would have to cross four small roads and one main road, and it was a whole mile. The roads on the same side as the school were easier to cross, so I would leave the crossing of the main road until last, nearer to home.

Someone must have left the gate open, so I started off. But I must have spent too long on my mental preparation, because it was now near the end of the break, and a teacher intercepted me in front of the school. I had got a good twenty yards, but it was some way short of Steve McQueen jumping fences on his stolen motorbike in that film they used to show every Christmas.

I found the sums easy enough at primary school level, but of course there's more to education than that, in particular the socialisation aspect. This comes in two main packages, namely religious indoctrination and peer group pressure. The teachers just try to squeeze in the odd bit of wisdom, through the cracks between these twin edifices. They do a pretty good job, I must say. I still remember Mrs. Parker's favourite saying, "Great minds think alike." How wonderful that humans occasionally agreed on something!

As far as religion goes, looking at it now from the perspective of a grandparent who has attended a nativity play at school, it's basically a framework for teachers to put a bit of a show together, give the kids a chance to speak up and to sing, and to include a bit of moralisation for the rest of the year. When you consider the vast open spaces in growing minds, needing to be filled, anything that helps top up the school day's content is welcome.

I'd already begun to see it like this, morning assembly just being a chance for teachers and pupils to settle down and contemplate the day ahead. Whilst droning on about God being immortal, invisible, God only wise, I think it was. Like Superman, but with invisibility powers added, and no susceptibility to green Kryptonite.

Obviously this was totally unfair to anybody else, such as mere humans. Even Superman was pretty rubbish as a superhero most of the time, as in 'I'll just use my indestructibility and breathing in space capability, to stop this meteorite,' or 'I'll just use my flying at incredible speed, and strength, to catch and stop this runaway train.' It doesn't work, from a dramatic point of view. You've got to have weaknesses.

I'm not sure how much we were bombarded with the concept of a punitive God as such, but there was a fair chunk of Lucifer and the poisoned apple in there, and probably a lot of purgatory seeped through from Catholicism. In any case, I was already aware that I had almost certainly lost the redemption game, because of all the wasps. A bit like sliding down to square one on a snakes and ladders board whilst God is on square ninety-nine with a dice that has a figure one on each of the six faces. Nobody likes a smartarse, but we were expected to toe the line.

Having discovered that escape from the institution was about as feasible as space flight, even when somebody had left the gate open, and that my mum didn't want me at home all day anyway, I moved on with my development.

So far, the main thing I had found out was that a worrying proportion of humanity would probably comply with instructions from a Nazi officer unless there was somebody bigger than them who said otherwise.

The other life lesson I carried forward from primary school came during a mealtime. The food, in retrospective view, was better than gruel in a Victorian workhouse, or the odd treat of rat in a Japanese prisoner of war camp. However, at the time, I viewed it as pretty poor. We would generally get the basic meat and two veg', followed by tapioca ('frog spawn') or the appallingly unpalatable sago. An advert of the era showed a grey-pullovered urchin (not surprising on black and white TV) eagerly looking at the proffered dish in front of him, transfixed with delight.

'Cor, sago!' he intoned, as if it was a rare delicacy from an emperor's banquet. What was he usually fed, pigeon droppings? Ugh.

The meat was usually fatty lamb or stringy beef, the potatoes always mash, and the green veg' often cabbage. Oh, and you might get a splash of gravy, too thin or too thick, to disguise the sorry mess. Goldilocks was nowhere to be seen.

One day, dispirited by the ration of lukewarm, watered-down milk at morning break, and weakened by the desperate struggle to separate the lean lamb from its labyrinthine tendrils of fat, I became aware of a teacher leaning over my shoulder. I had eaten little of the meal thus far, with only the mash seeming remotely palatable to me. On a scale of tastiness, the mash reached the dizzy heights of 'neutral blandness', to my mind. The lamb, cabbage and gravy were all, on this particular day, profoundly negative in desirability.

I would often picture the two mounds of mash as Swiss mountains, and use my spoon to carve the precipitous helical curves of a perilous road upon their flanks, the foray into civil engineering a blessed pause before I instigated the calamitous storm which would result in the avalanches that swept away half the mountainside. Before it disappeared, via my spoon. Into my mouth. Tastelessly.

On this particular day, I had made little progress, still being preoccupied with the carving of a particularly elegant stretch of mountain road, which was currently threatened by a raging torrent of gravy from God's spoon, pouring down the flanks of the Matterhorn. So I thought it best to humour the teacher as she sought to help me, and hope the intrusion into my Alpine universe would not take up too much time.

Thankfully, she didn't home in on my disgust with the horrible lamb, the lean meat of which would have barely yielded the amount of calories expended in separating it from its fat. Like all teachers, she assumed I hated cabbage. I did, but not as much as I hated lamb fat.

She spoke, encouragingly. The sentence has remained ever since, engraved in my brain. An indelible maxim by which one's life might be guided.

'If you mix the cabbage up with the potato and the gravy, you won't taste it.'

'Yes miss.'

With that, she continued on her rounds, keen to ensure that other children were benefitting fully from the provender.

I was left alone to experiment. This would certainly be worth trying. I abandoned the Swiss mountain scenario in favour of a vague notion of white-coated scientific empowerment, as I began to stir the three ingredients according to the formula that had been so generously entrusted to my young and eager mind. The prescription should cause a chemical reaction to take place, and eliminate the taste of cabbage altogether. The teacher had said so. What a useful bit of scientific knowledge this would be!

When I tasted the mixture, I could clearly taste the cabbage. I knew this wasn't a result of getting the comparative quantities of the ingredients wrong. The cabbage, with its taste, was still there in the mouthful, just in smaller pieces. No chemical reaction had taken place at all.

The 'scientific wisdom' had been nothing more than an utter barefaced lie. From an adult to a defenceless child. An out-and-out, provable lie.

But what a life lesson! What a gift that teacher had given. It should be built in to the curriculum somehow. Just think, how many times countless hordes vote for an obvious charlatan, based on hollow promises and false charisma.

'I thought he was the best thing since sliced bread.'

Adults lie, mate.

'He says the cheque is in the post.'

Adults lie, mate.

'He said he needed money for materials.'

Adults lie, mate.

'He said he would build a factory that provided hundreds of jobs.'

Adults lie, mate.

'He said everything would be better for ever and ever, and we would have a future where our destiny was in our own hands...'

Mate, taste the cabbage.

Bittern

I was a bittern, once.

The bittern is an elusive bird which lives in reed beds. It is very hard to spot there, with its perfect camouflage colouring in shades of brown, light brown, and the most uninteresting shade of yellow from the pallet of possible yellows offered by natural selection.

Birdwatchers prize a sighting of the bittern. It could be said to be a bird of such elusiveness and skill in concealment, that it should be elevated to the pantheon of truly great birds. Or it could be said to be so invisible, that it contributes nothing, blending in to the extent of being a nobody, a non-achiever, a makeweight.

Every once in a while, a bittern will make a honking noise from deep within its extensive reed bed. This may assist it to acquaint itself with another bittern, and, later, smaller bitterns may ensue. They will grow up in the reed bed environment, seeking to one day make their own occasional honking noise.

They may look up at the big sky, thinking, that is big and that is blue. When it is not overcast. They may think that their reedy domain is somewhat damp to say the least, and they may think that it would be nice to find a sort of Hollywood environment for talented bitterns, where they could flaunt their rare feathers as supporting actors to peacocks and parakeets. But it's likely that they don't think like this, and that they accept the inevitability of their adaptation to their surroundings, and stay all their lives near a windy estuary, looking at reeds, exhibiting a vaguely defined stoicism. Like the bit-part actors trapped in a grimy, terraced Salford in a nineteen-sixties Albert Finney movie.

These days, I am no longer a bittern. I have wandered far and wide, I have seen great canyons, mountains and oceans. I have travelled by train, boat, plane, and army truck. I have crossed the Golden Gate bridge. I have been in California, Mexico, and in Wales. I have driven racing cars, I have won prizes. I have navigated the foibles of human society in order to contribute very slightly to its overall betterment. I have experienced many aspects of culture, heard fine music and seen great art, and read accounts of human life within great literature and within the Daily Mirror.

I do not feel that life is lacking one particular great experience which would make it complete. I can always find something which amuses, entertains or educates me.

I do not live in a reed bed.

I did not choose to be a bittern. Nevertheless I made a choice which led me to it.

I was a schoolboy in Edgbaston, Birmingham. Trying, like some interplanetary visitor, to make sense of the human society within which I swam. I never did fully fathom it, but of course, realising that it is essentially meaningless is a good coping mechanism when confronting its enormity. Like a bittern looking up from its reed bed at the traffic plying across the Humber Bridge, and not caring or wondering about where any particular vehicle is headed.

Every week, our studies were punctuated by Games. More precisely, organised sports. Games sounds too much like fun.

It was mainly rugby. Soccer was a bit beneath them, I think. King Edward VI School, Edgbaston. Hive for the most promising minds in the Birmingham area. Future men of prominence, making their commute via New Street Station through the winter smog of the early sixties. A golden era, on the days when you could see where you were going.

There must have been cricket, though I remember none of it, save the day at my primary school when I stretched out my hand along the grass to intercept the rolling ball. The keenest player was rushing for it himself, not trusting me, the mere mortal, as a fielder. As he arrived in his flurry of haste, he trod on my hand. This involved blood, as he was the only player on the field wearing proper cricket boots. They had spikes in the soles, the better to enable expert practitioners of the cricketing art to display their skills. The mortals wore what we called pumps. Pumps were adequate exercise wear, the antecedents of trainers. Trainers are massively over-specified money earners for the likes of Nike and Adidas.

I was mildly annoyed with the keen player, because I was about to stop the ball successfully, and had no need of his presence. He felt that he had to do all the jobs on the field, because he was better than the mere mortals. He felt this because his father played professional cricket for Warwickshire. On balance, I felt rather sorry for him.

Rugby was colder than cricket, due to the seasonal nature of it. Nowadays the colossi of the game bestride the stadia at all times of the year, particularly in Rugby League, which appears to have become a summer endeavour. Surely Rugby League should feature nothing but heaving giants covered in mud, like Richard Harris in the film *This Sporting Life*, grinding slowly across the arena of a monochrome existence, rendered anonymous under the caked-on slime from the drizzle-soaked puddles of an almost grassless pitch under a dark, northern British sky. Shouldn't it?

At the age of twelve, there were notable discrepancies in size amongst the boys, due to variances in rates of development. The year cohort had three or four giants compared to the rest of us. These lofty specimens were divided between the teams, so generally the winning side was the one which featured the more committed sample of the big kids. One or two of them weren't really interested, like most of us, and just trotted about fairly aimlessly, enough to keep warm and not get shouted at too much.

Being of average size, I was usually allocated to the hooker or scrum-half position. Being hooker involved dangling between two taller boys in the epicentre of the scrum, trying to hook the ball backwards with the heel, after which you could relax for a bit. I have no idea what useful lessons in life could be derived from spending time as a hooker.

The scrum-half position, if the ball emerged from your team's part of the scrum, involved picking up the ball and passing it, after which you could again relax whilst running vaguely after the throng. Enough, you will have guessed, to keep warm and not get shouted at too much.

On rare occasions, out of boredom, I would become more animated and chase the member of the opposition who had the ball. One of the big lads was often to be seen wading over the line to score his try, slowed but not stopped by the two or three smaller lads who clung to him like limpets without quite managing to bring him down.

One day, he had got clean away and was steaming along the wing. He had half the length of the pitch to go, but there was nobody to stop him.

Except one, as it turned out. I set off on a diagonal path to see if I could intercept him. As I got near, it became clear that I wouldn't draw level with him, but I was close enough to launch myself into mid-air, just enough to grasp his trailing ankle with my outstretched hand. It was enough, combined with his momentum, to send him crashing to earth like a Fred Dibnah chimney stack.

'Now, that's how to tackle,' said the teacher, after he had got over the surprise. He had, in fact, taught us that grabbing the legs (preferably both at once) was the best way to get a man down. It stands to reason really. I don't know why professional rugby players don't try it more often. They seem, usually, to prefer the 'inept wrestler impersonation' technique.

The other time I gained stunned admiration was when a scrum parted like the Red Sea, and the opposition scrum-half, who was about 180% of my size, charged towards me, holding the ball, filling my field of vision. I do remember his unusual name, so we'll call him Smith.

Everyone from our scrum had sensibly run to the left or right, to make way for him. I don't think this happens in professional rugby. Being a stubborn sod at times, I didn't see why I should get out of his way just to make his life easy. I did, though, have enough of a survival instinct to duck down nearer to the ground with my back arched, like some sort of misguided armadillo.

He chose not to waste time going around me, and simply motored over me, at which point I pushed upwards, sending him to the floor in a surprised heap. I have no idea what happened to the ball, or about the subsequent pattern of play, but was aware of several lads standing motionless near me, open-mouthed, going, 'You tackled Smith, you tackled Smith.'

That was quite enough fame for one day. It didn't do to look like I cared.

It turned out that King Edward VI School Birmingham offered a second weekly opportunity to go outside in winter in shorts and a sports jersey, and run about to keep warm. Sorry, I mean participate in Games.

It was later in the week, Friday maybe, when this other activity was provided, out of the classroom. I think they just let us chase a rugby ball for a while, for a few weeks until we settled in, but it gradually became apparent that a choice had to be made.

We noticed, on these afternoons, that a sizeable contingent of the older boys was made to dress in khaki uniform. They could be seen on the main playing fields doing things like marching and forming into echelons of neatness, so that they were all the same distance from each other. You can imagine the kind of thing. The main recollection that stays with me, is of these drably-clad unfortunates, in their woolly, sticky uniforms in the height of summer, running in formation, carrying rifles (presumably devoid of firepower), and dropping to the ground, full length, before, as quickly as they could, pointing said rifles forward towards an invisible enemy.

I had no connection with, nor knowledge of, war, beyond reading the Victor comic and knowing that Germans were prone to saying things like, 'Pig-dog Englander, for you ze vor iss over.' My father had escaped military service due to being at university during the war. Perhaps they thought it was more use to have him learning physics rather than traipsing on a battle field, I don't know. He did tell me once that he had had to go on marches with army cadets. He would fall behind, swinging his legs at a natural pace, before overtaking the entire troop a few miles later when they had tired themselves out going left right, left right. Whether he would have got away with this if born in a country where he was christened Fritz or Nikita, rather than Maldwyn, is a matter for conjecture.

The older boys who flung themselves to the ground were called Combined Corps. They began doing Combined Corps in the third year at school. Until then, they were allowed to do Games on the Friday afternoon, for the first two years of their school career.

We were given a stark choice. Combined Corps, or Scouts. Scouts started now, no games on Fridays any more. The prospect of khaki and drill in two years' time was unthinkable. I became a Scout. Woggle, neckerchief, dull-coloured shirt, and shorts were obtained.

Scouts involved learning knots and doing arcane activities, possibly including swinging on, or climbing up, ropes. I remember hardly any of it, beyond going on a camping trip and having to do a race down a hill carrying a bucket or buckets of water whilst having to hold an "OXO" beef stock cube in our mouths.

When it came to my turn, I spat it out, using contempt, after a few yards. Like Frank Sinatra in his song. "I ate it up, and spit it out." How can you eat it up, *and* spit it out, Frank? It's one or the other. And I think you got the tense wrong as well. 'Kin 'ell, Frank, get a grip.

We were divided into little groups of six. They were called something like a patrol or a troop. I don't remember. They had a leader, a second-in-charge, and four others, going down the age range. Obviously, you were the youngest of the six when you started.

The leader would be relatively jovial, with a hint of fierceness in case you didn't do as you were told, but for the most part predictable, normal and boring. Probably destined to be an accountant, solicitor, doctor or tory MP.

Our second-in-charge was a bit less boring, probably headed for a life as a dodgy businessman. His job seemed to be to relay the instructions of the leader, show us how to tie knots, and to mention wanking.

I don't remember the other three personnel, but surmise now that the one immediately above me would occasionally exhibit the characteristics of an excited puppy, overjoyed to no longer be the youngest.

These groups of six were given designated names, drawn from the available wildlife of the UK. One hoped for something tough and solid, like a badger, or clever like a fox. No. I was now a bittern. A honking bird nobody ever sees.

It meant that I could grow up in the comforting knowledge that such a thing as a bittern existed. A vast number of UK residents outside the bird watching community are unaware of the bittern, I feel. Somehow, they manage to live their lives in perpetual ignorance, watching East Enders, going to parks and leaving litter, aspiring to, and eventually perhaps driving, a Mercedes; all without ever knowing how enrichment could be provided by a bittern, as it honks from its reed bed one day after they have parked their Mercedes and wandered near a windy estuary in search of poetic inspiration.

Scouting was started by Sir or Lord Baden-Powell. He had a first name which I have no chance of remembering. He came from a time when Britain fought Boers in South Africa and, in the process, invented concentration camps. I always meant to look up who had actually won that war, if anybody. At twelve years old, one seeks a sense of certainty in things. I never did get around to it. There was a sense from somewhere that things hadn't gone altogether swimmingly. There was also a sense that, if Britain had in reality lost a war, you wouldn't find the words 'Britain lost the war', within any school textbook. You would have to divine it, like solving a devious crossword puzzle which floated just out of sight beyond a Mad Hatter's tea party in a misty woodland glade.

Although our bittern second-in-command was clearly interested in wanking and mentioned it quite frequently, the opposite seemed to be the case with Baden-Powell. In his book *Scouting for Boys* (Baden-Powell, 1908), he discussed the subject, but without daring to mention penises. My recollection is that he couldn't even mention the word 'masturbation', although I could be mistaken. I think he called it 'self-molestation', or similar. Disgusting. A wearing, draining activity, to be resisted. A vice which would weaken one's stamina, stamina needed for trekking through woodland enjoying flora and fauna, or, if in South Africa, for trekking across veldt, conserving energy so as to be able to shout convincingly at Boers after reaching one's destination.

In order to combat the demon self-molestation, cold showers were recommended. Fuck's sake, man! The whole of puberty to get through, attending a boys-only school, when the main viable image of womanhood was Emma Peel in a leather catsuit on the TV, and all that Baden-Powell could come up with was a cold shower.

My days as a bittern were to end after two years. My father was quite high up the ladder at Lucas, in the Research and Design department. I found an employee chart years after his death, showing him just below Doc Arrol, the director. So he was in fact, second-in-charge, though being in a world of non-bitterns, he almost certainly didn't use the position to mention wanking.

We knew that there had been, within the bounds of civility, a slight clash. My dad had thought that Doc Arrol only wanted a yes-man to assist him, and told him so. He was amused that Doc Arrol's response to the suggestion was, simply, "Yes."

To move up somewhere, therefore, dad changed his job.

We used to holiday in North Wales. My brother and I would put towels on our heads, held on under rubber swimming caps. In nothing else but our trunks, we would charge down from the top of the high dunes near Harlech, towels billowing behind us, impelled by some nebulous Lawrence of Arabia fantasy, whooping and laughing without care.

Our friend christened the game: Indian scallywags. 'Wanna play Injun Scalls?' We didn't, at that age, quite grasp the concept of the various racial stereotypes which we had concatenated into one simple, if bizarre, costume.

Dad was offered an appropriate job based in Cardiff. Mum vetoed it, feeling that she would be trapped in Wales for the rest of her life.

We ended up in Manchester. The prediction of my form teacher at King Edward's, that some of us would feel a psychological shock if finding ourselves near the bottom of the class (having sailed along easily near the top of the class at our primary schools), had come true in my case, and my general work was sketchy at best. I was accepted at Manchester Grammar School, a similar type of establishment to King Edward's, on the grounds, I was told, that the High Master of MGS (you read that right) was an old boy of KE. The old boys' network at play. It was like a favour, and hopefully my work would improve. It didn't.

MGS, thankfully, didn't feature Scouts or Combined Corps. So I was free to focus only slightly on my studies, putting off homework on top of putting off homework, sinking into utter misery on Sunday afternoons with the thought of school the following day, nothing on the TV but Dickens serials. They depicted a world prior to the advent of the internal combustion engine, a world full of people in stovepipe hats and waistcoats and long-tailed jackets, often called Quilp. A world so completely and irredeemably depressing that it sometimes drove me to attempt some homework instead.

I have never quite shaken the thought that, had I possessed a crystal ball in 1963 and foreseen the future, I could have elected to do Games on Fridays instead of Scouts, and then escaped to Manchester before Combined Corps started. Two years of enduring Scouts in order to avoid Combined Corps, which I would have avoided anyway.

As mental scarring goes, it's really meagre.

And being a bittern turned out to be survivable. I don't, after all, live in a reed bed, but rather, in a comfortable suburban house, for which I am profoundly thankful.

And I've hardly ever had a cold shower in my life.

Spaceship Brian

I used to walk up the hill from Trent Poly towards Wildman Street. Or down, if it was a suitable time of day to want to mingle with some random swathes of humanity.

Going up, you had your choice of forking left, towards Wildman Street, or staying on the main road and then turning right into the arboretum. The arboretum was nice, if you were on acid. There were green trees, random foliage, and cages nearby with cockatoos. And a sky dome that filled with jumbled letters of the alphabet, ever present in their infinite hundreds, forming no words, dancing, twirling, pulsing in their giggly-worlintudiousness, in front of the pink and blue canopy. Always pink and blue, as you gazed above, and walked upwards, staying at the centre of the small world which held you, like a tiny being on the floor of a Christmas snow dome about to be taken from the mantlepiece and shaken.

You were in your Afghan coat that someone had sold you because she could see that you didn't care about being seen to be such a woolly woolly hippy boy, in your bubble. Members of normal society wore sports jackets and ties, and didn't bother you, unless they were lecturers from your Design course wondering if you were still enrolled. And even then they didn't bother you.

Whereas, once in a while, a long-haired deadbeat hustler, or a merely lazy long-haired daydreaming unemployed person, would stop you for a chat, about the state of the universe or whether you'd got a fag. A fag was generally known as a 'straight' in such circles, distinguishing it from a joint primed with psychoactive substance, Afghan Black on a good day, more generally Lebanese or Moroccan. Moroccan, always the Moroccan. How could you get blasé about it? Even the Moroccan seemed an improvement on bare reality. Someone somewhere must have gone to Morocco for it. Some of them thought it would change the world but it never really did. It just got you talking to sketchily educated street hustlers rather than accountants. A marginal improvement? Probably not, but no accountant was acquainted with Spaceship Brian, as far as I knew.

Nattering to the guy who had stopped me on the hill to bum a fag, he asked me if I knew Spaceship Brian. I didn't, really, I had to admit.

'You need to meet him. He can call up a spaceship. He can make a spaceship appear.'

'Oh. Wow. Could I have my matches back, please? Ta.'

'Yes, you need to meet him.'

'OK.'

Needless, really, to say, I didn't meet Spaceship Brian as a result of this conversation. The power of coincidence, the vibe, the flow... it wasn't evident in the days that followed. Clearly it wasn't destined, at that time, that I should encounter Spaceship Brian, with his special powers. I was also that little bit sceptical, speculating that a) spaceships might not be all that common near Nottingham; b) Spaceship Brian might have exaggerated his special powers to my casual friend; and c) that Spaceship Brian was probably stoned out of his tree most of the time and might have damaged his brain at some point.

About seven years later, I was in the USA, hitch-hiking around. I got a lift north, towards Oregon, with a guy in a VW Golf. They called it the VW Rabbit in the States for some reason. The reason probably being that Golf is a really, really ridiculous name for a car although nobody actually noticed. Which makes it a genius name. I digress.

We drove through the redwood groves. He had some very potent hash, which we smoked as we moved between these giant trees at dusk and darkness, perfect jazz from the group Weather Report on the stereo. I had done little of note with my young life, but the years of practice, sticking Rizla papers together to assemble a serviceable joint, at least paid off during this blissful and almost transcendental interlude.

He was the scion of a rich family. Oil money in Texas, if I recall. I listened to his declaration that he would use his inheritance to buy a second-hand submarine, and use that to help the green political cause by torpedoing some whaling ships. We were in 1978, halfway through Carter's presidency. Carter seemed like a reasonable man, yet on my trip I was given lifts by a salesman who told me that he was determined to escape to Argentina as soon as he could, a married middle-aged man who told me that he was gay, and various fundamentally unsatisfied souls. And they hadn't even got to Reagan yet.

By comparison, the Golf/Rabbit guy, Heinz, seemed more content, less prone to nagging existential angst. Even though his purpose involved probable multiple deaths of desperate roustabouts who only wanted to earn some good bunce to take home to have a good time with their girl. Who would never see them again as they were swallowed by icy Arctic waters. Maybe it was the dope. Luckily, I never saw in the news later that any whaling ships had been torpedoed by Captain Heinz and the crew of desperate hippy roustabouts possessing submarine skills that he would have had to recruit.

I think we found a motel and collapsed into respective psychedelic stupors, involving clinical despatch of whaling ships on his part, and unsurpassable perfection of redwood immortality on mine. But I can't be sure.

The next day I had a good lift in a pick-up truck with Mike, a decent, regular sort of guy. He was heading for Portland, but had to drop me in Eugene, a university town he said, due to having to make a delivery on the road north, later on. He probably wasn't supposed to carry passengers, I don't know. We stopped at a Christian community he knew of. He chatted to them. They weren't prepared to put me up for a night because they didn't know me. He was disgusted. They were supposed to be good Samaritans. Hypocrites.

Whether it was because of his disgust with them, I don't know, but we stopped at a bar and had three or four bottles of beer. I was trying not to booze on the trip, it wasn't in my budget. But Mike had been okay with me so I shared beers. He had to go, and left me outside a supermarket in Eugene.

'They're okay round here. Somebody'll help you out.'

There was a wild guy outside the supermarket, bothering people. Who, in turn, ignored him. He was long-haired with an Afghan coat. I was dull-witted from the booze. Lifts dried up. He said he knew somewhere. Nobody who was okay showed up like a good Samaritan. When the actual advertised good Samaritans don't come through, where does that leave you?

Eugene, Oregon, on an early sunlit summer evening. With the sun going down.

I went with the wild guy to an area some way from the supermarket. Overgrown, grassy concrete. There was a big old hippy bus nearby. We went into it and he chatted to a guy who was sitting in the bus, who didn't seem overjoyed to see him. There was a diner nearby, where we stopped briefly. Not a very busy place.

We went for a walk to a grassy bank near a stream. Met his mate. We got stoned and stared at the stars. When he wandered off, his mate said that the wild guy was a Vietnam vet. Although he didn't look like a soldier now, it could have been true. There were a lot of damaged people in the States as a result of that faraway conflict.

The Vietnam guy returned. He extolled the virtues of his mate. When it got fully dark, his mate had the power to call up a spaceship. Really. It could actually happen that I would see it.

His mate's name was Brian.

I looked at some more stars with them for a while, then got up, hooked my rucksack over my shoulder, and said I would go for a walk. They seemed disappointed.

I ended up back at the diner. It was an all-night diner. I asked the girl at the counter if I could stay there. She said okay. I ordered a coffee and settled down.

In the morning, after breakfast, I got a lift to Portland, of which I have no memory. Mike had given me his address. I found it, and stayed there for a couple of days with Mike and his girlfriend. Good people.

I sometimes look back, on very rare intervals, over the years. Contemplating that grassy bank in Eugene. Wondering whether I would have woken up the next day.

Probably. But I've never been quite so keen on the possibility of seeing spaceships, since that particular time.

A Brush with Religion

I would recommend history as a worthy subject. After all, how can we learn from the past if we don't look at it?

If you want to find time for just one book that presents some history in a readable and interesting way, try Elisabeth Asbrink's *1947 – When Now Begins* (Asbrink, 2018). She follows, here, many strands of human activity that, even from so far away in time, still affect us significantly today. And, if you think about it, it's only one or two generations ago, depending on how you define generations. My parents were married in 1947. And now there are children who call me grandad. So is it three or four generations? Still not that far away.

Of the pivotal events in 1947, those surrounding large scale resettlement of certain populations are some of the most shocking. In particular the irresponsibly rushed fumblings of the Grand Narcissist Mountbatten in India, and the desperate search for a peaceable way forward in the face of the clamour of Jewish refugees to settle in Palestine. 13 million on the move during the partition of India, Hindus and Muslims drowning, burning and otherwise massacring each other. 750,000 people in flight in Palestine, villages where everything was left behind except the keys to the abandoned homes. Snipers, bombs. The massacre at the village of Deir Yassin.

Hasan al-Banna, the founder of the Muslim League, lived, at age twenty, in a house in Ismailia. There were Jews renting rooms on the ground floor, Christians on the first floor, and he and some friends living on the top floor. He saw this as some kind of metaphor, Asbrink tells us. Presumably because his own religion occupied the top spot. As you do...

Asbrink lists what Hasan al-Banna loathed. As well as women's emancipation, singing, music and dance are included. Not exactly a libertine, then. I suppose there is more time for seething if you don't sing and dance a lot.

There was plenty to seethe about. The injustices pervading the issue of the resettlement of Palestine were gargantuan. Railing against the greed and imperialism of the West, and the suppression of free speech and thought at the heart of Communism, seems a fairly reasonable stance to me, yet it's puzzling that only Islam seemed to be allowed to lay claim to the Creation of the natural world and all its wonders. And when, in the turmoil of that post-war chaos, the notion of holy war is stirred by al-Banna and his successors after lying largely dormant for centuries, it was still a bad day for the world in general. Permission for proponents of violence to murder and hate.

The counterpoint of hate is love. Most religions talk about it. Perhaps they should focus less on the love of their god, and more on the love of their fellow human.

I had a tentative foray into the founding of a modest little religion, or at least, a bit of preaching, back in 1972. My initial spiritual quest began after reading *The Politics of Ecstasy* (Leary, 1970) by Timothy Leary, a would-be LSD guru and rabble rouser of love, dare I say. He was a doctor of social psychology before his conversion to psychedelic drug proselytizer. I read some of his social psychology stuff in the university library, years later. Way too complex. Masses of diagrams categorising people's characteristics to the nth degree and disappearing rapidly up their own kaleidoscopic arse. No wonder taking acid was freeing for him.

His motto became "Turn on, Tune in, Drop out". Lacking in some precision, perhaps, but snappy. A potential future of counting bricks, as a quantity surveyor after leaving school, was never going to compete with that. I tuned in to an opportunity to turn people on, in Nottingham, after I dropped out of Trent Polytechnic. It involved going down to London and buying some LSD tablets from somebody in a flat, whom I'd never met before. Obviously, somebody I knew had told me their name before I set off, so there was a business plan there. Somewhere.

Twenty-four tablets. Something of that order. Half were 'Purple Haze' and half were 'Strawberry Fields'. As if they were a reliable brand and not something knocked up in a kitchen by an idealistic hippie chemist. I'd never thought of people who were drawn to chemistry at school as being of idealistic nature, but I suppose if you take a big enough chemically skilled sample, there must be the odd one. Say what you like about big corporations, but if you were buying your acid from, for example, Nabisco, you would be reasonably assured that it had undergone enough testing to show that it wasn't going to poison millions of people shortly after their breakfast.

I was determined to adopt an ethical approach to drug smuggling, and sampled one of each type. Quite pleasant, actually, in each case. Goodness knows why I had got this far along the illegal drug guinea pig road, though. My first acid trip had been transcendent, yet horrendous in its latter stages, after I had taken two tabs in a fit of completely unjustified bravado. From bliss to unavoidable persistent visions of whirling blades chopping my existing inner world into tiny,

tiny pieces. And nearly two solid days of comedown before I felt even vaguely within a state recognised as normality.

Maybe I'd just been bloody minded after that. Feeling I'd seen the worst side already. All my weaknesses laid bare. Not fun. It couldn't be as bad again, surely. And it wasn't, though I could never claim it was wise. Just a personal choice.

I sold a few of the tabs individually, after my product testing sessions. The remaining ones were punted for me by a lad who lived in the house at Wildman Street. He was a more gregarious character than me, knew more people around the college. Overall, I roughly recouped my outlay, so couldn't be accused of profiteering. Let me be clear, this was coincidental, rather than of high motive. I ruled out a career of Howard Marks proportions, after analysing the evidence.

Howard Marks was an Oxford graduate, very bright, an enthusiastic consumer of high-grade cannabis, whose life turned towards drug smuggling and just kept going in that direction. His talent seemed to lie in being charismatic and charming, and in having enough spare brain capacity after the use of said cannabis, to organise the procurement and sale of it. You can read all about it in his book *Mr Nice* (Marks, 1996), which is quite jolly. I recently read his other book, *Mr Smiley* (Marks, 2015), which covers later days, after serving time in the USA, and becoming involved with MDMA, otherwise known as ecstasy, in the late eighties and nineties. Whilst having indubitably 'trippy' qualities (I am relying on Marks' description for this), I believe MDMA also has an appreciable amphetamine ('speed') component, hence its association with the all-night rave scene in Ibiza, and so on. I believe it was originally developed as a slimming aid, and you may find speculation that it was used by troops. It's fairly certain that it was first synthesized by Merck in 1912, in Germany, and was never made commercially available.

Mr Smiley is worth a read, but it left me feeling a little empty, rather sorry for the protagonist. The scene it describes appears devoid of any wish to find purpose or enlightenment, driven almost totally by pure hedonism. Not always a bad thing, but the days of psychedelia in the seventies incorporated a shred of idealism somewhere. I say a shred advisedly. One didn't have to go too far up the cannabis supply chain in Brighton, where I lived for a while, to come across tales of London gangsters, tooled up with guns, muscling in on deals. Nowadays, cannabis seems to have morphed into far more addictive and damaging variations like skunk.

If only Nabisco had been allowed to take it all on... (Other multi-national corporations are available).

Where was I? Having ruled out drug pushing as a career move, I had the brush with preaching which I mentioned. It came about when I had a birthday party at Wildman Street, where five of us lived in a large, skimpily maintained, house. My friend, the one who had helped me punt the small batch of acid, asked if I was having a party, when I mentioned my birthday was coming up.

'Could do, I suppose.'

Three of us were still students, after all, and what do students do? Have parties.

'Have you invited anyone?'

'Er, not really.'

'I'll see what I can do.'

He spread the word, and on the night, there mustn't have been much else going on, because it felt like half the student population had come through the door. We each had a bed-sitting room in the house, and there were three storeys, so, plenty of room normally. Nevertheless, crammed, or in the modern charming vernacular, rammed, on the night.

Around this time, we often used to play The Who's concept album *Tommy*, which was entirely concerned with the story of an evangelist/guru type who becomes enlightened and starts his own cult. The pinball wizard persona is essentially an allegorical framework around which Pete Townsend expresses his thoughts about what happens when people become preoccupied with the quest for quasi-religious fulfilment. The album was blaring from the top floor as I began to wander through the premises.

The normal convention would be for the host to politely circulate amongst his guests, enquiring as to whether they were having a good time, and wondering if they needed anything in particular. This approach was difficult, due to the degree of ramming of said guests, particularly on the ground floor. I also felt inhibited by the fact that I knew hardly any of them, particularly on the ground floor. I decided on a more radical approach. Or, I would venture to say in this case, the acid tab I had taken earlier, decided for me.

I am not given to the idea that someone can suddenly find themselves bereft of their own volition, and especially not when implying that a mere chemical could itself be possessed of any independent decision-making power. That would be ridiculous. Nonetheless, it felt that way. Perhaps the messianic connotations within *Tommy* had something to do with it. At each room, I stood calmly, and loudly proclaimed.

'I love you. I love you all.'

This doesn't look much in print, but at the time felt to me as if I was standing in front of thousands, naked (apart from an invisible heavenly comfort blanket) on the stage of the Albert Hall.

The inhabitants of the house on this evening could be divided into three clear factions, I saw. Those downstairs were drinking, those on the middle floor were mostly smoking joints, and a fair number of those on the top floor I knew to be on acid, lying around listening to Roger Daltrey singing "I'm Free". The counterpoint to Hasan al-Banna's house of division and potential hate. A house of love, where I loved everybody.

With my senses peeled, I saw instantly that the messianic declaration of love meant different things to every individual. One constant was that nobody really wanted to talk about love, except for one guy who followed me for a bit, thanking me for prompting him to declare his homosexuality to the world. That's good, mate, but I'm on about spiritual love here, just at the minute.

The lack of any prepared speech, after the first seven words, was also a discouragement to continued interest. Most people merely blinked for a bit and waited for me to go to another room. There was a continuum from slight hostility to smiling acceptance, correlated with how high in the house I went. My very own metaphor/allegory, to contemplate as I wished.

I realise now, reflecting with the perspective of the years, that, whereas my grandfather, the Reverend Robert Roberts, was able in his sermons to talk about love quite freely, in a prescribed setting, I did not quite share that freedom in Wildman Street. This was because he would have been wearing a dog-collar and had the title of Doctor of Divinity. In my case, I was wearing a scruffy green jumper and had the title of Bloke Who Happens to Live Here or Somebody Who Was Possibly Just Wandering By. It's all about image.

The encounter had a profound effect on my future plans. I was able to strike several categories off my list of possible career paths.

Cult leader without pre-prepared speeches offering potpourri of pseudo-spiritual guidance.

Rabble rouser of love.

Doctor of Divinity.

Performer of anything whatsoever in front of crowd of any size whatsoever.

Over-keen psychedelic drug user.

Instead, in my search for spiritual advancement, I would become a wanderer of the Earth, much in the manner of the Samuel L. Jackson character in *Pulp Fiction*. I would make sure, though, that I had access to suitable transport, usually lorry or van, with which to wander. There's a limit to barefoot dedication.

If you cannot be like Tommy, ultimately trying to foist your own cult upon whomsoever might be amenable, there is always the route of joining a pre-existing cult.

I had an option for this when I was in San Francisco a few years later. Young, idealistic sounding folks were handing out leaflets around Fisherman's Wharf. Come to a meeting. I can't remember what they gave as a reason.

I went along in the evening, for a bit of a break out of the hostel. I think there was the odd bit of food and drink. Maybe just drink. Take your shoes off at the door.

This was just a ploy to put you at a psychological disadvantage. I don't remember the carpets being particularly opulent. Many years later I married a woman who likes visitors to take their shoes off at the door. This is just a ploy to welcome you into suburban bliss. She's never admitted to anything else, anyway.

The hosts were probably the Moonies. Or, if not, a similar set-up. They weren't Korean, but had a certain indefinable idealism about them. A chap of about my age talked to me for a while. It felt like a cosier version of a time-share sales pitch.

They had a farm. Self-sufficient. What was my background? The talk turned to religion. My grandfather. His ears pricked up. What did I do? Truck driver. They had a truck. Maybe there was a job driving the truck. What was the wage?

Wage? Oh no, there was no wage.

Now where did I put my shoes? I'd like them back now please.

Don't worry, I'll maybe come and see you again.

Not.

From a technical, objective point of view, I think the guy could have plugged the 'nubile women looking for a partner' angle, a bit more heavily. He got distracted by the religious idealism branch of the sales talk.

It wouldn't have made any difference, though. Not when wandering the Earth was an available option.

Peak of My Powers

I went out and got a job one day. I can't remember why. Maybe just for a break from getting stoned and reading Carlos Castaneda, wondering if it was indeed possible to reach other planets using only the power of the mind. When you got hard-headed about it, it seemed far more feasible than using an actual, physical spaceship. Astronauts from the physical world were encumbered by heavy suits, breathing apparatus, and the need to take a shit now and then in a capsule the size of an overgrown baked bean tin. And with a range of... the Moon.

The cartoon world of indolence and psychedelic drug use existed alongside the routine world of everyday drudgery and regular people going to and from work in clattery, grinding buses. It was possible to slide from one world to the other at will, since there were no borders as such. Functioning in one world with a mindset from the other was sometimes a different matter.

It may have been a whim, it may have been a suggestion from my girlfriend, on the lines of leading an animal to water hoping it would drink. Most likely, it was the Jobcentre, which was called something like the Employment Exchange in those days, realising that I had a driving licence. I did like driving and had some skill in doing it, so that was OK. It had nothing to do with the concept of ambition. I think boys at the school I had attended were expected to bring some sort of ambition to the sixth form equation, perhaps via some sort of osmosis within their family, or by talking to the careers master, whoever he was, and waking up. Neither of which had happened to me whilst I was looking.

I became employed at a firm called Redgate, delivering lemonade and soft drinks in their lorry. I say 'in', but although I had a rickety cab, the load was exposed at the back. It wasn't exactly a flatbed, because the wooden boxes containing the lemonade were stacked in tiers on a sort of triangular sectioned structure, so that the ones at the top of the framework sat further in, towards the centre line of the truck. A sort of elongated pyramid of pop.

The boxes were held in place simply by gravity. It would have been completely impractical to strap them, given the amount of deliveries to be made. The saving grace was that the shelves sloped inwards, so that the boxes were tilted, reclining back towards the spine of the vehicle like smug holidaymakers on their loungers. But woodenly. As long as you didn't go too quickly round a corner.

It was on the third day that I went too quickly round a corner, in a moment of impatience. Luckily, the wagon was provided with a standard issue broom and dustpan, so it was merely a matter of stopping and sweeping up half a dozen broken bottles after hearing the smashing sound.

The soul-destroying aspect of the job was that it was impossible to deliver all the drops, which I discovered on day one. They sent out a lad from the office, with me, to show me the route. He was about eighteen and I was about twenty, so I felt infinitely older and wiser. He wore a cheap suit, which perhaps meant that he was possessed of ambition. Or perhaps his mother had frogmarched him to the Redgate nerve centre upon leaving school, I don't know. At any rate, he was a miserable sod.

At the end of the day, I explained to the boss, who wore a more expensive suit and drove a Jaguar, that we had done our best, but there were some boxes yet to be delivered. I hadn't even had time for lunch. The boss just grunted and made a slight harrumphing noise, so I gathered that it would be OK to turn up for work the next day.

On day two, I said to the lad in the suit that I would be stopping for lunch, whatever the schedule. Some of the pubs and corner shops might have to wait for their pop. He made a harrumphing noise. I stopped in a town square, maybe Heanor or Ripley, one of the many small satellites around Nottingham which we supplied, and got some fish and chips. Humping wooden crates of bottles all day demanded fuel. I said to the lad that he might as well have something. He decided to spend the time sulking instead.

The route was a different one, so this time we failed to deliver a portion of the load to a different set of corner shops and pubs. I had no idea how Redgates fulfilled the deliveries to the various establishments which had been missed each day. It didn't seem to matter, because it was still OK to turn up for work the following day.

The truck was one of those weird-looking BMC things from the sixties, with a rounded cab and unusual windows down by your feet. Either an enlightened attempt to eliminate a manoeuvring blind spot, or an attempt at a Fritz Lang futuristic gleaming deco *Metropolis* vibe as it plied through the mundane and sooty towns of the East Midlands. Take your pick. The somewhat wacky bulbous cab was not enhanced, unless you were a fan of surrealism or Micky Mouse cartoons, by the addition on the roof, of a sizeable replica of a farm gate, in wood, painted red. Red – Gate. It served no purpose other than to enhance the driver's awareness every time he approached a low bridge. And to do what we now call marketing. Red – Gate. And, so that nobody would forget it, to sit on top of the cab, sticking up, looking really, really stupid.

The third day was a Saturday, around Nottingham itself. The lad wasn't with me this time. I was glad about the easier atmosphere, and glad it was the end of the week. In spite of this, the smashed bottles had been caused by a degree of frustration. Despite my lunchtime disregard for the unachievable workload on day two, there was still an irrational sense of negativity about the whole setup. If I was going to work, it would be pleasant to be able to feel some sense of success at the end of the day, however small.

When I went in on the Monday, there was a difference of opinion. I remember telling the boss that the job was set up to be impossible, and that he was paying me a pittance whilst driving around in a new XJ6. Was this an outbreak of latent communism? I generally had no sense of politics back then, other than to feel that during Ted Heath's three-day-week period during the miners' strike, being unemployed had denied me the pleasure of having a couple more days off per week.

At any rate, there were no repercussions at the Labour Exchange, or whatever it was called. Did the name imply that one would exchange one's time and sweat for simple remuneration, or was there a deeper agenda somewhere? My father said to me once that employers were keener to recruit married men, especially those with children, since this meant the responsibility would make them more reliable. Probably so, but the other side of that coin was to see such responsibility as a key component in some sort of semi-slavery contract, with the employee less able to walk away from the proverbial Jaguar owner and his harrumphing.

I did like driving, though, and gravitated towards it as a profession. Driving has a similarity to writing, insofar as many people feel that they can easily do it, but relatively few can do it well. Which is why you should choose a skill, if you are so inclined, whose practitioners are rarer. The niche market. After all, you never see experts in Moral and Social Philosophy queuing at the dole office, do you?

But wait. In 1988, Hull University was going through a sticky patch, and looked towards making some lecturers accept 'voluntary redundancy'. A philosophy lecturer named Edgar Page refused to accept the redundancy, seemingly showing that there was nothing voluntary about it at all. There ensued a very long legal wrangle, resulting in the decision that the university was an "eleemosynary corporation governed by a system of private law", and that the decision of the "university visitor" (to give Page the bum's rush) would stand. So there. The whole case had important implications in the weakening of the principle of academic tenure; we now see academic institutions with paying students, insecure lecturers, and a significant increase in higher level degrees being given away in exchange for cornflake packet tops.

I remember Page being interviewed outside the Jobcentre by the local TV channel. He had probably arranged to meet them there. He declaimed, somewhat haughtily, that the Jobcentre 'haven't got any jobs for specialists in medical ethics, have they?'

So maybe philosophy isn't so secure a niche, then. It can be a terrible subject, frequently taking lengthy detours via its own backside, but I would always defend its right to exist. A society which would expunge it is no longer a free society.

Van driving had no need to justify its existence, being firmly rooted in the physical world. An item would be delivered and someone, somewhere, had a day that was a little bit better for it. Although, had I ever delivered the Jean-Paul Sartre quotation that I had copied out and pinned to the wall as a prime example of pseudo-meaningful gibberish, their day would almost certainly have felt momentarily worse.

I had spells delivering flowers and dry cleaning. Anything to stay mobile and not spend too much of the working week indoors, though I did baulk at the van driving job at an abattoir, being a sensitive and hypocritical meat-eating soul. Sometimes it was necessary to compromise and do things like packing or labouring in order to spend at least part of the time out on the road.

Thus I found myself working for a Stockport firm as a packer/driver. Stockport, along with Luton, had been a big centre of hat manufacture in its heyday. The factory produced leather bands to go inside traditional hats, and peaks for various types of cap. These were pressed out of sheets of semi-flexible synthetic material, using 'bumping' machines. Sometimes these peak shapes would go direct to companies in Luton, and sometimes the crescent shapes pressed out from a glossier, black, laminated material would be decorated at our own factory before being shipped to far-flung outposts. Have you ever thought who made the peak for your Peaky Blinder fashion cap, as you set it to a precise degree of jauntiness before setting forth? Well, you should have; somebody's got to do it.

I worked there through the best part of two years. During most of that time, a very large wooden crate sat in the corner of the packing department. From time to time, a small batch of shiny black peaks, decorated with fancy gold sculpted bands joined carefully to their front edges, would be brought through from the factory floor, when the women had found some spare time to do whatever they did to finish them. I thought the crate would never fill up, but in the end, in the manner of thousands of football pitch sized areas of clearance adding up one day to a non-existent rain forest, the inexorable march of finalised peaks had filled the crate.

The packing crate was labelled to go to Uganda. Kampala, I think. This gave me pause, on the philosophical rather than the packing technicality level. There was a song in the sixties released by Donovan. *The Universal Soldier.* Without the ordinary foot-soldier, how would [insert name of despot/dictator/general/emperor] have won his wars? In other words, if nobody signs up, nobody gets bullied or hurt. Naturally, the real world doesn't lend itself to such simple theories, and I've worked with ex-soldiers who are decent people, if often slightly brainwashed in certain aspects of political awareness.

But when it all goes awry, there are those who sign up with the despot and those who don't. Were the peaks vital to the process of brainwashing, part of the machinery of state, the gold-braided peanuts rewarding the trained rats of the military? You never had to wrestle with these moral questions when dropping boxes of flowers off to a shop. In the floral world, most people were chatty and jolly, and not in fear of a vicious militia.

Although I had not made the peaks myself, and Harry, my packing mentor, had taken it on himself to load the Uganda crate, I still gave the matter some thought. Idi Amin was portrayed in the British tabloid press as something of a clown, but he was undoubtedly a racist despot whose violent misdeeds had begun without the massive order for dress uniform cap peaks, and would continue whether they arrived in Kampala or not. He might even have forgotten that he had contacted Stockport in the first place, to support his aggrandisement.

So I took my hands to be clean, especially when the bulky crate disappeared one day when I was out on a run to North Wales. The company had diversified into making garments from Welsh wool, so I plied there and back to the tourist outlets and to Trefriw Mill, delivering garments and bringing rolls of wool back. Many middle-aged women became smart and happy.

The vehicle was a Vauxhall Viva van, technically called a Bedford. It seemed to be one of those motors that had ended up with a happy blend of tolerances when the engine was assembled. Quite nippy. I daydreamed, imagining myself as Jacky Ickx, amassing Le Mans victories, as I swept through the Welsh bends and curves. Although it was the blazing summer of 1976, with the Hunt v Lauda Formula 1 battle in full swing, fancying myself as the playboy Hunt seemed just a tad immature. I was, after all, twenty-four. Ickx was all right, though.

If I'd wanted to get into Formula 1, I probably should have started at around the time that I was penniless and drug-addled in Nottingham a few years earlier. Instead, I later settled for a seat in a Bedford three-ton truck at Smiths Engineering, a mile or two away from the cap peak factory. One of Smiths' main products were what they called crane barrels, basically the pulley wheel for a mobile crane, the drum around which the cable was wound. I took them to Coles Cranes, which had works in Sunderland and Grantham.

Jack was the driver before me. He also did the accounts in the office. A dual role of a kind rarely seen these days. Gradually I took on most of the truck driving. Jack was a friendly mentor. He advised me that a sea cruise was just the thing to alleviate stress. This arose from his wartime experience returning from the Burma field of conflict, after hostilities had ceased. The long sea voyage had done a lot to calm him. He was one of those who would never countenance buying one of the Japanese cars that were finding a foothold in the British market in the seventies. I could see his point, but after I bought a second-hand Toyota Supra nearly twenty years later, I was quite taken with the product, and thereafter viewed Japan as a giant toy factory sending me things to play with. The get-out clause was that I never bought a new one, being generally the fifth or sixth owner of whatever jalopy I could afford.

It was when working for Smiths that I found myself in Grantham, with time to spare for a leisurely lunch before the Coles factory was ready to unload the cable pulleys. I parked the truck and settled down in a Chinese restaurant, which was busy with punters enjoying the special lunchtime menu.

I was joined after a while by two men in suits, since there were no empty tables, and mine was the only one with spare seats.

'May we sit here?'

'Sure. No problem.'

We fell into a conversation of sorts, after one of the pair began by griping about the cleanliness of the tablecloth. I hadn't noticed any issue with it.

'Just like everything in Britain. Dirty.' He curled his upper lip, contemptuously.

Since I was British, I thought this was rather an insensitive remark, but let it pass.

'Where are you from, then?'

They turned out to be Swiss, and were putting up with the provincial backwater of Grantham in order to negotiate an armaments deal. They made it sound like a very cloak and dagger operation, although some brief research reveals that the

Grantham firm of BMARC, a manufacturer of munitions, was a subsidiary of the Swiss armaments company Oerlikon at around this time (1971-1988).

'I thought Switzerland was a neutral, peace loving sort of country.'

If it was possible to sneer and laugh simultaneously, he managed it.

'You'd be surprised.' He carried on a bit, without going into any detail. It was apparent that the high moral ground adopted when Europe was in flames, and thenceforth, was no bar to making profits from weaponry, and perhaps even an advantage. What did I know, after all? I was only a truck driver sitting there by some whim of fate.

His mate didn't say much, but was, I think, quietly complicit in the sneering. On my rare trips abroad, I've always thought it polite not to express, to local people, any overt feelings that their surroundings are despicable, but that's just me. I'm just a wagon driver, not a respectable businessman.

The truck went quicker once the load was off. I liked taking the picturesque route through the north Derbyshire Peak District. I used to muse upon what the crane pulleys would have a part in loading and unloading, in their future working life. Components to build roads, bridges, railways, warehouses, food factories? Consignments of timber or logs, or Nissan cogs? Crates of food for Africa, crates of rifles for militias? Crates of medical supplies with urgence, smuggled rockets for insurgence?

And maybe the odd crate of hundreds and hundreds of shiny peaks, to fit onto military caps, to be part of a dress uniform, to be worn when parading as drilled, in identical detail, to make them feel like part of an invincible unit, to make them feel better about crushing and persecuting their less fortunate countrymen, to enable a psychopathic despot to live in splendour with his young wife with her many thousands of shoes, until she tries to become head of state after his death at the age of ninety-eight and is then shot like a dog while the people have a party in the muddy streets outside their corrugated shacks and bars.

World trade is a wonderful thing and it's great to have had a career where I was involved.

Considering Gayness in the Tropics

Stayed in San Francisco for a few days. Recharge. Fisherman's Wharf, hills, the Golden Gate. Perception filtered through a Jefferson Airplane sun.

I went up a tall building and looked out over human creation, like God taking pleasure from the deal he got on concrete. Reinforced concrete, famously pioneered by Julia Morgan, the architect of Hearst Castle. Earthquake proof. Take that, nature. Until the next big one, anyway.

I was staying in a backpackers hostel that was mentioned in the Rough Guide book. Not too far from the centre of town. Some evenings there, I chatted to Gary, an English guy. He had come to San Francisco to study sexology and become a sexologist. They didn't do courses for it in Stoke-on-Trent. He was affable, and good company.

One evening, enthused by his chosen subject, he posed a question. 'What would you do,' he asked, 'if you were marooned on a tropical island where the only other castaways were a ninety-year-old woman and a young, good looking and well-proportioned man? Which one would you prefer to make love with, even though you're not gay?' I'd never thought about gayness in those terms before. Suggesting that our sexuality extends over a continuum does seem healthier than having a world where people bury certain proclivities under a layer of seething denial.

Gary went on to tell me that he had been conducting his own studies into sexual responses, after having delved into the realm of behaviourist psychology. He wondered whether it was possible to train a human to alter, or at least add to, the range of stimuli which would provoke their sexual arousal.

At this point, I was still four years away from a serious study of psychology at university, and thus not readily versed in the differences between Pavlovian (Classical) conditioning, and Skinnerian (Operant) conditioning. Therefore, I merely listened with interest as Gary outlined the structure of his experiment, rather than questioning its scientific validity. Nevertheless, I did feel it to be just a little bit outlandish.

He had enlisted a subject for his experiment. Someone guaranteed to be co-operative, available and on standby at any hour of the day or night. Somebody not afraid of pushing boundaries in the cause of the advancement of knowledge. Somebody with the stamina to see it through.

Himself.

Of course, that's a great idea. It is not unknown in the annals of science for brave pioneer scientists to undertake potentially risky experiments, using themselves as the first subject. The ethical dilemma is solved, since, if it all goes badly wrong, the experimenter has only turned themselves, rather than some hapless underling or student, into a slavering monster of a Mr Hyde or Incredible Hulk.

A downside is that the experimental sample is rather small. One, in fact. Therefore, generalisation of any findings to the rest of humanity is a long way from being proven. But you've got to start somewhere. And this particular experiment, being quite radical, might struggle to attract willing subjects.

The idea was for the scientist (Gary) to condition the subject (Gary) into a new way of thinking. Specifically, to expose the subject to a pictorial stimulus and try to condition him into attaching sexual connotations to it. In the light of knowledge later gleaned, I feel that the methodology veered more towards classical conditioning than that of the Skinnerian operant conditioning tradition, though it could be debated. I would venture to suggest that it was more than a tad unusual, whatever the theoretical background.

At a suitable moment, the experimenter (Gary) would ask the volunteer (Gary) to begin masturbating, with a view towards bringing himself to a climax. Did I mention stamina? Oh yes, I see that I did.

I forget now whether the journey towards orgasm was aided by the use of an arousing photograph, perhaps of a young lady in alluring and probably flimsy apparel, or whether the volunteer (Gary) was expected by the scientist (Gary) to work from his own unaided imagination. In any case, at the moment of orgasm, a photo of something different was produced for the hard-working subject to view. It is unclear, in the circumstances, whether this photograph was quickly unveiled by the experimenter (Gary), or grabbed in a trembling frenzy by the subject (Gary). Perhaps both, if it didn't fall from the table during the confusion.

This, let's call it the neutral or second photograph, was a picture of the object to which the volunteer's sexual feelings were going to be attached, or fixated, if the experiment succeeded. I did say earlier, I think, that I felt the methodology to be somewhat beyond the norm of run-of-the-mill Pavlovian research.

One might surmise, given our earlier conversation, that Gary's experiment would involve the castaway from our tropical island, the tanned, muscular, well-toned young man, probably naked or clad in a mere banana leaf. So that after many sessions in the lab, the subject (Gary) would end up being measurably gayer than his baseline gay reading taken at the start of the research. Or was that too risky, the scientist (Gary) harbouring a secret fear, despite his avowed open mind, that the subject (Gary) might become irreversibly gay with no way back? A raving Mr Hyde, dashing out of the lab in the direction of the gay bar, refusing to countenance a course of further experimentation which might reverse the process, bringing him safely back to the naked virtual bosoms of the young lady in the first picture.

The thought is an intriguing one, but in fact we need not concern ourselves with it. For Gary had gone to the opposite extreme with his experimental design. The second picture contained nothing remotely sexual. Or even human. He had deliberately selected... a house brick. If the subject, after the experimental sessions, experienced arousal when looking at a house brick later on, this would surely prove... what, exactly? That sexual preference could definitely be trained into somebody? Or that Gary's experimental technique was a danger to the world?

Why would you want to condition somebody in sexual preferences anyway? Perhaps to over-ride anti-social ones. In any case, it didn't work. After he had outlined the bizarre scenario, I put forward a possible snag which could arise in the erotic house brick world.

'Aren't you worried that if you saw a particularly attractive wall, that you might find yourself greatly aroused, to the point of debilitation?' We laughed, in the knowledge that we were unequivocally safe from architectural erections.

Having a clear week in the backpackers hostel was like having a vacation from the job of hitch-hiking. I had a wander round, looking at the sights, taking a boat trip. One day I stopped in a quiet bar to indulge in a rare beer. The barman confided in me that everyone there was gay, except me. 80% gay, given that there were three other punters. They all looked very ordinary guys in their forties, nothing flashy or ostentatious in their clothing or demeanour. We could safely say that they weren't a noticeably different species of humanity, neither was I about to be seduced towards the sultry tropical island paradise of Gary's gayness continuum by the presence of a young, handsome, musclebound Adonis.

The use of the word 'gay' had become fairly common parlance by this time, 1978. At some stage, its earlier usage, in describing someone as being "light-hearted, lively, cheerful, merry" (Cassell Popular Dictionary), has become impossible to deploy. It is now set in stone, or perhaps in the mortar joining some of Gary's bricks, that gay means homosexual. The complete appropriation of the word is, in a way, rather sad.

Whilst it is certainly possible for a homosexual to be light-hearted and cheerful, it is not an intrinsic component of the sexual preference. Thus, someone can now be morose and gay at the same time, a condition which would seem ludicrous to the ears of an earlier generation.

If we accept that gay now means homosexual, which seemingly we must, faced by the overwhelming simplicity and shortness of its syllable, where does lesbianism fit into this nomenclature? Surely it is a subsection of homosexuality, of the condition we now call 'gay'. But that creates a dilemma, an anomaly.

How do we describe male homosexuality? The population at large are unwilling to tackle the five syllables of 'homosexual', and have replaced them with 'gay'. Asking them to use the term 'male homosexual' is therefore a non-starter. Leaving us with nothing. Except 'gay'.

From a starting point of having a category of homosexuals, which encompasses male homosexuals and female homosexuals, we now have a category of gay, which encompasses lesbian and gay.

Which is nonsense.

It's like saying that humans consist of females and males. So we will describe them as females and humans.

What utter, shabby, lack of effort. All because nobody came up with a single syllable word to describe, in a non-pejorative way, a male homosexual.

If only male homosexuals had, in a previous era, flocked to a preferred Greek island, the male equivalent of Lesbos, there to be charmed by the poetry and philosophy of a charismatic gay male figure, we might have been saved from the linguistic decadence into which we have now fallen, with even our feeble-minded over-used acronyms beset by logically inconsistent precepts.

These ubiquitous acronyms fill the modern media, rarely pausing to tell us their full credentials. We are left to 'Google them' if we seek precision, or even basic understanding.

LGBT I can cope with, despite the questionable provenance of the 'G' bit, as discussed. But they proliferate, within themselves as well as like a species. We now have LGBTQ, and, I think, some other appendages. What does Q stand for? Is it Querulous, or perhaps even an ironic, unashamed Queer, proud and priapic?

I can't tell you. I don't speak Acronym well.

If we take the LGBT genre to refer to, let's say, those of more minority sexual preference or of ambiguous physicality, then the counterpoint is the folk of heterosexual, non-ambiguous physicality, coincidentally in the majority.

To call this latter group mainstream, or normal, is to step onto shifting sands. Why should being a member of a majority group confer, upon anyone, any greater value as a human? That is a dangerous path. So far, so reasonable, I hope.

Hence the need for a new category for those who are *not* LGBTTVQXYZ.

Cisgender. It derives from a paper by a German sexologist. From a German root 'Ziss', possibly. I don't even know how to pronounce it. And neither, at the time of writing, do 99% of the population. I haven't verified this figure scientifically.

Cisgender.

Yes, that's helpful.

Gary, did you qualify eventually?

Come back, I need help.

Bring your brick. Not to throw, but as a representative of calm and measured reason.

Sid

My father, always a keen cyclist, became very involved with the Moulton bicycle club after his retirement. The engineer Alex Moulton had produced a radical bicycle in the sixties, which featured proper suspension and unusual small wheels. Although there was a much later high-tech design, an all-singing shiny alloy delicately-tubed creation with an appropriately four figure price tag, the original steel-framed sixties Moultons could be found for small change by comparison, and dad had quite a number of them in the garage. As you do.

Once a year, various 'Moultoneers' would congregate at my parents' house, and a ride into the Cheshire countryside would ensue, featuring a civilised lunch stop at a pub or at the home of one of the other members in Bollington. After the return leg, my mother and Anne, another non-riding wife, plus usually my visiting aunt, would be ready at our house with tea and the joviality of scones. My brother would often have invited a couple of mates along. There was no exclusivity about it, you didn't have to bring a Moulton bike. I had the luxury of simply choosing one from the garage.

On one of the rides, I fell into conversation with a chap who wasn't one of the regular bunch. We compared notes about life. He was involved with driver training, specifically HGVs, in other words, lorries. This was a coincidence, as I had trained for an HGV licence in Stockport back around 1979, 1980. We were now in the early nineties I suppose. It seemed like half a lifetime ago.

The fellow remembered my instructor, John.

'Oh yes. John.' He recalled John's surname, which I had forgotten. 'They never liked him at the test centre, did they?'

The cyclist chuckled.

'He had a great big sticker on the truck, saying I HATE YORKIES, didn't he? Probably not the wisest move.'

I ruefully concurred. The Yorkie reference pertained to a well known TV advert of the day, wherein Rowntrees' agency had decided that associating their chunky chocolate bar with a macho truck driver was the way to go. Look out, Cadburys, with your prissy Dairy Milk and its hints of genteel femininity. You would see the trucker, in his check shirt, climbing into his tall cab, getting ready to dominate the highway. He would then lean slightly out of the window as he bit decisively and manfully into the substantial bar.

Anybody with any sense would have simply broken a chunk off and put it in their mouth, thereupon to suck contentedly, but that wasn't an option for the Yorkie bar eater. No matter that the thing was twice as thick as a Dairy Milk; it had to be chomped. No doubt the trucker, at the end of his heavy-duty ride, would use his indestructible gnashers to pull the top off his beer bottle before retiring to his sleeper cab with his girlie magazine.

Of course the guy was some male model desperately hoping he wouldn't lose a filling, and it was laughably bad, but the British population was now firmly imprinted with the knowledge that the Yorkie bar existed, and, moreover, with the lingering feeling that it might sustain them over the course of a long day, for a few miles further than one of those thin and effete Dairy Milks. Which probably had at least the same volume of chocolate in its thin wideness. Genius.

Having a sunstrip on the truck windscreen saying I HATE YORKIES probably wasn't genius, though. Sorry, John. I must admit to a twinge of unease when I first saw it, but I had made an arrangement, John had turned up, and it would have been churlish to turn and walk away at this point. We had conversed on the phone and I was happy with what John had said. And his price was reasonable. Any training of this nature ran into hundreds, even in those days, so it was a large commitment. John was a one-man band, although he had an occasional colleague, Doug I think he was called, who took me out one Saturday for a second viewpoint. There were a couple of other operators who ran several trucks, but they were considerably more expensive.

Hindsight is a wonderful thing. The cheapest isn't always the best choice.

There was nothing wrong with John's tuition. And we got along well, the days in the truck were fun. But, as my new acquaintance said, they didn't like him at the test centre.

It was quite unjust. A skill should be judged as a skill, not by who exhibits it. However, human nature is a many splendored and often crassly biased and prejudiced thing.

John's sunstrip might as well have said I AM A DETERMINED NONCONFORMIST. And driving examiners, to some extent moulded or even attracted by the very nature of their job, tend to be conformists.

As we took a breather, waiting for the group of cyclists to regroup, amid the leafy splendour of Lyme Park on a beautiful autumn day, my companion had another thought.

'Do you remember Sid? Was he there when you were doing the test?'

Ah, yes. Sid. Indeed.

'I wonder if he's still alive? Probably not, with all that was wished upon him.'

I knew exactly what he meant. I think there was a permanent staff of four examiners at the Stockport test centre, and Sid was the terror, the short straw, the one everybody dreaded. My cyclist friend told me that somebody once got a re-test after the way Sid had treated him. The candidate had been on time, but due to a mix up in the paperwork or a change to the schedules, Sid had formed the impression that the lad was fifteen minutes late. Sid was wrong, and should have been aware of the change. He tore into the bloke with such verbal ferocity that of course, the guy was a nervous wreck before they even set off, and almost inevitably failed. A test result cannot be changed, but the chap was given another test free of charge at a later date. Almost unheard of.

So that was Sid. Probably the holder of an Olympic medal in the sport of unfriendly gruffness. And that, it would seem from my friend's story, was on a good day.

So you could argue that it was a tactical error on John's part to mention Sid's reputation to me at some point during the training. Why make someone more nervous than they might be already? But when you're together all day long for a solid week or two, what do you chat about? The whole topic underlying it all is the actual driving test, after all.

In general we had a good laugh, as I've said. One day we had a run out somewhere south of Alderley Edge, in the countryside. At a roundabout, instead of the second *main* exit, I took the second actual exit. This turned out to be a country lane not much wider than a single track in places. The truck was an articulated unit, known as a Class One in those days. If you passed the Class One test, you automatically got the licence for the Class Two and Three rigid trucks as well.

So, we didn't want to have to back up for any reason. Luckily, the only thing that came the other way towards us was a Bedford Rascal van, just about the narrowest thing on four wheels at that time.

Regaining the main road, we motored through a village.

'Do you think you did anything wrong in that village?'

I thought hard.

'Well, I saw the speed limit. I checked my mirrors and slowed down. Before the parked cars, I checked my mirrors, I signalled, checked my mirrors and pulled out. After passing the parked cars I checked my mirrors and came back to the left. At the end of the speed limit, I checked my mirrors and then accelerated to forty.'

'So... I don't think I did anything wrong.'

'Did you see those two old ladies on the pavement?'

'No. I must admit I didn't.'

'Did you see the big puddle that they were near just as you passed by?'

'Ah... Oh dear.'

Since I had observed neither the old ladies or the puddle, it was a bit like an unobserved tree falling in the forest and making no sound. John might have been having me on. But probably not.

Many years later I was walking from my flat to start my shift at the taxi office. There was a massive expanse of semi-flood water in the road to my left, and a railing to my right. A Morris Ital was heading towards me at speed. He would probably move out and go around the giant puddle. I didn't have time to climb over the railing.

The Ital didn't change course. There are many, many gallons in some puddles. I turned round and went back to the flat to change.

Karma.

Most of the time we frequented the roads of south Manchester. We were coming along a pretty, leafy road through a stretch of park, no traffic around. Two sparrows had rather imprudently left their nest – if they had one; they might have been first time buyers – and were twittering and interfering with one another on the roadway ahead of me. I deliberated for a split-second, then checked my mirror and drove around them.

'Bloody hell. Don't do that on your test if it crops up.'
'Well, there wasn't any traffic.'
'Even so...'
'OK.'

The next day we were in one of our regular cafés, the one near the test centre. It is a law of physics that there is always a café near a test centre. Various truck drivers, trainers and test candidates were engaging in banter, mainly about how the mark of a fast driver was if they could keep up with a bread van. Bread vans, it was well known, were always driven by the fastest lorry drivers in the land.

At the time, the film of the book *Watership Down* was showing in the cinemas. A tale of a tribe of brave rabbits undertaking a perilous migration to a promised land habitat which had no bulldozers.

The conversation turned away from bread vans for a while, touching on matters within the ecological domain. John nodded towards me, and announced to all present.

'Nature boy, here, yesterday, drove around two sparrows that were shagging in the road.'

Instantly, a tuneful voice piped up.

'Bri-i-ght eyes, burning like fire...'

The test day dawned and we presented ourselves at the centre. The normal pre-firing-squad atmosphere. Well maybe not quite that bad. A 75% chance of not getting Sid.

I got Sid.

Gruffly we did the paperwork and gruffly we walked to the truck. And, after answering the gruffly presented questions about the truck couplings and suchlike, gruffly did we begin.

The test centre was in Bredbury, about a mile away from Stockport at the top of a hill. We started by driving down into Stockport, where we came to a small junction controlled by traffic lights. I had to turn right off the main road which would have taken us back up to Bredbury.

I moved forward on the green light, but there was traffic coming towards me from the Bredbury road, so I had to wait. It dawned on me that this rig wasn't going to be able to quickly nip through at the end of the light sequence like you could in a car. I had to pray that the oncoming traffic would finish and still give me time to get turned and out of the junction. I had cocked up by getting the cab over the stop line.

Not being religious, praying had never worked well for me. Too much oncoming traffic materialised and my goose was cooked. Although not blocking traffic, the cab was well forward of the stop line. As we waited for the next green, Sid spoke. He said something like...

'Mnnrrrgh. Nmm. Grumblegrumble. Mumblemumble.'
'What?'
'Hrrmph. Hrrmmmm. Huh!' Dismissively.
'What are you saying? Stop mumbling!'
'Huh. Hrrumph. That's not the way to do it.'
'Well I've done it now. Anyway, you're not supposed to say anything. All you're supposed to do is give me directions.'
'Hrrr. Huh!'

OK then. The rest of the test looked like it was going to be a barrel of laughs.

He took me to Cheadle, where a tricky right turn onto a dual carriageway was included. You were supposed to do it as a single manoeuvre, but the amount of traffic on the 'Kingsway' could have you sitting waiting for a week. John had told me to go halfway if there was no complete gap in the traffic after a long wait. In fairness, the centre reservation was so wide, at that point in the road, that almost the whole length of the vehicle could be accommodated. Sure enough, the scenario played out that way.

This provoked a grumbling expression of disapproval from Sid. By his standards, the growled comment was almost in the category of affable feedback.

'That's no way to do it, is it?'

'My instructor told me to do it like that if I'd been waiting a long time.'

'Huh. Hrrr. Grrrh.'

Eventually the purgatory of feedback collection was over, and we were back at Bredbury, where I handed the test form to John. The obvious junction misdemeanours were noted, along with several ticks under the 'making progress' section. Making progress meant getting on with it, up to the speed limit if possible. The lorry was a mid-range Bedford lacking in newness, and would prefer to make progress in its own good time, but what did I know? I didn't think I'd been especially dawdling.

A re-test followed, after some more training. The next examiner was more correct, without the disparaging soundtrack, just giving the directions. I didn't discern much humanity beneath the robotic façade, but it was nevertheless a relief after Sid. The one thing the tests had in common was that I didn't 'make progress'. I wasn't aware of much else wrong, but the result was the same. And the confession of failure, and the bitter rant for my friends' patient ears, in the pub, was the same.

Doug backed up John's feeling that my driving was of the same standard as other candidates. We discussed the 'making progress' issue. I was beginning to feel that it was a catch-all category, if they couldn't get you to drive over a kerb or get stuck in the middle of a junction. Doug thought it possible that the right 'impression' counted. The right demeanour.

Maybe the Yorkie-style lumberjack shirt wasn't enough. Maybe the longish hair and habitual louche, Byronic pose outweighed it, in a negative way. Maybe I had not exhibited enough gruffness when answering the questions about coupling the cab unit to the trailer.

I read one of my wife's chick-lit novels recently, for a break, and out of professional curiosity. There was a part in it where one of the protagonists drifted into drug abuse, and was held hostage by a drug dealer, who wore a 'dingy wifebeater'. What was this, some kind of style of jacket? Eventually, it dawned on me. It was a vest! What they used to call a singlet, or later, a tank-top. The kind of vest, once white but now grey, that was accompanied by tracky bottoms, beer drunk from a can, and a hapless stepchild sitting blankly in the corner of a threadbare room whilst the vest wearer stared at daytime TV.

That was it! Short hair and a wifebeater vest, with a growling but unshakeably confident attitude. Eliminate the slightest suggestion of cultural sophistication or tendency to read anything deeper than the Sun newspaper.

I never did try the experiment of course. The robot guy turned up for the third test and watched as I put the rear wheel just over a kerb in Stockport. I was by now completely demoralised. Not a sentence you see too often in autobiographical writing.

My rant in the pub was more of a sulk by now. I had formed the opinion that the whole set-up was a stress test, and that the antics of people like Sid were done to prod you, to test whether you could stand up to the rigours of strapping down your load and dealing with the odd puncture. I began to wonder whether I was indeed of the right stuff to be able to handle retiring with my girlie magazine to the confines of my sleeper cab on godforsaken industrial estates all over Europe.

After prevailing on the doctor to prescribe waiving the charge for a taxi-driving medical, which helped my glum mood, I was at least able to start work again. And later I asked John to get hold of a rigid truck, in order to at least get a Class Three licence out of the whole debacle. Of course, since he hired the truck, it didn't have the I AM A DETERMINED NONCONFORMIST sticker on the windscreen. Coincidentally, the examiner was a different guy who actually had a bit of general conversation with me and treated me like a human being.

Many years later, I became involved in driver training myself. Around this time, in the late nineties, there were a few changes to the format of driving tests. One of them was a sort of statutory requirement for the examiner to try his or her best to put the candidate at ease.

Hilarious.

I wonder what Sid would have thought?

Gordon

'Good job you've got Gordon with you,' said Gordon.

I glanced across at him, briefly, not wishing to take my eyes off the road. It wouldn't do to run over one of the various bricks and stones that were lying scattered in the carriageway.

I didn't need to glance at Gordon. It was just a sort of polite reflex. I already knew that he was a middle-aged man of about five foot three inches, with receding hair, and of average weight for his size. Not the type to inspire immediate caution in the mind of any ruffian we might encounter in the next few minutes. They probably wouldn't expect him to have a black belt in judo.

He reminded me about his black belt in judo. I nodded, focusing on keeping near the middle of the road. Most of the piles of broken glass, and most of the bricks, were nearer to the pavement.

'Yes, you'll be OK with Gordon here,' he said.

When I first met Gordon, he had been standing at the bottom of some steps which led up to the front door of a house, brandishing an umbrella. Memory is a little hazy after all these years, but I think the woman who lived in the house had thrown the umbrella down after him, thus enabling the brandishment to commence. For her part, she stood in the doorway, ranting, and cursing his uselessness.

The row was noisy, and unusual for Cheadle Hulme, normally a quiet middle class Manchester suburb. Nonetheless, it didn't feel like the kind of altercation that might escalate into violence at any second.

During a moment when they had both paused for breath, I ventured to interrupt.

'Gordon? You wanted a taxi?'

'Yes, but she's got my briefcase in there.'

'OK. Well, I'll be waiting in the car, mate.'

After a while, he came over, and left his umbrella with me in the car.

'Now. I won't be long. I just need this briefcase. You're with me, now, aren't you? You're working for me?'

'Well, I'm driving the taxi.' I felt it wise to imply that my remit did not include assistance in umbrella brandishment, or indeed any incursion into the domain of the harridan at the top of the steps.

Eventually the tirade from above waned sufficiently for him to get up to the front door again. I had the impression that a goodly portion of humble pie had been consumed during his ascent. He re-emerged holding a briefcase, insults once more rending the customary tranquillity of the Cheadle Hulme air behind him.

'Thank you. Don't worry. She'll calm down in a bit. You needn't say anything about this. I'm with Special Branch...'

'OK. Where to, then?'

I got to know Gordon a bit better during the trip, and by the time we got to Fallowfield he had painted a fuller picture, although I still wasn't sure if the woman who had thrown him out was a suspect in an international drug smuggling operation or merely a disappointed member of a tempestuous love triangle. What was clear was that Gordon was quite high up in the police, in an undercover role, and had previously been in the secret service. He attested to the painfulness of having one's fingernails removed under torture, behind the Iron Curtain, so it must have been true. I think they had grown back, mercifully.

Back at the office, Mo, the telephonist, asked me how it had gone with Gordon.

'Oh, alright. He was about four different people during the trip, though. Not so much a schizophrenic as a quadrophenic.' I knew that the study of schizophrenia encompassed more detail than the title of an album by The Who, but it was a decent soundbite. Not telling the latest driver about Gordon seemed to be some kind of initiation ritual. That and taking the nervous Mrs Jones from Bramhall to Altrincham. One chap had driven her all the way to Stockport in the wrong direction, waited for the Altrincham bus to set off from Stockport Square, and followed it all the way. No, he didn't last long.

Gordon was a regular customer, so we didn't mind picking him up from nearer Manchester, to return to the Cheadle area. He'd often been visiting one of his women friends, although I don't remember any more umbrella brandishing episodes. I knew the women only by repute. They tended to be feisty, capable types, high up in the police force in undercover roles, the kind of women who would have been a handful for most men, but not Gordon of course.

And I did feel safe driving south out of Manchester towards the Moss Side area that evening with Gordon, but it had less to do with his superpowers than the fact that we seemed to be somewhere on the edge of the rioting, rather than the epicentre. Perhaps they had just gone to take the looted items home, and to fetch more bricks.

We had strayed from Gordon World into Thatcher World. It was incredible, and surreal, to be driving through a modern, so-called civilised society, in the city where you had grown up, with it looking like a war zone. Disadvantaged people wandering about looking for the next rioting session to start.

We were guests at the beginning of an over forty-year-long experiment into exactly how much the great British public would tolerate. Even some of Thatcher's cohorts from her time in power were later prepared to admit that she didn't seem able to muster a thread of empathy for those who couldn't climb off the bottom rung of society by use of a bicycle. That's if you were prepared to conceptualise such a thing as society, which she famously didn't.

The Poll Tax did for her in the end, about nine years later. More rioting, bookending a reign of strife. It's still shocking all these years later, even after a summer of Black Lives Matter marches and a spot of statue toppling for embellishment. South Kesteven District Council recently pushed their luck by agreeing to underwrite the unveiling ceremony of a statue of the lady who wasn't for turning, to the tune of 100,000 pounds, in her home town of Grantham. Yes, that's the unveiling ceremony, not the actual statue, which seems to have been a fair bit more.

Will she be for toppling, if not turning? Who knows? They apparently put her ten feet up, to deter such vandalism, which doesn't show a lot of faith that she's loved by all. A 300,000 pound petrified idol, at a time when some members of the population are reliant on food banks. Staggering.

Maybe they'll get Gordon to infiltrate one of the likely statue-toppling groups. He must be still alive, like James Bond, about to enter his seventh incarnation. He could use his five foot three inch charms to seduce a 'Woke' young activist, start bringing up a family with her, under deep cover, until assigned to the next undercover operation, later to be prosecuted under an alias for use of false identity and wrecking somebody's life.

I could go back to the taxi driving, be his handler. Choose a persona based on the latest TV thriller, or, better still, one from the sixties. There would be plenty of spirited women on hand, just feisty enough to make the chase interesting, but willing to put up with a playful slap on the *derriere*, as Sean Connery or Roger Moore would have administered in the days before it was recognised to be an assault.

I can feel myself drifting into Gordon World, here. There's a danger of being trapped forever in a domain where women throw umbrellas at me from the top of some steps.

It would be better than Thatcher World, though.

Fucked by Vulcans at the Skill Centre

Do they still have Skill Centres? Big single storey buildings on industrial estates where young men learn to be electricians, plumbers, plasterers, welders, mechanics and bricklayers? Last night the news mentioned that some occupations of this sort of, shall we say, non-esoteric nature, needed recruits, and that immigrants would be considered to fill vacancies. If the immigrants felt that the land of Brexit was worth a punt, presumably.

So maybe they don't have Skill Centres. Or at least, not enough. Back in 1982, we were still pre-Big Bang at the Stock Exchange, and there was a presumption that basic skills, of making and decorating the physical structures in which daily life took place, had a value and a worthiness. That the people who could do them weren't just there to serve the whims of Porsche owners.

I'd been working for a local taxi company after the one I worked for earlier had folded. Bill couldn't offer a lot of regular shifts, but it was better than nothing. I was waiting to hear from two universities. Who knew what might happen?

I knew a bit about mending cars. Rudimentary mechanical stuff that I had picked up. I was running an old MG which had enough issues to provide learning experiences. I figured that if I could learn how to do bodywork, I could somehow be a more well-rounded moderate mechanic. The plan wasn't 100% foolproof but it motivated me enough to ask the Employment Exchange to send me to the Skill Centre course at Trafford Park. Automotive Bodywork.

Trafford Park is different from Old Trafford. Old Trafford was where a small proportion of skilled footballers became rich skilled footballers. Trafford Park housed a Skill Centre and a number of industrial premises where people earned an adequate living. Since those days, it now also has a gigantic shopping mall (with elements of Rococo style and Egyptian motifs) where people spend what's left over from their adequate living.

The bodywork course began with a week or two carrying out mundane tasks at the bench. Access to panel beating tools and actual paint was a world away. There was a requirement to file a piece of steel into a rectangular shape. It was a rite of passage and an opportunity for the instructor to stare over your shoulder from time to time whilst you wished he would go away. It also gave him the opportunity to conduct his own personal psychological assessment of the would-be craftsperson, to determine whether he or she (we were all 'he', though) would be fully accepted into the instructor's meticulously guarded fiefdom.

He was amused by my efforts, and seemed gratified that I had not achieved perfection. The piece of metal became smaller, somewhat on the lines of shortening a table leg, whereupon the other three become too long, you then shorten those three, one of them is too short, so you have to shorten three others; and so on.

After about a week, he deigned to offer some rudimentary advice. How to hold the file, whatever. There's not that much to it. The work wasn't terrible, but neither was it perfect.

'It's funny. You're obviously a clever lad. You would think someone like you would have the... nous, to get a better result.'

The best I could do in response was to consider how many millimetres I should raise my shoulders in a shrug. Too many might be seen as insolent, too few a sign of not caring. In truth I wasn't excessively devoted to the bit of metal. It was beginning to bore me somewhat.

The instructor had touched on a truth: that people possessed what we might now term, different skill sets. He was wrong, though, in suggesting that someone of above average intelligence should be able to demonstrate a more manual skill easily, as if it was a lesser accomplishment. Human cognition is more interesting than that.

In any case, he could barely disguise his glee that I had taken this long to pass muster. I began to wonder how I would fare when it came to rubbing down body filler, an activity that would offer an infinite continuum of microscopic degrees of smoothness with which he could find subjective fault.

The other lads on the course were alright. The usual mixture of Mancunian working class gruffness and jollity. I'd spent the previous few years working in small factories, packing and labouring when not driving the works van or lorry. Working with ordinary folk. A working life which happened to most people most of the time. They weren't academic hothouses, but they had their own little bits of wisdom and banter.

'Where are you going in the truck, today, Dave?'
'Hyde.'
'Where do the flies go in winter?'
'I don't know, Jim, where do they go?'
'Through Denton to Hyde.'

I still tell that to my wife when we go towards Stockport on the M60. It has got to the stage where she speaks before I do, when we see the Denton sign appear ahead.

'Time for your joke, Dave.'

There is a certain comfort in predictability.

Back in 1982, I was still looking for some surprises. Having no idea where my life was going had a certain frisson to it, without being unduly strenuous. I would drift through the world like an observer, day to day, unencumbered by the future, except for occasional random plans to try my luck at something different, like a university or a Skill Centre. Nowadays you look at people's Facebook profiles, and a lot of them have been to the 'University of Life'. I think it's quite a good uni., but how much study did they put in?

The more literate of the lads at the Skill Centre would study their copy of The Sun newspaper. This was the infamous period during which it proclaimed "Gotcha" after the General Belgrano was torpedoed during the Falklands War. The instructor entered into eager debate with some of his longer serving, favoured lads. Of course, the demise of any 'Argies' provoked a more light-hearted mood within the discussion.

'I heard that a Marine downed an Argie jet with one shot from his rifle.'

Yeah, right.

An actual war. Real people getting killed on both sides. Not quite on the same level as WW2, but it was Thatcher's chance to be Churchillian. Without the 'fighting them on the beaches' bit, though. Argentina was a little too far away to worry about that.

The expedition across the globe had included the bombing of Port Stanley airfield, to prevent its use by Argentine fast jets. An incredibly complex logistical exercise involving mid-air refuelling of Vulcan bombers from tanker aircraft. A spearhead of two Vulcans took off from Ascension Island on the final leg towards the target, but one had to pull back after a faulty seal meant it was impossible to pressurise the cabin effectively. The sole remaining plane dropped twenty-one bombs, one of which wrecked the end of the runway. Which was enough. A very fine line.

'What's the similarity between Mr Spock's wife and Port Stanley airfield?'

'They've both been fucked by Vulcans.'

I quite liked that one. Nobody was killed in it and Argies weren't mentioned.

The Vulcan, a Cold War bomber, was virtually obsolete. The tale is laughingly told, of a vital component languishing in the Officers' Mess, performing the function of an ashtray. Without it, one of the planes would have been unable to fly.

The technology can be looked at as a development of WW2 era stuff, the cockpit more reminiscent of a Lancaster than anything modern or digitised. It's an awe-inspiring aircraft, huge and menacing. Looming out of a distant past, even viewed from 1982.

The achievement of getting even one Vulcan jet to the Falklands cannot but be admired, but the whole thing is also rather sad. It was like sending a capsule to the Moon in the late sixties. Men in a cockpit at the end of a thin gossamer spider thread of cleverness and calculation, depending on the fragile connection to eventually bring them home. Perilous journeys at moments in history when they seemed to have a purpose, yet now look almost like propaganda exercises. Were they like the Dambuster raids, which have been said to have had more value in boosting home morale, compared to the physical damage done to enemy installations?

If you argue that the Falklands War might have been lost if that airfield had not been rendered unusable (to fast jets at least; transport planes were still able to use it after the Argentines effected some repairs), then where would that have left the Thatcher government? Many more British lives lost, a retreat with tail between legs... Not very good planning and preparation, to have to rely on a less than 5% chance of a bomb landing where it was supposed to. From a highly skilled crew in an obsolete aircraft. Naturally, there is more to the full tale, and some other missions were later launched, using Vulcans. Here, though, we are able to argue from the actual result, and the version of it which has been encouraged to pass into legend.

Of course, everyone was relieved when the Norland ferry, converted to troop carrier, docked on its return, and brave lads were able to hug their families once more. The wartime spirit was called upon, filling each broadcast with joy and triumph.

Guess what? It's still called upon, when convenient. Not overtly, but the Farages and the Rees-Moggs didn't mind one bit, when a tragically ignorant pensioner broke down in tears on the TV in 2016, as he sobbed that, after the Brexit vote, we were 'free at last'.

I survived the discussions about the Falklands War by saying very little. I suppose I like to think that I would go down fighting if we did end up with a fascist dictatorship, but the cost/benefit equation around discussing peacenik viewpoints with a few average lads who could be bothered, and an instructor who was mainly concerned with whether a Rover 2600 or a Ford Granada was better for pulling his caravan, looked like a lose-lose option to me.

I think it was in the second week, that the caravan owner had me practising with the spray gun in the area set aside for painting. I wasn't allowed paint though. Just water. Whilst I practised my technique. The technique is simple in principle. The spray gun needs to be kept at a constant distance from the panel as you move along. That's it. Don't stand in one place moving your arm in an arc, or the result will be different at the far ends of the arc. Simple. And fair enough to practise the technique with water. But not for most of the day, surely? You will only get feedback from your efforts if you use actual paint on an actual panel.

One or two of the more thoughtful lads would pass by on their errands.

'What's he got you doing that for?'

'He said just to practise the technique.'

'Fucking hell.'

I think it was into the afternoon before I was released, and he found me something else to do. I maintained affability, but inwardly thought of it as Sisyphean bollocks.

In the end, I got to sit down in the office with him. Well, I might have been allowed to sit down. I can't remember.

Here we go.

'This isn't for you, is it?'

'If you say so.'

What he meant was, I wasn't for him. He had categorised me as 'clever', which, in his world, qualified as a threat.

I've met one or two people like this, over the years. Is it a British disease, I wonder? Probably not, exclusively. Probably more common amongst insecure people who have worked their way up to caravan ownership and view their undoubted skill as something to be jealously guarded, rather than shared. Maybe British after all then? But not exclusively, as I say. That would be forgetting the countless generals and dictators in banana republics. Leaving out the skill bit, unless you count low cunning as a skill. Oh, and there's Stalin, of course...

The good thing about my demise from Car Bodywork was that I would now get to choose what trade I would like to do instead. I was allowed to tour the Skill Centre, explaining, to the instructor in charge of each section visited, that I had been given the bum's rush from Car Bodywork

I soon received affirmation that I wasn't necessarily completely useless at filing a bit of metal.

'Another one from Car Bodywork, eh? Not unusual. This is what we do here...'

I started by ruling out Plastering. I knew I hadn't got the reserves of Zen patience to ever make a plasterer. The instructor who ran the Plastering section was an ebullient character whose off-duty hobby was hot air ballooning. His balloon canopy was black with a white skull and crossbones. Once he had to bring it down during a trip and selected the large yard of a brewery as being the best place to land. Climbing out, he greeted the manager who marched towards him, by singing the refrain from a TV beer advert of the day.

'Ah've cum from miles an' miles away, all to sup your beer...'

They weren't impressed.

Anyway. Plastering. No. Same for Bricklaying. They probably both appealed to people who had enjoyed making mud pies as kids. But with the addition of skill. That's where my interest waned.

Carpentry was the same. I knew my efforts during the rare woodwork classes at school had been poor, because my mother still had the ropey tea pot stand I had constructed, on her kitchen table, as a proud reminder. So 'no', to Carpentry.

In the end, rejecting Draughtsmanship, which I would have been allowed to do, after demonstrating brain power during a short interview, I narrowed it down to Welding, or Plating. Plating is also known as boilermaking in part, in other words, making shapes from metal plate, bending and welding them. So I would get to do welding within Plating, rather than just welding in Welding. Potentially more interesting. In fact, I've still got the notes somewhere in the garage, in case I ever feel the need to manufacture a metal cone.

Jack Buffey ran the Plating course. We got along fine. He had run his own company erecting buildings with steel frameworks, and had none of the insecurity that characterised the Car Bodywork guy. I got the impression that he didn't need the job, but enjoyed imparting his knowledge to another generation, rather than sitting around at home all day. A genuine man who was easy to respect.

We learnt how to draw patterns for the gusset plates that form the junction with the steel joists that make up the skeletons of the giant sheds which are now seen all over the modern landscape. They don't have a great line in imposing magnificence but are pretty good at functionality and almost total lack of adornment. Hard to argue with, even if Fred Dibnah probably wouldn't have been impressed.

One day we had to do a 'height test', which involved climbing a ladder to a tall platform outside the building. Jack said I needn't bother with it, sensing that I wouldn't be keen. Nevertheless I gritted my teeth and went up, just to say that I'd done it. In no circumstances would construction work far from terra firma be part of my future, though.

Eventually, I got the news that I could take up a place at the University of Hull, so it would be a question of treading water for the summer. Since being at the Skill Centre was equivalent to being on benefits, it would probably be easier, bureaucratically, to stay on a while longer, rather than leaving and having to find a temporary job, or, more likely, re-sign on the dole.

I told Jack about the situation, even though I probably would have kept shtum if I'd still been with the Car Bodywork guy. Jack was pleased for me, and had no issues with me wanting to stay on for a few more weeks. We didn't let on to any of the lads, and he found me a few different things to do.

One of these was gas welding. I don't know if it was on the Car Bodywork syllabus, but I was doing it now. Ha ha. I found it completely absorbing. Here at last was the Zen task that put me at one with the universe, or, specifically, a small pool of molten metal moving from one side of my field of vision towards the other.

The younger lads noticed my preoccupation, and asked me if I would help modify the exhausts on their two-stroke motorcycles. The thing to have was a silencer which consisted of a cylindrical body, cone shape at each end, and from the rear cone, a small tube like a glorified peashooter. This was supposed to encourage the gases through faster, on the lines of a venturi. It probably enabled them to annoy the neighbours on their housing estates more effectively, whatever the tuning benefits.

I would draw the shapes, they would cut and roll them, and then I would practise my welding assembling them, manufacturing a real-life useful artefact at the same time. Then they would fit them to their bikes during the lunch hour and ride along the concrete area outside the building, past the height tower, over and over again. I emphasised to them that they shouldn't test, in an empirical spirit, the very small addition to the very small amount of original horsepower. So they were probably only conducting empirical research into the amount of loudness and the amount of annoyance capability that their bikes now had, as they buzzed to and fro, to and fro, past the open back door of the workshop. Until someone would come out of the welding workshop next door and shout at them, concluding testing for the day. I remember it fondly.

The other thing I learnt at the Skill Centre was how to move an item of large machinery around a tight corner using a gang of helpers. We were called upon to help move the old guillotine from the Plating section to the Welding section next door. A useful diversion from watching a pool of molten metal move along a join, however virtuous the Zen benefits.

I knew some of the principles, from being involved in moving lathes at the engineering company where I had worked. In principle, the machine is jacked up enough to slide stout lengths of round steel bar underneath it. It is then moved across the factory floor using muscle power and lengthy crowbars, or, if you want to be more sophisticated, a winch and cables, anchored to a part of the ancient building which would not part company with the rest of the ancient building. At Smiths Engineering, the winch was a long silver box holding some mysterious pulleys within, and a cable coming out of each end. It was tapered, suggesting the usage of a larger and a smaller pulley wheel, and it had a protruding lever over which could be slotted a longer tube, to operate the ratchet mechanism.

It was known as the Turfer, as used in the phrase, 'Get the Turfer'. As I fetched it one day, I glanced down and saw that its maker had provided a nameplate. TIRFOR. Presumably a trademark. One day in the future, whilst idly meditating, I realised the coincidence. Aha. TIRFOR – Turfer. Amazing. Had a winch always been known as a Turfer around Stockport, as in the phrase, 'Just turf the bloody thing out', with the makers capitalising on this colloquialism in a canny coinage? Or had the company merely been oddly named, or come up with a six-letter acronym, its details lost in the mists of time? With somebody at Smiths, or a similar company in the tightly-knit heavy engineering fraternity, then picking up the device and declaring, 'Here's the Turfer', to a foreman who was about to move a lathe?

Chicken or egg? I spend chunks of time pondering things like this, which is probably why I was a labourer and driver for an engineering company, rather than an accountant or manager for an engineering company.

Moving the guillotine followed the same pattern as at Smiths, except that Smiths used to be more efficient. There were about six of us clustered around to provide pushing power (Indians) and two or three instructors (Chiefs) to supervise actions. Forgive the colloquialism. This rose to four or five Chiefs once the machine had exited the Plating workshop. Jack was wise enough to quietly bow out of proceedings once the thing had moved beyond the threshold of his domain.

The entrance to the welding shop was awkward. We had come along an aisle that was bordered by the workshops on one side, and a collection of lathes for the 'Turning' course on the other, in the big open area in the middle of the building. About the size of a couple of Five-a-side pitches, end to end.

Manoeuvring into the Welding workshop proved to be impossible. Very nearly possible, but not quite. The senior Chief issued many instructions, but nothing quite worked. We always needed about three inches more, of space instead of a wall.

The guillotine, in plan view, was like a letter 'E' with the centre bar missing. Getting round with the back of the 'vertical bar' part near to the 90 degree wall at the welding shop entrance had proved impossible. They even came back, went past the far corner of the welding shop entrance, and tried to turn in from there. Same problem.

There was a wide aisle between the two '5-a-side' areas where the lathes were. At a suitable moment, when enough Chiefs had paused for head scratching, so that I could be heard, I made a suggestion.

'If you come out again, go along to the wide bit between the lathes, and use that to turn it right round, you can come back along, you can turn it in with the side with the arms on facing the corner, and it will probably go round easier.'

There was a very brief pause, for thought.

'That'll never work,' said the chief Chief.

We messed around for about three quarters of an hour. To and fro. To and fro. It was fairly evident that none of it would work, because they were still using the principles which had failed.

Eventually the chief Chief decided to use my suggestion, and off we went along the aisle. It wasn't too far, and soon we were back at the entrance with the machine the other way round. Of course it was all the chief Chief's idea now, because enough time had passed since I had spoken.

The guillotine went round the corner without problems. I must admit I was pretty gratified. Thank goodness the chief Chief's idea had worked before the end of the working day.

I went off to university feeling that the psychology course might be a pleasant interlude, a bit easier. If I were to accidentally appear to be clever, maybe nobody there would be too bothered.

Life of Crime

Experiencing Hull in the early eighties was akin to being adrift in a mythical kingdom, a looking glass world where things didn't happen in quite the normal way. My status as a mature student with a reasonable grant, on which I could survive, probably had something to do with this. Without having to earn a crust, I could appreciate the slow rhythm of the place at leisure. My world view was coloured by coming from a job as a night shift taxi driver, where my televised cultural input consisted of afternoon programmes such as *Camberwick Green, Trumpton* and *Cloppa Castle* (work of genius), as I gradually worked my way from waking up to full consciousness, preparing to go to work when most people were coming home.

The chronicler of the new domain was the stalwart Hull Daily Mail, its finger firmly on the parochial pulse. Amid the gritty realism of shoplifting and benefit fraud, there was a regular section devoted to the unsettling crimes perpetrated by a would-be super villain who inhabited the low-lying Badlands outside the city. Like Piltdown Man, he had probably been found in a peat bog on the area of the map which featured nothing, absolutely nothing, except blank whiteness, labelled 'Thorne Waste'.

Now, raised from slumber, his mud caked, superpowered form would shamble menacingly at night around the hinterlands, terrorising or at least worrying the normal citizens.

Goole Man Accused of Theft. Goole Man Charged with Arson. Goole Man Held After Night Club Incident. How they held him was unclear, with his peat encrusted body being so slithery. Goole Man Released. Shocking.

In Hull itself, the villains seemed less likely to slip through the fingers of law enforcement, if reports were to be believed. This was until the front page spread highlighting an armed robbery at a bank. The bank was on Hessle Road I think, where the trawler fishing communities used to live, lots of parallel streets with terraced housing.

The perpetrator had entered the bank, drawn a pistol, and demanded cash. He was dressed in a boiler suit, rather than the standard uniform of leather jacket and stocking over the head. He had brought a bag with him, probably a plastic bag from a supermarket. What I used to call a 'Hull briefcase'. It wasn't big enough to hold all the money, and the bank staff had to help him by finding a sturdy bin liner from the back room.

He then escaped on a push bike, 'down the tenfoot'. This was my first encounter with the term 'tenfoot'. It referred to the alleyways behind and between the rows of terraced houses. Ten feet wide, naturally. He pedalled away down the tenfoot and was not seen again.

The front page of the Hull Daily Mail that evening featured a photo of a policeman mounted on a horse, looking forlornly into the distance. Presumably waiting for the other riders in the posse to join him. It was like the Lone Ranger, except that the horse stood on an urban wasteland where terraced homes had earlier been razed to oblivion, rather than a picturesque boulder-strewn canyon somewhere above Los Angeles.

A number of years later a man, who lived alone with his mother in a council house in East Hull, was arrested after going out one day to buy a Maserati with cash. My theory is that it was the same guy. Fancy getting away with it for so long before cracking. You're not allowed to have a Maserati, living in a council house in East Hull. It doesn't compute, it's like a crack in the universe which has to be sealed.

Maybe the guy was only blessed with deft bank robbing skills. A narrow skill set that couldn't be easily translated to more mainstream endeavours. So sad. If you can't do time, don't do crime, they say. Or at least don't go out with a bagful of cash to buy a Maserati.

Another who wound up with a bagful of cash was one of the taxi drivers I later worked with. His mate had worked out that an office bloke from an industrial company used the same route at the same time every Friday, returning on foot from the bank with the wages. My colleague was enrolled, and they waylaid the unimaginative clerk, with the briefcase duly changing hands. A proper briefcase rather than a plastic bag. The prising tool was the threat of a cosh rather than a replica pistol, but the effect was the same.

A couple of days went by, and they seemed to have got away with it. Then Steve (let's call him) got home from a taxi shift, and his wife told him that the police had been round looking for him. The game seemed to be up. He contacted his mate, and they decided to spend the money before eventually facing the music. Decamping to London, they got through several thousands of pounds on a hotel, casinos, booze and women.

When they got back, unburdened now by wealth, Steve asked his wife if the police had been round again.

'Yeah. It's only about a parking fine though.'

At least they hadn't gone to the Maserati dealer.

The Prophet

Some people think the public road in front of their house is territory to be defended. Our next door neighbour was like that. Had to park his car in front of the house at all costs, and went bananas if I parked mine there. The principle of road tax cuts no ice with such folk.

When I did park in front of my own house, he used to use my car as a buffer in the struggle to squeeze into his sacred spot, even though there were usually three empty spaces a few yards away along the terraced street. I didn't really care too much when I had the Vauxhall, as the bumper was the same height as the one on his Morris. All my cars are well into their life story when they fall into my hands. Later, though, I had a small Austin, semi-classic though hardly pristine, with chrome over-riders, so-called, on the bumpers.

When the neighbour was parking one evening, I heard the familiar rev, rev, bump sequence for longer than usual, and asked my housemate if I might look out through her front bedroom window to see what he was up to. When he got the Morris bumper stuck under the Austin's, and pulled forward, tugging the over-rider off with a loud clang as it dropped on to the road, I exclaimed in triumph.

'Right. Got him red-handed.'

I marched to the front door. My housemate was probably thinking that I was as bad as the next door neighbour, and that she could happily do without a territorial skirmish while she tried to do her exam revision. On the other hand, it was a break from the books, and she would have a good view of the mini-drama.

We had a good yelling match, running out of steam and oaths around the time his wife came out of the house to join in.

'He's got angina. Leave him alone. He's got angina.'

I supposed it was more likely for somebody to develop heart issues if their insecurities were triggered by so petty an issue as a parking space. After that I left the car out of his way, even though I was the innocent party. It wasn't worth the aggro.

Also, I knew he had a gun, and sometimes you never can tell. I reasoned that a quiet life is preferable to an reckless death, although there may be examples in the field of human conflict where the principle breaks down. But not for about fifteen square yards of tarmac. I was thinking more of a heroic stand against the forces of totalitarianism. That sort of thing.

I smoothed the waters a bit. He wasn't too bad in some ways. In fact, after a while, he kept inviting me in to look at his prophecy charts, when he realised that I was doing a psychology course. Psychology is OK, but it's 'man's knowledge', you know. That was his angle. What chance did it have against prophecy?

On the other hand, I wasn't desperate to know what would provoke World War Three, or how the Russians would lay waste to the Lebanon in precisely nine and a half years' time. That would work out to somewhere around 1993 if you want to check out what they did or didn't do; I can't remember. Maybe the chart meant Syria and got the date wrong.

No, I preferred, and still prefer, to maintain at least a smidgeon of hope regarding humanity's survival. Despite the ever lengthening odds.

And I'm not interested in a ticket to the Last Judgement, whatever happens. They're probably even harder to get than ones for the Olympics or a Little Mix concert, even if I was bothered.

I passed the time, then, when I saw the prophet, by talking about earthly things like Cortina camshafts. Anything for a quiet life. I never told my housemate about his gun. She was a little bit wound-up in those days, taking her exams seriously, so I figured there was no need to stretch her nerves any further.

I needn't have worried though. She found out herself in the end when she went outside to the back yard and found him in full-on *Starsky and Hutch* pose, wide-stanced, arms forming a V with the gun in both hands directly in front of him, taking pot shots at her cat. She gave him a right mouthful of telling off, which reduced him to sheepish embarrassment. Not much you can say as a rejoinder when you've been caught *in flagrante Starsky and Hutch* fantasy.

He probably went back inside to peruse his charts, and plan to avoid infernal cats and their mistresses in future.

Takes all sorts to make a world, let alone prophesy what's going to happen in it.

BENEFIT FRAUD WHEN INNOCENT

My housemate was, at one point in her life, a compulsive list-maker. There were lists scattered all around the house. Most of them seemed to say similar things, but I didn't want to pry. I could just see at a casual glance, that they didn't involve complex plans for world domination. More like item 5. cauliflower. That sort of thing.

I suppose there is a crossover point where someone might spend more time making compulsive lists than actually doing the things on the lists. I didn't think she was at that point, although she was feeling a lot of stress. So I didn't make a thing of it. One day I wrote a list of four things on the back of a used envelope, and asked her if she wanted anything from town whilst I was there.

She asked to look at the list, out of curiosity.

'You've not put down that you're going to the bank. It should be five things.'

'Going to the bank is the main reason that I'm going to town. These four are extra things that I don't want to forget whilst I'm in town.'

'You'll never make a compulsive list-maker.'

There wasn't much in the bank, in those days. I had been doing a few car repairs and small-time deals to get by, watching the reserves dwindle. After seven weeks of waiting, I finally got a giro cheque. This was in the late eighties. I've just been reading that Universal Credit, the current system, requires people to wait "at least five weeks to receive any money, sometimes far longer." I don't know what that says about the politics, apart from the fact that unemployment is rarely high on most people's lists of desirable options, in any era. Not long before, I'd finished a university course. They had a careers office, implying that young students would want some sort of progression in their life. Nowhere did they list 'skid row on a giro' as an area to consider.

I had some experience of the benefit system, from when I lived in Nottingham a few years earlier. That was the seventies. It wasn't that unusual to be sitting in the cubicle for your interview, to find it interrupted by a fracas in the adjacent cubicle. They were only separated by a wooden panel. Bang! The sound of a fist on the desk would be followed by a rant from the claimant, and occasionally further commotion leading to the light fitting above the cubicle swinging wildly as the claimant exited the premises under his or her own power, unrewarded.

A friend of mine worked within the system, apportioning the state's largesse to those who had fallen on hard times or merely grown up in them. In his office, there worked a legendary clerk, who wore pebble-lensed spectacles, such was his short sight. He was in the habit of bending forward to within three inches of the desk, to complete his paperwork. One day, he bent forward as usual, just before an axe flew through the air exactly where his head had been two seconds earlier. It embedded itself in the wooden panel behind the cubicles, as he carried on working.

Despite these interludes, my experience had been generally positive. In exchange for being scrutinised, you generally got a giro before too long. Not a bad trade off, and the wait sometimes had its share of drama, as I've said. So, comparatively, seven weeks was poor, even for the Thatcherite eighties. I would hate to imply, though, that the later Universal Credit fiasco led to an improvement in service.

I set off to collect my benefit by cashing my giro at the post office. I don't know whether that happens now. They would probably like to implant every claimant with a computer chip and make the transaction cashless. The technology, I'm told, is just around the corner. The guy in the post office, in the eighties, told me that the giro wasn't cashable there. Despite me specifying that office for payment. I boiled up and raised my fist up, and slammed it down on the counter, which was the nearest inanimate object. I noticed a woman at the next counter looking at me as if this was a bit unusual.

Hitting the desk calmed me down, and then the clerk explained that I could pay the giro into a bank. I thought this to be a good idea, and thanked him. Problem solved. At this time I had one pound and ten pence left in the bank. What had wound me up was the prospect of having to chase round half the post offices in the area to find out where the giro *was* cashable. They would put a number on the giro which corresponded to the correct post office. Security reasons in case you got your giro pinched.

Except they would get it wrong sometimes. Like this time. Or putting the code of a post office that no longer existed. That had happened before. Once, I went to cash a giro for my list-making housemate, when she was laid up with illness. She couldn't remember where she'd specified to cash it, so I tried three post offices at the university end of town, starting with the one that had refused me this time. At the second one, I asked if they knew which office the number corresponded to. No way. They only knew their own number. Security reasons. It was at this point that I began to feel somewhat felonious.

I persevered, to Newland post office, which wasn't on Newland Avenue where one might expect to find it, but somewhere else. The natural quota of surrealism in the ether of Hull was beginning to seep into my day. No joy there, anyway. Running out of ideas, I ended up at the dole office itself, and asked them. They couldn't possibly divulge such information, even though my housemate had signed the giro authorising me to cash it. I exited the premises under my own power, growling, gnashing my teeth, and generally giving the impression that I was about to have some sort of a fit involving the destruction of a wooden panel if one presented itself in my path. I was followed out by a character who'd clocked the commotion.

'Hey mate, do you want to know where to cash that giro?'
'Well, yes. I could do with a break.'
He looked at it.
'They put numbers on which say which post office it is.'
'Yes, I know.'
Pause.
'It could be Beverley Road, maybe.'

Which was nowhere near the university or where we used to live last time we had giros. The guy just wanted to sound clever. He had nothing better to do. Somehow I'd expected him to have a mental list of every post office in town, I don't know why.

I had another idea, and went to a post office near the old house. I explained that I thought the giro might have the number of the post office near our old house which had since been demolished. The post office that is. We weren't quite that downmarket.

The guy behind the counter grunted and cashed it. Which was quite a relief, as I was beginning to anticipate a 'felt collar' at one of the next few post offices I tried. I could've explained it all, officer. Not like the claimant in Manchester who got a giro for his electricity bill, payable directly to NORWEB (North West Electricity Board). He signed it N. Orweb and waited patiently whilst the clerk went into the back room and phoned the police. You would think that someone with the nerve and creative brain to sign a giro N. Orweb, would have sussed that something was awry when the clerk didn't cash it straightaway. Apparently not, as Mr Orweb was still there when the law turned up.

I got the envelope out of my pocket, looked at the compulsive list, and crossed out item 3. Steal a giro.

CATCH 22

After I got the Class Three licence, one of the UK's periodic recessions took hold, and there weren't many truck driving jobs available, whatever class of licence or girlie mag you held.

The few that were advertised insisted that previous experience was required. So how could you get the previous experience if you didn't already have it? It was around this period, early days of Thatcherism, that I had a go at a computer test. There were openings in programming, and I was sure it would make a steady and more profitable career than taxi driving, even though I didn't mind the taxi driving too much.

The test, which I found to be easy enough, got me to an interview in Liverpool. Serious stuff. An actual journey to another town.

'You haven't worked in an office before.'

'But I want to work in an office now. I can get along with all types of people. You have to be able to get along with people when you're driving a taxi.'

'But you've not worked in an office. We don't know whether you could work in an office because you haven't worked in an office.'

'Well, I want to work in an office.'

It was like an endless loop, a chain of unreason leading always back to the pre-existing starting point, that they were always looking for ways to whittle down the candidates to whatever their target was.

I can't remember, in this case, whether there was a CV involved, or whether I was there solely through passing the test. If it was just the test, and I proved not to be a Martian upon actual acquaintance, why couldn't I do the job?

I found more of the same thing later on, after spending four years studying at university. Once more setting foot on the Escher-esque spiral staircase of pre-conceived attitudes, always coming back to the same thing.

'You haven't worked in an office.'

'But I want to work in an office now.'

'You've had solitary occupations.'

'Well, driving a vehicle can be a bit like that, by the nature of it. But I want to work in an office now. I can get along with anybody.'

'Hmm. You've always had solitary occupations, you see.'

Yes, I see. And you should see also mate, because IT'S ON THE FUCKING CV. Why the FUCK have you got me here for this interview when you've convinced yourself before we start that it's not going to happen? Did you think perhaps that I had Henry Kissinger along as co-driver on the international summit truck driving trips, or attended management guru seminars whilst waiting for my taxi customers at the conference centre? More likely it might be a licensed victualler shindig watching naked women fuck each other with a dildo on stage, waiting for it to finish so that I could take the punter to north Manchester. That, yes.

One of the best ones, best as in surreal, was the interview to be a manager in a biscuit company. My first interview during the last year at uni., part of the so-called 'milk round', the milk-supping cast presumably being the young graduates wishing to suck from the metaphorical teats of

British and multinational industry. After several years of studying psychology, I felt somewhat psychologically satiated, so to speak, and was looking at some less specialised jobs, sorry, career paths.

'What would you do if the production line broke down?'

'How many production lines are there?'

'Two.'

'OK. Well, maybe send the production down the one that was working whilst the other one got repaired.'

That was it really. I have no other recollection. Sometimes I felt like Meursault in *L'Etranger* (Camus, 1942), drifting like a hedonist, detached from normal humanity. If I got a reasonably paid job, I could maybe get a house, a girl, an easier life than scratching about patching up old cars to sell. Then walk along the sand like Meursault, enjoying the sun but not killing an Arab. Was that actually too much to ask? Too ambitious a plan?

Or was it not enough of a plan? You were expected, I think, to offer some notion of a career path, show an interest in the intricacies of biscuits, however false.

The interviews were a way for them to see what you were made of, the cut of your proverbial jib. Inherently ageist, given the circumstances, they also had antennae acutely tuned to the possible presence of an I AM A DETERMINED NONCONFORMIST sticker on your forehead, despite averring their dedication to the pursuit of fresh and ground-breaking new ideas.

One of them came up with something a bit more original.

'You're a psychologist. How would you use your psychology to deal with the unions?'

You're not really a psychologist until you work as a psychologist, I would say, but the question was a good effort on his part, so I didn't argue the point too much.

Use my psychology, though? Good grief, I had spent four years picking holes in it. I was hardly a card-carrying believer, though I saw some merits in the scientific viewpoint.

I think he meant, how would you use your psychology to trick, deceive and get the better of the unions, from his tone. Not 'reach out to them', as we might say nowadays if we were American.

An awkward one, given that we had been to lend moral support on the miners' picket lines not too long before. Four of us in the car, two men two women, out in the car to West Yorkshire in the dark early hours, telling lies to the police about where we were going, when they pulled us up on the motorway for no vehicle-related reason.

Perhaps that interview was my chance to hoist my inner psychopath to the fore, and show how I was willing to use any means, foul or foul, to further my own, and by extension the company's, aims. But I was ill-prepared for the question, I confess, and I do not recall what I said, or even what company was interviewing me. And it would be another forty-four years until I read Jon Ronson's *The Psychopath Test* (Ronson, 2011), which was, although fascinating, a little late to help.

All in all, I wasn't too good at management-speak. The jargon and bullshit. Thinking that the public sector might offer a bit more reason and open-mindedness, I applied to the Prison Service. Assistant Governor alias office junior. A three-day interview at Wakefield jail! This would be a one-off effort, all or nothing. No way would I go through such a thing twice.

Gary from the psychology course was amused.

'So, Dave, if I end up in jail, you're going to beat me up?'

'No, Gary, I would be telling somebody else to beat you up.'

You can see from this that I was willing to abandon all my principles in order to advance. Sell my soul for a few years, save up some decent money, start some sort of business.

In actual fact, at that point in evolution, the devil wasn't paying anything for souls. He might, in those days of rampant monetarism, say that he was prepared to take your soul off you if you paid him to do it. A bit like cheap steel killing the scrap market.

In reality, I was probably under a misconception anyway. It may well be the case that the only deals available are a once-only option. In other words, selling your soul 'for a few years' might not be on the table. No leasing plan, full ownership only. It doesn't sound too flexible.

I pondered these things as I stood in an assembly hall at the prison. It was nearing the middle of the third day, and we were about to be finally released back into the outside world. The group of about thirty candidates was instructed to queue up for expenses cheques. As the others milled around, I thought I might as well nip to the toilet, to be ready to set off straightaway at the end. I returned and joined the back of the orderly line.

One by one they trooped to the stage, where a severe looking middle-aged woman examined the claims and signed the cheques. My petrol claim from Hull was meagre compared to the journeys of most of the others, who had come from all over the kingdom to vie for this rare prize.

Finally I climbed the steps and crossed to the desk for my pittance. The woman looked at me without an iota of interest or any effort to smile whatsoever.

'You're last,' she said, releasing me to my future life. It was as if the entire pantomime of tests, interviews and written work was just a charade, and the candidates had in fact merely been chosen according to the subtle pecking order demonstrated by their queueing aptitude, in this last, secret, test. Thirtieth of thirty, I was not the slick motorist, ready for off, not needing to stop on the way, but rather the runt of the litter who had shown no interest at all in wanting to elbow the competition.

Well, that was how she made me feel, anyway. Maybe her smiling muscles had just worn out.

Back in Hull, I fell into conversation with a friend one evening in the Students Union building. She had been one of the crew when we had travelled to the miners' picket lines. Also a seeker of employment, she had been trying to get something in the field of social work. She felt she came from the same category as the people she would be helping, after seeing a lecturer chalk a diagram of social strata on the blackboard. Whereas most of the other students and lecturers were from middle class backgrounds. And she was unable to get on with people she used to work with, who thought that social workers were middle class by definition.

Caught between two worlds and uncomfortable in both, she thought that her presence at university, one of the relatively few from the working class, according to that blackboard, was the excuse that the system was working OK. It seemed strange to me, that someone should feel so deeply about the psychological shackles of the British class system, but then I hadn't been raised in the back streets of Rotherham, had I? Of course it suits the ruling establishment just fine, that bright people from the bottom rung find it hard to muster the confidence to climb off it.

Predictably, I wouldn't have the choice whether to sell my soul regarding the prison job. I did have the choice not to apply to the Prison Service ever again, though, and took it. My professor opined that the Probation Service might offer a more 'optimistic' environment. A reasonable thought.

So reasonable that I filled out forms for that career route for three years running. A psychology degree and experience of life. That ought to do, surely? It seems, looking back, that they wanted aspirants to do voluntary work, and I became more preoccupied with scraping a living, as the university days faded gradually behind me.

The social workers I met appeared to be a hand-wringing lot on the whole, saying things like 'we need to try and change things politically'; whereas my preferred option in those days would have been to see Maggie Thatcher herded through Barnsley on the end of an electric cattle prod. Perhaps a bit radical for some tastes.

I once saw a social worker execute a genuine miracle. This was Gareth, who had done the same Sociology and Politics course as my friend Bob, and gone on to work for the local social services. He was a wiry, slightly gangly chap, down to earth and easy going. The latter a good quality in a social worker, I would think.

We were in East Hull. God knows why, we never went to East Hull. I think we had been to a party. Gareth came out of a fish and chip shop holding a very large portion of chips in a paper bag, with a giant haddock perched precariously on top. As we chatted, the haddock slid off the chips and commenced its plummet towards the mucky and gum-trodden pavement of Holderness Road. Barely pausing in his conversation, Gareth dipped his body down, extending his right hand. With the chips still balanced in his left palm, the haddock was intercepted in his right, within about six inches of the ground. Miraculously, the long fish stayed intact. Neither front nor rear end of it broke away as Gareth calmly returned it to its designated spot atop the chip mountain.

Gareth wasn't a sporty type, but if Ian Botham had executed the catch, it would have been re-run on video for evermore. Clearly, he had drawn on a higher power.

This was the power of 'ravenous ordinary human being accessing cat-like reflexes due to not wanting to lose haddock'. Had he paused to think for even a nanosecond, the haddock would have reached the ground. Even then, it had been the closest-run thing imaginable. Gareth seemed to suddenly realise the astounding nature of his feat, before briefly smiling in a self-effacing way and resuming the conversation.

So, the moral of this little tale is, don't over-think things. Probably a lot of social workers over-think things, and become weary as a result. Gareth hadn't done so, and as a result cemented his status as a truly admirable fellow.

By the time of my third application to do a social work course for a year in order to work for the Probation Service in order to earn a decent wage in order to afford to sit back and have time and luxury to choose what I really wanted to do with my life, it had become a sort of bloody-minded routine. I wasn't prepared to spend unpaid time doing voluntary work when it might make no difference to my chances anyway.

The thought of sitting with social worker types (not Gareth) on a semi-academic course, as a means to an end, didn't appeal a lot, in truth. The black humour joke of the time, in the wake of the Cleveland 'child abuse' scandal, was: What's the difference between a rottweiler and a social worker? You can get your kids back off the rottweiler.

Probably expressing the opinion that Dr Marietta Higgs was 'obviously out to lunch' didn't help my chances at an interview for a job at a bail hostel, either.

I had actually done a bit of voluntary work whilst on my university course. The Student Union ran a group called the 'Pooh Bear Reading Society', or something of similar wording.

Its purpose was to send undergraduates out to local schools to help individual pupils who were struggling with their reading. I enjoyed it, and spent an hour or two each week at a nearby school.

I was assigned two pupils. A shy girl whose name I don't recall, and Darren, a more confident lad. They were about eight years old, plus or minus two years. I've never been great at children's ages.

The girl had a certain cleverness about her, deep down. If she couldn't read a word, she would sometimes conjure another word to replace it in the sentence. It would make good sense in the context, but looked nothing like the original word. An educated guess, you might call it.

Young Darren, on the other hand, was more of a plodder. They both made progress in their own way. Darren was more conversational outside the task at hand.

One day, he asked if I was from the university. It was only a short walk away from the school. I told him that I was.

'We go round there at night, stealing bits from the bikes.'

I thought about this. Darren was a pleasant, sociable lad. I felt I had a duty, as someone benefitting from a higher level of education, to point out the antisocial aspects of his nocturnal expeditions. And to indicate to him that there was a higher moral compass which could be followed, with attendant benefits for his fellow human beings. And to subtly suggest, of course, that following a worthier path in life would undoubtedly bring with it a warm glow, which he could enjoy.

I did not know it at this point, but this instance might represent my one chance to intervene and steer someone away from a life of crime. In view of the fact that the prison and probation systems would later, misguidedly, eschew the use of my undoubted talents.

I marshalled my arguments carefully, distilling them into an unanswerable case, a concise prescription of how he might move forward as an honest and respectable citizen.

'So, have you got a lot of good bits on your bike then?'

'Oh yes. Lots.'

'So. How would you feel, then, if somebody came along and stole one of the really good bits off your bike?'

'I'd just go and get another one from the university.'

Checkmate.

I'll get my coat.

Ergonomics Explained

I signed up for an extra year, after my psychology degree, to do a diploma in occupational psychology. I'd already done enough to get a good degree mark, and the big attraction was another year in academia whilst I figured out what to do next. Morally dubious? Quite possibly, but the opportunity would only come around once.

It turned out to be quite relaxing, most of the time. The department occupied a big old house on a leafy street opposite the main university, and I sat at a desk in an attractive high-ceilinged room whilst plotting titles for stories that I would never tell. "The Manic, The Depressive and The Schizophrenic." Not quite Sergio Leone. And it wouldn't be nice to talk about my acquaintances like that, anyway.

Our course had been partly spoilt by a character who joined just for the year, along with a few others from the outside world. He'd run his own company, apparently, actually selling psycho-babble jargon to those who would pay for it, as far as I could make out. It wasn't a skill I had, though he didn't arouse jealousy in me. I presumed he was taking a year off from charging corporations exorbitant fees, to add to his legitimacy with the diploma.

The trouble was, he was such a bullshitter, knew everything about everything. So we'll call him BS for short. He said that his wife was a ninety-eighth percentile, and other such things. I tended to laugh, whereas my friend Mark, another mature student, tended towards audible seething every time that BS opened his mouth.

On this particular day, the lecture was on ergonomics, conducted by the Greek postgraduate student, Sophia.

'What do you consider,' she asked, 'when you design a seat?'

BS starts. The back support should be S-shaped, there should be support for the bilateral pectoral inferadiggeral muscles at the base of the spine, plus the pelvic nerve and the bifederal asymmetrical didactic dendritics should be considered and... on, and on for about five minutes.

At length, Sophia gets a word in edgeways. 'Fine,' she says, 'fine. Does anyone else have any ideas?'

'It should be comfortable,' says I.

'As Dave says, it should be designed to minimise muscular strain.' Meaning, we don't want to hear any more of your terminally boring bullshit, BS, and now I can progress with the lecture. Brilliant.

Of course, it got worse. We went through the palaver of designing a device, a video keyboard or something.

'What is the target population?'

The answer was obvious from the elements of the lecture that had gone before, but nobody, not even BS for once, wanted to be the class bore and actually say it.

So some bright spark pipes up to break the silence.

'The people who are going to use it.'

Er, quite. But Sophia wants her cue, she's a bit like a schoolmistress in her approach, making sure each minutely boring point is understood.

She sees my friendly face. Amazingly, I took her out for the evening once, but it was apparent we weren't suited. I liked her, but she was ambitious, hard-working and dedicated, and I was a vagabond. Never mind. She addresses me.

'Dave, you have good ideas, what is the target population?'

'You design it for the ninety percent in the middle and ignore the ten percent of other poor sods who are too big or too small to fit.'

'Dave is exactly right.' She can see I've grasped ergonomic principles. Easy. Trouble is, everyone's bored out of their minds by this time. At least I might not be the only one who's done no work for this course, I'm thinking. One guy has already walked out.

Just as a ground swell of paper-rustling starts to build up, an unspoken group statement of intent, to say, 'We've been here long enough,' a keen European student asks if we apply the same principles to the designing of a car cockpit.

This sets Sophia off again, discussing, in particular, the gear sticks.

'Yes, the design of gear knobs is a good example of ergonomics,' she proclaims. 'I have seen knobs of many different shapes and sizes. They can be long or short, thick or thin, depending ... Philip, why are you laughing?'

The room gradually fills with more murmuring, suppressed laughter as she carries on, oblivious to the connotations in the rich slang of the English language.

Soon, the continued great detail about the shape of knobs is too much, and Philip emits a semi-stifled guffaw. Sophia's ire flares and she suggests that he goes home to laugh, still without a clue about the reason for the outburst, poor woman. After Philip's red-faced exit, BS the bore starts on about how modern American and Japanese cars have computerised seats that adjust to fit 'the wife's dimensions.' He should know, he's got one. An American car.

If his interjection is a gentlemanly attempt to divert the discussion away from the knob topic, rather than a simple desire to boast about his car, it's ruined by his chauvinistic subtext.

Sophia launches the point that seats could adjust to fit the boyfriend too, meaning that women are allowed to own cars. Good for her. He responds with the rejoinder that men have to sign the documents. How could such a smug, supercilious dingbat be taken seriously? A woman at the back shouts, 'Crap!' Good for her.

When all that dies down, BS starts coming out with some more garbage, upon which Mark just stalks out without even waiting for an opportune moment.

Then BS turns round and demonstrates his knowledge of lathes. Has anybody here worked with them? The controls are designed to let the operator walk to the end and get exercise, talk with his mate.

Not where I worked, they weren't. But then it was a satanic mill type of place. Nobody cares anyway. They all want to go home and who can blame them?

Well, that's most of the subject of ergonomics covered. Who knew it could be so involving?

I'll never forget Sophia.

Mechanical Frontiers

I was first introduced to Bob by the lady from Rotherham, who was on the same course as he was.

'You would get on well with Bob. He's interested in vehicles too. He's just bought a van that he's fixing up.'

She introduced us in the Student Union bar one lunchtime. Her intuition proved perspicacious, since we're still friends now, well over thirty years later. Bob was a keen biker, so I'm not quite sure where the van idea came from. Perhaps he just fancied being dry for the winter. It was a Ford Escort van, and there was a problem with the brakes. Our friendship was cemented over a brake bleeding session outside my terraced house. One person pushes the brake pedal, the other grapples with rusty bleed nipples, brake fluid, a short length of flexible, ideally transparent, hose, and a jam jar on the floor ready to be knocked over when half full.

Bob was, like me, a mature student. He was a good self-taught mechanic and I was a moderate self-taught mechanic, so we had a certain amount in common. The next time I saw him, we were in the Union bar again. Having come from a regular working life, I viewed the opportunity to indulge in lunchtime drinking in this convivial place as something akin to a sojourn in paradise. It was even funded by a reasonable grant, in those pre-Blair days. Making scrounging ne'er do well students pay for their degrees must have been quite low on Maggie Thatcher's list of people to attack, at the time.

Bob told me that his van was playing up. Probably an ignition problem. We discussed a few theories.

We next bumped into each other a couple of weeks later. In the Union bar, hub of all wisdom. He told me, in a matter-of-fact tone, that he had crashed the van. It involved planning to be on a roundabout at the same time as a lorry, whose driver had decided to use the bit of road that Bob had earmarked for himself. Nobody was hurt, but the van was fatally crumpled.

'Oh. You got it running OK, then?'

As time went on, our mechanical fates became frequently intertwined. The first project we shared involved a Mark Two Ford Escort. This model has become a sort of elusive unicorn for retro rally enthusiasts, but was just another second-hand car at the time. It was a white, two door model. Slightly the worse for wear, as the previous owner, a young student, had driven into the back of something, due to the brakes being iffy. More rusty nipples and jam jars, then, as well as the front bodywork. Quite a good counterpoint to the arcane texts of academia in one's regular week.

I think we gave the lad 200 quid for it, 100 each. The aim was to realise 800, but there was quite a lot of time and energy involved. I remember driving back from the scrapyard in my MG Midget, with Bob supporting a white Escort bonnet over his head in the passenger seat. I don't think we were as lucky with the whiteness when we got the other panels, the front one and the right wing, as we had to buy new pattern parts. I had a welding kit by this time, having got into the habit of repairing the odd jalopy during the summer holidays, but spraying kit was a distant dream, so I presume we used lots of rattle cans when it wasn't windy.

The only exterior panel, forward of the windscreen, that we didn't change, was the left-hand wing. We must have done something right, because the first punter who turned up, after we finished it, pointed to the left-hand wing, adopted a disparaging tone, and dispensed his expertise.

'That wing's been changed.'

Anything else and you'd have been right, mate.

The other fond memory is of Bob turning up at the house with the car, to do one or two 'minor' jobs on it. On the day, Hull was treating us to one of its howling gales direct from the North Sea. Icy wind cutting to the bone, sleet arriving horizontally into our faces. We would work for approximately three minutes, then dive into the house for ten, crouching by the fire and supping barley wine to supply heat from the inside. Then out again for three minutes, back into the survival capsule (terraced house) for ten, back out for three, and so on. Since one of the jobs was brake bleeding, the torture was doubly intense. When we finished, the car was back on the road for another two weeks, until we bit the bullet and got a replacement master cylinder for it.

Later, Bob moved to a house in the same vicinity, although it didn't have the demolition-ravaged wasteland, opposite my terraced house, that had failed to shelter us from the pitiless wind as we bled brakes on Fords from time to time. His new residence featured a tenfoot passageway, at the back, wide enough to get a vehicle along between the walls. It was effectively a dead end, due to the presence of a railway line one house away.

At any one time, up to three vehicles would be accommodated, various projects that needed off-road storage, usually owned by an impecunious student or former student, waiting to see if Bob could fix them. One ragged and immobile would-be hippy van took up de facto resident status, and changed hands three times during its time there, without ever moving.

Another shared project of ours occupied the third slot for a while. The slot furthest from the railway line, which meant that it had a vague chance of seeing the road again within the century. In fairness, things did come and go slightly more frequently than that. Except for the would-be hippy van. The tenfoot became known as 'The Web', since the casual visitor, myself included, would pop by for a coffee or to discuss the purchase of a component, and leave two or three hours later, having become embroiled in taking the engine out of somebody's Transit van, or the ilk. Heavier engineering than they had envisaged for the day, at any rate.

The shared project was a Lada, another car previously owned by a young chap of Bob's acquaintance who had abandoned hope of using it again. It needed a replacement back window and an engine repair. It was the top of the range Lada model, with twinned headlights. Posh. Hull was full of Ladas at that time; the main importer stored hundreds of them at an industrial estate on a former airfield near Bridlington. Most of the taxis in Hull were Ladas.

Bob rebuilt the engine. He was full of praise for its simplicity. The Lada bodyshell was descended from a model of Fiat, but the Russians had replaced the Italian powerplant with a single overhead camshaft engine of 1300 or 1600 cc, designed for durability in Russian conditions. Even the 1600 in ours wouldn't have challenged many cars in a race, but it had the virtue of being easily maintained with the most modest set of tools. Within a few years, the tide of Ladas that had swept through the streets of Hull was ironically reversed, and Russian sailors were busy doing deals in local scrapyards for

Lada parts and even complete cars, to take home to a second life.

Our own Lada's second life was to be with Mike, a taxi driver with whom I had worked. I was living by now in a flat in Pearson Park, a lovely green space surrounded by a perimeter road and tall, elegant houses, from one of which Philip Larkin, the famous poet and University of Hull librarian, used to contemplate the comings and goings of humanity below.

Mike thought he could do better by owning his own taxi, rather than the arrangement at the firm we worked for, where the boss owned a few Datsun Sunnys. I'd always preferred the set-up of using somebody else's car; although your share was less, it seemed less permanent, with the option of stepping off the treadmill on a whim.

The Lada was ready, and Mike was keen to begin his new life as an owner-driver. Twin headlamped, at that. It was a beautiful summer afternoon, and I sat on the grass outside the flat, waiting. Mike had been negotiating to raise some of the purchase price with a businessman he knew, let's call him Mr Burns. When he arrived, he was impressed with the car, which sat gleaming in the sun. But there was a small stumbling block. Could I provide something in writing for Mr Burns to see, which guaranteed that the car would pass the taxi test?

Well, there was no reason why it shouldn't, as far as I knew. We hadn't had to address any major issues with it, after the engine and rear window were sorted. But saying that in writing was a different matter. It smacked of potential further involvement and never-ending obligation. What did the guy think I was, a car dealer?

When Bob called by a little later, I had finished rolling on the grass and beating the ground with my fists, in frustration. We had to wait a little longer for Mike, poor devil, to convince his acquaintance that a return on his investment was going to be safe. It was only a few hundred quid, but to some people, that's a lot of money. A serious commitment to a treadmill.

My friend and I had made a modest profit on our shared terraced house, at the cost of living in a shabbily decorated shell of a place without a useable bathroom, the extension containing the bath having been built by a previous owner whose grasp of building regulations had been less than thorough. But the showers at the university had been a luxuriously hot substitute, if somewhat distant.

Now I was renting again, and living in comfort, if not splendour. My view was of Queens Road behind the park, rather than the lofty Larkinian vista that the wordsmith had enjoyed from his flat at the far side. Neither were my artistic efforts on a par with Larkin's, being confined for the most part to drunken ramblings moaning about the inability of car customers to fit in with my world view.

There were four lock-up garages behind the flat, reached by a tenfoot that emerged parallel to Queens Road. I rented one, and eventually two of the others to expand my empire, from my landlord. The third garage became home to the bodyshell from an MG coupe, a BGT as it was called. It had been a donor vehicle for a kit car, and I was going to repair it and install a V8 engine from a Rover. There was always something else to do first, though.

I was keen on Rovers at this time, having progressed to a P6 model with the V8 in. This was the late sixties, early seventies model, prior to the big pointy-nosed SD1 five-door hatchback that came along during the British Leyland years. A shonky V8-engined version of the P6 could be picked up for a couple of hundred pounds then, and the smaller-engined models were in similar 'classic banger' territory. I had several of them through my hands, and sold one to Gary, a fellow drinker in the Queens pub on the corner near the park.

'How long is the guarantee?' he laughed.

'The thing is, Gary, it's guaranteed for five minutes, or until you drive out of the park. Whichever comes soonest.'

He laughed, and set off. A little while later the bell rung at the flat. There he was, without the car.

'I think it's out of petrol, actually.'

'Oh. Well, I know there wasn't a lot in it. Which way did you go?'

'Round the far end, and out towards Beverley Road.'

'Anti-clockwise? That makes it the second exit. You've invalidated the guarantee.'

Some time later, Bob joined the ranks of Rover owners. He didn't see it as man's best friend, though. It was one of the SD1 models, and had probably been chosen on the principle that it was very cheap because the person selling it had left it lying around for a long time and was desperate for a small amount of cash to leave town with. I don't know. Whatever the reason, Bob didn't even like driving it. It was a gas guzzling automatic, and had the 6-cylinder engine, not the V8. They came in 2300 or 2600 options, and were a stretched version of the old Triumph 2000 engine. The 2600 didn't have a very good reputation for reliability. I think Bob had already done something to the cylinder head. The car was only seven years old at this time.

He would drive it to do an errand when he had to, after putting a pound's worth of petrol in it, then have to put more petrol in before its next outing, with whatever loose change was left in his pocket. Times were hard.

One day the unloved behemoth turned up at the working area behind my flat. Slow ahead, helmsman.

We were going to do a body repair on it, I think. Finish by spraying on some of the horrible brown colour that Leyland must have thought looked distinguished. It was, in fact, shit colour. Not '*a* shit colour'. Shit colour. However, we were thwarted by rain and adjourned to the Queens pub opposite. After we settled down, Bob began to lament the whining differential on his lumbering conveyance.

He had been informed by an experienced mechanic of a dodge to quieten the diff. There are all sorts of urban myths about quietening differentials before selling a car to a hapless punter, of course, but this particular one had aroused his interest. The experienced mechanic it had come from was known as De la Pole Danny, apparently an allusion to the local mental hospital, De la Pole, where he spent some of his time. I knew of him by repute, having seen his work a couple of years earlier. He had cured my friend's car's oil pressure problem by simply disconnecting the warning light wire from the filter. Luckily a filter change was all that was needed and it wasn't an engine issue, but that's hardly the point. It just shows how easy life can be if you have no scruples whatsoever.

As we warmed up and the Guinness took effect, we debated the Danny solution. It involved stuffing ladies' tights into the diff casing. Bob felt that it might be a more ethical solution than the usual unscrupulous tricks like sand, which was only good until the car had left the premises, hopefully reaching California or at least Driffield, before the abrasive substance had ground the crown wheel and pinion to oblivion, leaving the irate victim far enough away and stranded.

At least, went the argument, the nylon of the tights had some substance to take up some wear, whilst also possessing slippery, slithery qualities. Du Pont's answer to Slick 50, the latest wonder additive.

I think we went as far as we could on the merits of this idea, and were somewhere near the third pint of Guinness, when Bob moved the conversation to a more radical level. It had been very wet in the recent past, and snails were everywhere underfoot, especially around the grassy track that led to my garages. Snails, he said, might possess some of the greasy squidgyness to help with the problem. He had actually considered them, as an alternative to ladies' tights...

Cheaper too, I mused, mindful of his perpetual battle to find spare change for fuel.

My thoughts turned to a scene in one of Carlos Castaneda's books, where he was walking through Mexico City with Don Juan, his Yaqui Indian mentor. These volumes are thoroughly discredited now, but nevertheless provide the odd amusing philosophical conundrum. Castaneda bent down, picked up a snail on the pavement, and moved it to 'safety' near the hedge. Don Juan reprimanded him, saying that he may have placed the snail near some plants which were poisonous to it, and that, moreover, the snail may have had enough 'personal power' to have crossed the pavement safely on its own. Castaneda moved to return the snail to its starting point, but was told by Don Juan to leave it where he had put it – it was that snail's fate to have crossed the path of a fool.

I apprised Bob of the Castaneda scenario, before concluding that, in all probability, not even the most 'personally powerful' snail would survive an encounter with a whirling crown wheel and pinion. Which left us with the only conclusion to be drawn, that Bob had veered beyond the pale in his desperation. Although tights were still on the table, so to speak, the use of snails crossed a philosophically distinct moral frontier, and was environmentally dubious to boot. Any evaluation of the merits of the additional bulk provided by the shell fragments would be superfluous.

The lesser moral issue, of whether to use tights as an additive, mercifully avoiding the arena of snail murder, hinges on how viable an engineering solution it is. Might it last well enough until the rest of the car has expired in some terminal way, thus saving replacing the diff with a second-hand item, or, if possessed of various specialised tools, dismantling, overhauling, and setting up the whole thing according to factory clearances? If anybody has carried out this experiment, could they please write in?

In the end, this Rover was uncherished. It was a disposable item, to be got rid of before the rust came through again on the repair we were about to do when the sun came out.

Wait, though. Despite everything, the Rover came good in the end. One evening, Bob had with him a young lady. She wanted a light, and he had no matches. But – he was in the *Rover*. With its *dashboard lighter*! Salvation! And one thing apparently led to another...

It's not certain, though, that the workforce at British Leyland in the late seventies or early eighties would have appreciated any inference that their skills were mainly being used in the manufacture of mobile cigarette lighters.

Shaving

In the taxi office, the representative of normality asked if I was growing a beard. It dawned on me that this was a none too subtle hint that he had noticed that I hadn't shaved for three days. I had gone to the interview with good references and a stubble. Luckily the references were very good. A little envelope containing the headed notepaper letters from employers for whom I'd driven. A portable packet of credibility.

The patriarch dwelt on the references and made a decision. The luxury he enjoyed from being a mini Godfather. I got taken on and everyone was happy. It was an arena of life where the ability to do the job outweighed your external appearance. Just. After this narrow squeak, I remembered the shaving.

I'd been going through a phase where I occasionally bought the local newspaper just to find out what day it was. Somewhat bohemian, writing rants in a garret. Forgetting how important it was to meet the everyday public with a clean face. Or at least a consistent face. Responding to itchiness of chin only, is not approved.

I felt sorry for Bob Geldof, who always appeared on TV with designer stubble. He must, logically, have taken three days or so out of the public gaze after he had shaved, waiting for the stubble to grow back. I think they have special razors nowadays to achieve the look. I had missed another trick by not patenting the style, I thought; though in reality, how can you patent an appearance? It's like saying, I have exclusive rights on looking like a bum.

Nowadays we have designer jeans with a slit at the knee. Another missed opportunity. I used to create jeans split at the knee by crawling under cars a lot. Now corporations sell the look, although they don't seem to have yet cottoned on to the asymmetric style of one slit knee with the other rubbed a muddy brown, which was my original speciality.

There seemed to be a burgeoning market in anti-heroes at around that time. The time of raising money for starving people in Africa and singing we are the champions no time for losers at Wembley Stadium. I don't really blame Freddie Mercury, he was only tapping into a collective consciousness that was already there.

Below the George Michaels and the Duran Durans making videos on yachts, were the regular public, in vast hierarchies of tie-wearers, hoping their conformity would keep the boss off their back, and below them the non-tie-wearers hoping the tie-wearers would not bother them too much. But they were all allowed out at weekends and the tie-wearers could try to affect the air of a Geldof, but only had two days to accomplish it. Not enough.

At the base of the pyramid was skid row, if you were unlucky or misbehaved enough. There, you were allowed to have stubble like the Geldofs, but without the money. It didn't appear on the list of options in the university careers office, but did have the benefit of not needing to be interviewed for admittance.

I quite liked the higher rung of taxi driving, then. Remember the odd shave, and no need to wear a tie. I once went to a stag night and put on a tie in case it involved getting past a bouncer. It occurred to me that I hadn't worn a tie for about ten years before this. I sometimes thought that I must have been hanged, in a past life, so much did I detest the accoutrement.

I progressed in the mini-career at the taxi office, to the status of being seen as competent and friendly, which was all that was needed. I even stretched the boundaries of acceptability on one occasion, when they called on me to come in early before the evening shift, to cover a couple of jobs. I explained that I needed to change a battery on my car, and would be in my scruffy clothes, but this was OK, they said.

'Just cover these two jobs, then you can pop back home and get changed.'

It was no use carrying an old battery three blocks whilst wearing decent clothes. If there was any bit of acid lingering on it, it would eat through your pullover. I knew from experience. Therefore, I wore my pullover that already had a hole in it. The taxi office was near the car spares place, so I swapped the old battery and turned up for work. I could take the new battery home in the taxi afterwards.

The second fare was part of a famous music group that I had never heard of. Although I naturally apologised for being in my jeans and scruffy pullover at the start of the journey, in the end it was too much for him. He spent the first quarter of the journey to the famous studio, which I had also never heard of, saying how good it was to be in London a lot of the time, and the second quarter of the journey saying how life in Hull was now beneath him, and criticising my attire even though I reiterated my explanation of the reasons for it. The second half of the journey he spent walking, after sniffing at me and demanding to be let out because I smelt too bad. He did pay, probably in order to demonstrate that money was now beneath him, so that was alright.

When I got back to the office, they thought it was hilarious. They already knew what had happened, from his disgusted phone call.

'I did explain it all to him,' I repeated.

'Don't worry, Dave. We told him you would spend the fare on a shower.'

So, it turned out, the patriarch did have a sense of humour, and I had clearly got my feet under the table.

So much so, that I introduced Bob to them, as a potential driver. He was looking to earn a bit of money over the university holidays. They gave him a start, and things settled down. I allowed myself a sigh of relief, having been persuaded, if I recall, by Bob rather than the taxi firm, that this might represent a good career move for him. One of our friends in the pub was highly amused by Bob's working attire of leather jacket and aviator-style sunglasses.

'Bob's going through his New York taxi driver phase.'

The taxi office at that time was an old, long caravan parked in a small yard. There were two tenfoot alleyways to the yard, which lay behind the patriarch's house, which doubled as a bail hostel for lads on probation. He also ran a driving school from the premises, so there were plenty of comings and goings. Usually, the driving instructors and taxi drivers left the car on the street if they could when calling in. It was easier, even though three cars could be squeezed into the small yard at a pinch.

One day, Bob was instructed to come into the yard with the car, rather than park outside. It was a test really. I was in the caravan at the time, and said I would pop out and guide him. No, said the patriarch, let him do it himself. The turn in to the yard was very tight, and Bob's main experience at this time was on motorbikes.

One of the patriarch's sons was also in the caravan, standing up as they chatted. He was ostensibly the boss of the taxi firm, but the patriarch could rarely resist putting his oar in. There were a couple of other sons I think. It was a bit like the Godfather film, without anybody getting shot on the New Jersey Turnpike.

Bob got a corner of the car jammed on the caravan. He reversed and went forward, reversed and went forward. The caravan lurched and rocked. Then lurched again. We hung on to whatever static fixtures we could reach, like submariners in peril on an aquatic adventure.

Bob finally got the car free and parked it. He climbed the steps into the caravan.

'I suppose you'll be wanting the car keys back?'

'That's a good idea.'

Bob headed for the pub to spend his takings. We joined him later as he regaled us with the stories of his adventures during part of a week as a taxi driver.

One Friday evening I was waiting in between fares during a quiet spell. I parked in a square in the north part of Hull, Sutton Park if you were posh, Bransholme if you weren't. There was a parade of shops opposite, where a group of people stood talking. A youth detached himself from the group and walked over towards me. We normally ran around in Datsun Sunnys, but on this particular evening I had ended up with the Bluebird, pride of the fleet.

I got the window down, and spoke to him as he got nearer.

'I'm booked up mate, got a job in a bit.'

He stared at me wordlessly, came nearer, and kicked the door panel.

At this point, I was still law-abiding, nobody had been hurt, and it wasn't my car anyway. I decided that the sensible option was to drive away.

The office were OK about it. It was just one of those things, only a dent in the door. They asked if I would go to the police station the following day. No problem.

At the police station, I got to see the book of mug shots. Like they do in the films. These would be all the lads in Hull who had fallen foul of the law at some time, and been charged with some misdemeanour.

After a careful perusal, I couldn't see the lad who had kicked the door in for no apparent reason other than being bored in Sutton Park if you were posh, Bransholme if you weren't, on a Friday evening.

But I did see the faces of virtually all of my taxi driver colleagues.

Removal Man

I was a removal man for a day. Shifting people's lives from one phase to another and providing a bit of casual psychotherapy.

I thought I was the alcohol driven poet Charles Bukowski, sinking a bottle of whisky the night before, and being driven on the back of a flatbed to a hellhole job, wearing a flea-bitten coat, frozen in the coldest crack of dawn, writing about it all with verve and punch and the validity conferred by being a booze-sodden bum clinging to the bottom rung of society's ladder.

But I was actually a middle class lad who'd just done four relatively luxurious years of study at university, funded by a grant, who had written reams and reams of aggrieved diatribes mainly about not finding a job after all the studying I'd done. None of which was publishable except for the paragraph about Bukowski that you've just read.

For a day, though, I would be a professional person. Although it was a close-run thing involving an eighty miles per hour dash to Bridlington after realising the alarm was twenty minutes out. Made a bad impression, overridden by the fact that they needed a body, and the body had, finally, arrived before the pantechnicon lorry was due to head out.

The job had come through Bill, who was a friend of my friend John from the psychology course. They both worked for an employment agency. At last, networking had paid off for me. Holding an HGV licence seemed to have helped, in Bill's eyes, although on this day I would just be hired muscle. Have I really just written that? Hired muscle?

In fact, it was a good job I'd made time for the bacon sandwich, at the cost of being a tad late. The lorry driver told me that the hired help would often be a student, most of whom would wilt by about eleven o'clock. Age and reasonable stamina obviously raised me above the student category, in his estimation. We got on quite well, and got stuck in to the task. Having all the purpose designed straps and trolleys was a big help.

I'd had a few van driving jobs in the past. And the odd job on the side that came with them. 'Dave, you've got a van, haven't you? Any chance of...?'

One I remembered particularly well was the shifting of a piano in Brighton. I had the Transit, at the dry-cleaning company, and Pat, my colleague, had the Volkswagen Transporter van. You could get clothes in the VW, but not a piano. His friend, client, whatever the status, was the piano owner.

We manhandled the upright piano, with much puffing and blowing, down some steps from a large terraced property. Not possessing any straps of any sort, I wasn't confident that the piano would behave well, on its wheels, loose in the back of the van. I suggested putting the piano on its back, so that it wouldn't slide. This was probably disrespectful to the piano. However, with some hesitancy, the piano owner agreed to the manoeuvre. We managed to tip it, don't ask me for the details forty-seven years later. It wouldn't go right over, and we had to perch the top of it on the wheel arch within the load area. Not ideal, but at least it couldn't slide off, there wasn't enough flat floor between the wheel arches.

We set off from Brighton towards Hove; it wouldn't be a long trip. The nervous piano owner sat with me in the Transit. Pat followed in his own van. Gaining confidence after the first mile, I essayed a cautious and conservative thirty-five miles per hour on a dual carriageway section.

There *was* enough flat floor between the wheel arches. We knew this because, after a very slight bump in the road, the piano slipped off the wheel arch and went BBBRRRRRRIIIIIIIIIIIINNNNNNNNGGGG-G-G-G.

For a very long time. Reverberating. Then continuing to reverberate. For a long, long time.

'Er. Whoops,' I said to the piano owner. The piano owner didn't say anything.

'We had a slight mishap,' I said to Pat, when we got there.

'I know. I heard it,' said Pat.

I found, over the years, that there was almost always a degree of angst when moving things for people. Especially when the people, rather than just things, were moving as well. Changing their lives.

Almost always a moment when an item of pottery hits the ground and shatters, and the person moving from Brighton to Yorkshire, or Nottingham to Nottingham, wails in primal anguish as half their life's accoutrements sit in the van and half sit in the hallway.

'I knew this was a bad idea. I knew we shouldn't have done this. I KNEW IT.'

Yes, but the train's at the platform now. As it were. The best thing is, after a respectful two second pause, to pick up the next bit of furniture and carry on with the job. You're an agent of the tides of time, and they're flowing.

With the Bridlington job, we were moving a family from a nice detached house to a bungalow in Sewerby a few miles above the town. All because the grandparent had a heart condition and shouldn't climb stairs any more. The heart condition wasn't helped when an item of pottery hit the ground and shattered, and one of the people moving from Bridlington to Sewerby wailed in primal anguish as half their life's accoutrements sat in the van and half sat in the hallway.

'I knew this was a bad idea. I knew we shouldn't have done this. I KNEW IT.'

We finished quite late after a long hard day. Wardrobes, fridges and cookers, beds. A whole houseful, stuffed into a bungalow. One room in the bungalow was crammed tight with everything left over, that couldn't be fitted into the plan for the bungalow's main rooms. Filled so tight with surplus furniture that a cat couldn't get in, let alone be swung.

They would have to sort it out later. We had solved a storage issue and bent the laws of physics in so doing. They were grateful.

The tip paid for my beer and a nice hot bath finished the day perfectly. In contrast to my other occupations of taxi driving and selling second-hand cars, I felt that total trust had been placed in me. The item of pottery had been dropped by the client (which is normally the case) and we had moved everything else without mishap. Dispensed a little sympathy, had a brush with physical fitness, and moved on at the end of the day, uninvolved in future wailing.

Professionalism.

Small World

I looked down from the window of the flat. Beyond the wide grassy verge was Queens Road, where the traffic murmured along. At the end of it, to the left, was the Queens pub, where I spent many evenings with convivial cronies. It was good for mental health, if not the waistline. Opposite was the bail hostel where I had, in a group interview for a job there, expressed the opinion that Marietta Higgs, one of the doctors at the centre of the Cleveland child abuse debacle, was 'out to lunch'. And further along to the right was St Vincent's Social Club, where I would first meet my wife nearly twenty years later.

I used to think that if you stood for long enough on the corner of Queens Road, opposite the pub near the mini-roundabout, you would eventually encounter everybody you needed to meet in life. Everybody from whom you would glean little bits of knowledge, adding up to an eventual enlightenment. Why chase around the world, when it would come to you if you were patient enough?

I was on the corner one day, waiting to cross, when Brian, another mature student from the Psychology Department, came along. We fell into conversation, and after a bit, Bob roared up on his Ducati motorcycle. He stopped at the kerb, dug into his leather jacket, and handed me a wad of cash, about two hundred quid. Then said he had to dash, and roared off again. The money was connected to some car project we had going on, but I think Brian had started to form theories around more esoteric types of activity, by the time we parted company.

On another occasion there, I saw a girl I knew from the psychology course, Juliette, walking towards me, so we compared notes for a few minutes. She was doing a further degree, a Masters, in the area of social work. I thought the concept of being a master of social work was somewhat strange. The staff at the bail hostel had kept going on about being in the 'people industry', and were at pains to stress how stressed they were.

I told Juliette that I had recently tried to get a job as a bus driver, but they wouldn't have me. She looked puzzled.

'I would have had a better chance if I'd told them that I'd been in jail for the last four years.' She looked even more puzzled.

I explained that they didn't really want people with degrees to be bus drivers, even if their bus driving might have been the equal of any other bus driver. Even perhaps giving them a chance of becoming, in the words of Bob Newhart, "one of the all-time great bus drivers."

She was young, and didn't really appreciate that British people can often be very dogmatic in their expectations. Very class oriented, unable to conceptualise that somebody might want to move from one profile to another, in order to be employed for a while. Your life was expected to follow a rigid tramline, and the longer you stayed on it, the harder it was to get off. I had even found an article in a psychology journal about the idea, early in my course, which Professor Clarke had then referred to in one of his lectures. So it was a genuine academic theory, if fairly unsurprising when you thought about it.

I remembered when four of us from the pub had gone roistering into the Union bar one night, to play snooker, where I bumped into BS, the guy from the ergonomics lecture. He had his 'marketing manager' with him.

I didn't really mind BS in small doses; one has to be civilized. He told me there were jobs for occupational psychologists. I told him about the bus driver thing. The field of psychology, as a career, left me completely unenthusiastic. What it really amounted to, I suppose, was that I just had no faith in it. We adjourned to our separate planets.

Never mind, though. Things had worked out well in the end. Here I was, now, looking across from the high window, surveying the scurryings of humanity. I had a comfortable place in academia to go to, and a comfortable car to drive in. I finished my leisurely breakfast and walked down the stairs.

The Jaguar sat waiting, sleek and imposing. I cruised out of the park and wafted gently up Newland Avenue. The university was only a mile or so away, but I liked to take the Jag some days, purely as a bit of a pose. The trappings of success.

I got to the university and continued a few yards further, to another gate, where I turned in. Going past some buildings, I reached the car park. There were plenty of spaces available and I brought the big saloon to a gradual halt. Nobody was around, let alone anybody I knew. I tried to convince myself that I wasn't secretly disappointed, but lost the internal argument. Maybe the posing could happen another day, then.

In truth, I didn't want to bring the car every day. It would have been somewhat extravagant. I wasn't bothered by the gas guzzling character of the big automatic, like Bob had been with the land-yacht Rover, but more by the squeal it made if I was insensitive with the braking. This was the reason I didn't take the car out of town on any longer trips. Twenty miles per hour on Newland Avenue was fine, with an alert driver, but I didn't really trust the brake pads with any heavier task.

'Brake pads' was in fact an optimistic term, since experience told me that they were probably nearly down to the metal in places. I didn't want to spend time servicing them, as the course I was on demanded at least a bit of work, and I owned the car only to turn it around quickly for a profit, without spending unnecessary time and money. Purchaser must bring trailer...

The car park was next door to the university, at what was then the Humberside College of Higher Education. I believe it later attained the status of polytechnic, after much lobbying, was then appropriated to become part of the University of Lincoln, was then later abandoned by the University of Lincoln when it hit a rocky patch, and now exists only as a nameless part of the University of Hull, who took over the buildings.

The course I was doing was called a Diploma in Information Technology in Business, on government funding, and was a good shelter from the rigours of the benefit system, for the motley crew of graduates who were involved in it. I always seemed to end up in a motley crew. I still remembered Trent Polytechnic from years earlier, where one of my cohorts was living in his Morris Minor. As you do.

Now I had a flat to live in, and a Jag that looked good outside it. From about twenty yards away. It had come from Hull Car Auction, a favourite haunt full of men in leather jackets trying to look seedy and disreputable. The auctioneer had a good line in patter, such as when he sought to burnish the appeal of a Lada by advising us that it would go forwards *and* backwards. Or exhorting the audience to bid quickly, before the MOT ran out.

Before I could try to casually exhibit my XJ6 at the college car park again, a man from Mansfield came and took it away. We quibbled briefly to 225 pounds, which was a good return on my auction investment of 175. I had explained about the brakes, in case you are wondering.

The other Jaguar I have had the pleasure of owning during my life was called, I think, a 420, from 1968. It was an immediate forerunner of the XJ6, slightly more compact, with a similarly styled front end, but the rear end similar to the older S-Type. Quite elegant though, taken on its own merits. It would have been nice to cruise plutocratically around town in it, had I got it running.

It did move whilst I had it, but only by courtesy of tow rope or trailer. It did this at least three times, between its original home in Ferriby, where I purchased it, various lock-up garages which I rented in the Avenues area, my friend Denise's house, and the flat at Pearson Park. The engine was so comprehensively seized that we never did get it to turn, despite soaking the bores with every known or reputed freeing agent, over time, and then eventually attaching an appropriate socket to the crank bolt, and connecting an eight-foot-long scaffold pole to the socket bar, with Bob and me hauling on the end.

Its final move was on a trailer to London, after a man parted with a couple of hundred more than I had paid for it, even after taking into account trailer hire. Such was the appeal of the 'classic' aura. Curious when you consider that the only slightly newer XJ6, if in chatty condition, was regarded as just another old banger, at the time. My recollection is that the 420 took me into the heady realms of a four-figure sum, selling for something like 1200 pounds. So, there you are, I never lost money on a Jaguar. Incredible. I would have liked to take Denise out of town to a swanky hotel in a Jaguar, but you can't have everything in life. It's important never to forget that.

The white whale (Jaguar 420) was installed next to Denise's house during its final phase with me. There was a hard-standing area alongside the end-of-terrace residence, with plenty of room for it. This was fine, I thought, until she decided to engage one of her network, of bohemian friends with building skills, to put up a perimeter wall. Chief amongst them was a Scotsman called Wilson, who was habitually primed with cheap sherry and allowed to pontificate for a couple of hours before starting work on whatever maintenance she had in mind. I tended to think it was a false economy, what with the sherry bill and the amount of time taken up getting these things done, but who was I to argue? Until the time I had to use my Rover to fetch two or three batches of bricks for him to finish her shed. Probably not a coincidence that something on the rear axle assembly cried enough, quite soon afterwards.

This entailed a trip to Jacko's scrapyard to detach a complete rear axle assembly from a P6 Rover, to replace mine. I was accompanied by a young lady who was one of the 'Giroscope' crowd. This was a housing co-operative which purchased and restored run-down housing for the benefit of unemployed, often alternatively-lifestyled, members. Very worthy. She had, at the time, attached herself to Bob in order to witness various mechanical projects and learn his skills by a sort of Zen osmosis. Thus, she was more than willing to lend me a hand and absorb the complexities of the De Dion suspension arrangement which was intrinsic to the sophisticated design of the P6 axle.

She had recently upped the bohemian factor by indulging in a radical crew cut hairdo. Which perhaps should have been a hairdon't, I thought, remembering her long flowing locks. Although she was in her early twenties, I could see why her haircut, short stature, and baggy clothes which hid her bosom, had fooled Jacko. He seemed to think she was a thirteen-year-old boy. Ambling up as I was making sure there were enough axle stands and old wheels under the car for our safety, he inquired.

'Is he alright? Will he be alright?'

'Don't worry, I'll keep an eye on, er, him.'

After this health and safety briefing was over, we spent the rest of the morning getting the unit off the old Rover. Using logic and some large spanners, the job was in fact straightforward, good preparation for when I did the same thing on my own Rover, followed by the reverse procedure of fitting the scrapyard one to it. And all because Denise employed handymen without transport who got a cheap deal on bricks.

I made sure I was out of the picture when the wall was built. They were different bohemian handymen this time and arranged the transport of the breeze blocks themselves. I knew the time for building the wall was approaching because the potentially glamorous Jaguar was in her eyes just clutter, and was about to become annoying clutter. This was signified when tolerance disappeared in the blink of an eye, as the result of no discernible stimulus immediately beforehand.

'When is that thing GOING?'

On a later occasion, her friend Maura presumably heard the same thing, out of the blue, after leaving an Austin Maxi on Denise's hardstanding for many weeks. I surmise that 'When is that thing GOING?' was said at lesser, more decorous, volume to Maura, but I can't be sure. They were both quite fiery of temperament, kindred spirits who were bosom pals for months on end until something was said out of line, or was thought to be, after which relations would freeze to Arctic level for long periods.

Was I interested in this Maxi, then? A mere machine was not a wrecker of relations, nonetheless it had to GO. Since I knew nothing about the condition of the car, my offer was a hard-headed thirty pounds. This was relayed to Maura, who deemed it to be 'less than generous', but eventually an acceptance trickled through.

The MOT involved only a top ball joint and some other small job. The faulty fail-safe device that stops the starter motor being operated unless the car is in 'Park' or 'Neutral' was by-passed with the use of a piece of bent welding wire to make a secure electrical connection. You will gather that keeping costs to the bone is a wise move when trading motor cars at this level of the economic ladder. Since the only significant threat was damage to the starter motor pinion, no ethical red lines were crossed, I felt.

The perspicacious reader may also have gleaned, from the description above, that the car had an automatic gearbox. Bizarrely, this made it somehow soothing, because the only really nerve-wracking aspect of a standard Maxi, the gearbox, had been removed from the equation. I quite liked Maxis, for their smooth ride, even though they were the epitome of 'uncool'. My father had about four of them at various times; he liked being able to get his Moulton cycles and other creations in the back, and I inherited the last one he had. I eventually, having the use of two or three other cars at the time, helped my next door neighbour's daughter out by selling it to her for fifty quid. For that price, she was happy to work around the complete absence of a working third gear. Or was it fourth, I can't remember?

The automatic Maxi, once again in the corporate Leyland brown colour, was similarly a car I didn't actually need, so I advertised it in a high-profile campaign using the windows of two Post Offices. It attracted strange characters with white beards or, at the very least, unkempt straggly hair, all of whom appeared to regard being poor as an art form. Whilst I had great sympathy, it eventually dawned on me that I was spending my afternoons standing next to a vehicle, talking to someone I had never seen before, and would never see again.

One day I drove across to south Manchester in it. It was legal and I had 100 quid 'in it', as the motor dealers liked to say. My brother Richard started using it, as his MG was playing up again. During my next trip over there I was mildly gutted to have to replace the front exhaust pipe. Twelve quid from the local Partco. Expenses were getting out of hand here.

Richard found a buyer for it at 200 pounds. I gave him a few quid for his trouble, saying that he could have kept the car if he had wanted to. I wasn't that desperate for 200 pounds at the time. But he had noticed that the fuel consumption was rather high in traffic, and fancied something more economical – like a Jaguar.

Fussy, or what? I quite liked the idea of obtaining a car for thirty quid and turning it into viable transport. Maxis could have been better sellers but were killed by a lack of ambition in styling, and dodgy manufacture. They used the same doors as the earlier Austin 1800 model, which may have saved a few quid but just perpetuated the Issigonis ethic that something box-like with rounded edges like a Mini would do for the majority, or even all, of the population. Being comfortable was regarded as disadvantageous for a driver, since it might result in drowsiness. This latter theory has relatively few adherents in the driver training industry, it should be said, presumably on the basis that fatigue, induced by fighting against inappropriate posture, is ultimately a greater threat to safety.

I don't remember Maxis being unduly uncomfortable, in fairness. They had the potential to be a decent machine.

The suspension provided a supple ride, the engines seemed to be reasonable. If they'd looked like a Renault or Citroen, they would have doubled their sales, just from purchases by teachers and academic lecturers. Who may have thought the gearchange was part of being 'chic'...

The Maxi had the British motor industry's first five-speed gearbox in a mass-produced car. Innovative, even on the world stage. If only it had worked properly. I had once driven one of the early ones. The boss of a taxi company had produced it after going to a car auction. I drove the 'bargain' once, picking up a party of four after their revelry at a hotel. Picking up speed in fourth, I remembered the high-tech feature of the gearbox and attempted to get fifth. No chance. These early Maxis had a cable gear change. Many modern vehicles feature a cable operated gear change, of excellent quality. Perhaps lessons were learned from the Maxi, about what not to do.

I lost speed, and tried to get back to fourth. I fished, I fished, I prodded and pushed. We had lost a bit of speed, so I decided to get third. I fished, I pushed, I prodded, I fished. We lost more speed. Second would be easier to find, then. No. It wouldn't. We had lost so much speed now, that there wasn't much point in flailing. I slowed to a halt from five miles per hour and said, 'I'll just try again from the beginning.' The passengers were as amused as I was.

It did occur to me to wonder, though. Did people turning up for a driving test in one of these cars get a head start?

My friend Colin had an Austin Allegro as a company car. Another 'state of the art' British Leyland effort. He was told he could sell it and put the funds towards something newer. I offered to take it round a few dealers for him, as I was between jobs at the time. I got three meagre offers. The last guy said I could take his phone number. I was sitting in the passenger seat after his test drive, and opened the glove box to fish for a bit of paper to write on. The glove box fell out. When I told Colin, he told me that the propensity of the hazard warning light switch to detach itself when operated, and fly across the cabin with rocket velocity, was equally amusing. Whilst he lay on his back on the sofa, gasping for air, helpless with laughter.

Colin had witnessed the ultimate party trick of the Allegro, when following one as a passenger in a minicab, going out of London towards the west. At a certain point along the A40, there was a slight bump in the carriageway. As the Allegro reached it, two hub caps, one each side, flew off the car with perfect synchronicity. The taxi driver merely shrugged, uttering the word 'Allegro' with such deadpan detachment that it was obvious that he witnessed this ritual occurrence, this symbol of the ultimate demise of the native British motor industry, on a weekly basis.

They never stood a chance really, between the complacent bosses, the stroppy unions, and the fragmented nature of the infrastructure. Leyland products were never near the top of my shopping list at the auctions, despite my affection for P6 Rovers and the odd MG. I looked for anything that was about 400 pounds, which might sell for about 800, and not cost me too much in my hopefully brief ownership. Thus, various plumbers and window cleaners were able to continue to ply their trade in conveyances which I had supplied, their only concern being whether they could fit a rack and carry their ladders, or sling their tools in the back of the Nissan 120Y estate car. It may have been old enough to be a Datsun, actually. I carried out a reliability trial by driving to Stoke-on-Trent in it, to see my girlfriend of the time, Julie. One of my drinking pals expressed the opinion that it would be good for her to see an example of the business I was in. Hmmm. He knew nothing about cars.

Julie had once seen a passport photograph I had, and expressed the opinion that, with my moustache, I looked like a 'San Francisco gay or a Mafia hit man'. I had hurriedly opted for the Mafia hit man persona. Surely, the guise of 'would-be disreputable denizen of the Hull Car Auction shed' could not dent her perception of me beyond what had already been forged?

Nevertheless, it wasn't too much later that my friendship with Denise took a more intimate turn.

The Datsun went well, to Stoke and back, and Chris the plumber was chuffed with it.

The Information Superhighway

The course on Information Technology in Business was an interesting distraction. It had to be better than scratching about with other people's vehicles behind the flat in non-industrial premises with non-industrial equipment for non-existent reward. That all ended when a young couple with an aged Volvo estate took umbrage at my failure to find any viable second-hand seatbelts for it, after spending all day in breakers' yards on their behalf.

'I'm sorry, but it seems that Volvo change the design every year, and I can't find any that will fit. Buy some new ones off Volvo and I'll fit them for you free of charge.'

'Oh, we can't do that.'

'Well, what do you want me to do, then? I've looked everywhere and they can't be found.'

'There's no need to be like that. I think we'll have to take the car somewhere else.'

'Please do. Take it now, and then I can go out of business in peace.'

I never quite worked out how trying to get them out of a hole by looking for safe used parts had made me some kind of a charlatan in their eyes. The husband was a student and it was clear they couldn't afford Volvo prices. Which, ultimately, wasn't my problem. Nevertheless, they couldn't get away from some sort of pre-conceived notion that anyone in the motor trade was predisposed to villainy, even though I had spent time for no reward.

Extortion, were one to practise it, would of course be better carried out from behind an uncluttered desk at the end of a walk across a massive glass-fronted showroom full of gleaming new vehicles. But punters at the lowest end of the spectrum seem to feel entitled to more righteous indignation per pound, if there's a snag.

The other occupation whose practitioners are viewed as modern day Dick Turpins, is taxi-driving. Hence it was relaxing to get away from vehicles for a while, back to the comforting embrace of academia.

The information technology course was a post-grad diploma, so the psychology degree was my passport to it. It had government funding, so income was about ten pounds a week more than the dole. Plush. The Thatcher government was bent on reducing the unemployment figures by whatever means it could, in a virtual if not actual sense. Various tricks were used to make the real figures seem less appalling, easy to spot if you had read Darryl Huff's book *How to Lie with Statistics* (Huff, 1954), as part of a psychology degree.

We now appear to have reached a point in the twenty-first century, at least pre-pandemic, where unemployment itself has been totally banished, so that government can sleep easily at night, without having to worry any more about graph manipulation. I assume that this is because

a: most of the previously unemployed population has been forced into delivering pizzas on an uninsured moped to scratch a living, and

b: those that are unable to do this, by reason of disability or lack of licence or riding skill, are forced to spend thirty-six hours per week actively searching for work whilst initially starving for at least five weeks due to having to wait for their Universal Credit payment to begin.

In all cases, if they are unable to pull themselves up by their bootstraps, it is their OWN FAULT for being morally degenerate scroungers, as defined by the terminally sour Mister Duncan Smith, who managed by some quirk of fate to amass a seven-figure fortune.

As you can see, back in the late eighties, things weren't quite so bad as they are now in the Duncan Smith era. Did I just say that? It was nevertheless a good idea, if you could, to take shelter from the tentacles of the benefit office and do something which might increase your employability.

Our course was founded on the principle that people could be trained to manage others despite not knowing the details of what those others were actually doing. A bit like being a choreographer when you didn't know how to dance. When I was young, a man called Leonard Lord was in charge of the British Motor Corporation. He was, would you believe, a production engineer. How handy. That sort of progression seemed less common in later years. I wouldn't say it was impossible for people from different fields to succeed in, say, running an engineering company, just that it's probably harder for them to have the credibility with the workforce.

But we were in the Thatcher era, and the workforce was regarded as a stroppy nuisance in many of the older industries. As far as information technology went, you weren't expected to be able to program a computer, just to be able to design a system in principle and then tell programmers to implement it.

It boiled down to being an *analyst*, and an analyst was further up the chain than the programmer. Upon whom he or she depended. Oh well, have it your own way.

We were given a book about relational databases. I don't think it ever said in so many words that it was about relational databases, but it was. I think the authors preferred a bit of mystique. A bit like when you ask a computer nerd how to do something on the machine, and they loom over your shoulder, their fingers whirr over the keyboard, and the problem is solved. They go 'There you are,' unable to hide at least a degree of smugness, and you go, 'Er, OK, thanks,' thinking, I've learnt absolutely NOTHING, so asking him (almost invariably a him) for help was utterly, utterly pointless, and next time I'll just sit here fuming and hacking about to see if I can solve it myself instead of asking that smartarse anything ever, ever again. As a good team player.

Nobody amongst the twenty of us on the course could make much sense of the book about relational databases. If anybody did, they weren't saying. If you tried to ask the lecturers, they tended to avoid the question, saying we should read the book and not be lazy. This was because, I thought, they either didn't want to read it, or had read it and, like us, failed to come to grips with it.

The book was trying to address the concept that data consisted of 'entities' rather than actual physical counters like beads on an abacus. The computer would be instructed to go to a file called, for example, Handbrake Cables, for the name of the part, and another file for the price, or for the vehicles it fitted, whatever. It shouldn't have been complicated, really, but everything was wrapped in arcane terminology. I thought of 'entities' as being amorphous dollops of slithering alien slime in a film like *The Blob* with Steve McQueen, or columns of mysterious sparkling mist like in *Star Trek*, about which Mr Spock could declare, 'It's life, Jim, but not as we know it.'

You can see that I tended to drift off a bit, at times. I did try, though, to up my credibility by enrolling for a COBOL computer programming course at the local 'Tech' college, not to mention a typing course there as well. My typing did improve, nearly thirty years later when I needed to type a book I had written. The COBOL programming gave me a bit more confidence, but at a terrible cost in time. COBOL is, or was, a business language for the computer, in other words, oriented towards the accounting side of computer usage. As such, it has limited parameters and is one of the simpler codes. We were shown how to do a fairly straightforward program, of about ten lines. I did my version, but it simply wouldn't work no matter what I tried. Eventually, after about two hours staring at it, I asked the lecturer for help. He had a look, and saw that I had put a zero in, where there should have been a nought, or vice versa. They are quite close on the keyboard.

I'll never get those two hours back...

One of the highlights of the course, for me, was in the refectory one morning, where we were sitting on our break. One of our bunch brought the subject of philosophy into the conversation. We were all graduates, remember. My friend Andy, in order to clarify the boundaries of the discussion, asked, 'When you talk about philosophy, do you mean the theories of Kant, Hegel and Wittgenstein, or do you mean, life's a bitch and then you die?' I think we can all take useful guidance from that statement.

The course wasn't too difficult to pass, after which we drifted to the four winds, or, in one or two cases, to the St. John's pub on Queens Road. This was handy for me as it was just along from the Queens pub to which I have previously referred. Erudite company is always welcome.

I did play the game, of trying to gain employment. Yet again. Although I felt it to be a game, I was in fact serious about wanting to be an earner of a respectable wage, rather than a bottom feeder in the murky pond of the bleak economy. As such, I was prepared to start anew in a far outpost; Ipswich, Newcastle, wherever.

Somebody from British Telecom, in Ipswich, asked me what I would do if I was in charge of a coastal town and a tsunami came along. If only... if only I could, in a split-second that lasted hours, have jumped forward in time... jumped forward to Oregon in 2018, when my wife and I motored down the coast towards California. In one town there was, in the dock, a large block of concrete, perhaps the size of a small lorry. It had broken away when a tsunami hit Japan a few years earlier, and had been left in the dock as an exhibit. It had floated all the way from Japan.

The consciousness of the reality of the tsunami phenomenon along the Oregon coast was something that surprised us, in the sense that we had never really thought about it before. Of course, there is a realisation that the San Andreas Fault is not too far from both Oregon and California, and any large 'quake might certainly provoke a tsunami. There were frequent road signs. Tsunami Route. Basically, the advice was simple. Drop everything, and head inland to higher ground.

Yes, if only I had known that. If only... So simple. Drop everything and head to higher ground.

Back in Ipswich, I sat imagining that I was looking out at the English Channel, in Brighton where I had once lived, and a tsunami was coming. In the English Channel. I had, possibly rashly, assumed that the interviewer from British Telecom meant that I was in charge of a British town, since their name wasn't International Telecom.

I suggested to the interview guy that getting the police and the radio stations to spread the word to get out of town to higher ground might be a good idea. If only I had known then what I found out in 2018, with my wife.

I could have said to him, 'My town in the English Channel would have already been well prepared earlier. I would have spent the council money on having many signs put up, saying IN THE EVENT OF TSUNAMI, DROP EVERYTHING AND GET OUT OF TOWN TO HIGHER GROUND.' I would not have said to him the extra part about kissing your arse goodbye if you couldn't get out of town. He was a bit serious, as an interviewer. Consequently, I would also have avoided the temptation to say, 'What the fuck has a tsunami in the English Channel got to do with telecoms?'

OK, I never actually said that, but I am fairly sure he could see that I was thinking it...

Yes, I would have kept it serious, got the job, gone to Ipswich, and almost certainly never met my wife and gone to California on a road trip to see her relatives.

Time travel is weird.

From Master to Pupil, featuring Glamorous Women

I had a lucky break after the tsunami washed away my dreams of a new life in Ipswich. Another post-grad information technology course was going to run, again with government tenner, this time at the proper university next door to the college of higher education. And it was an M.Sc. this time. Master of Science. Master of my own destiny would suffice, thank you. They made an exception for me, in granting the funding, due to it being a higher qualification. It was like hopping from dry island to dry island, across the ever-raging river of Thatcherite structural unemployment policy, and I was appropriately grateful.

The course wasn't bad, actually talking more about the world of computing than management-speak bullshit. The operating systems part seemed way out of date, and I never quite overcame the difference between what the word 'imply' meant in normal English, and what it meant in the type of logic used in artificial intelligence programs. I don't think it has affected my life too much, thankfully. Now, over thirty years later, artificial intelligence appears to consist of Facebook knowing that you like to see posts about something that you are interested in, because you have looked at posts about that subject before, and Alexa occasionally getting your shopping list correct.

The really good thing on the course was that the opportunity existed to learn programming in a proper sense, rather than asking a passing underling to do it. And at the end of the year, we were sent out to the real world, in twos and threes, to do some actual work for a company. My partner was a young chap who was a bit of an archetypal nerd, if I dare say. He owned a personal computer (PC) and thus knew how to plug in a PC and stay up at night doing god knows what with it. I didn't own a PC, but my contribution was to own an old Rover in which we could get to work, across the Humber Bridge.

We designed an information system and estimating system for the company, who installed industrial electrical equipment. The engineers were fairly macho and liked to talk about how their BMWs had anti-lock brakes and would thus protect them from harm whilst driving inches from the back of the car in front, in sleet and thick fog at eighty miles per hour. They called my partner 'Brains' because he looked like Brains from *Thunderbirds*. This was a handy distraction, preventing them from spending time discerning that I had, at the age of eleven, according to my schoolmates, borne a resemblance to the character 'Professor Popkiss' from *Supercar*, another Gerry Anderson TV series. It's rarely a positive, when old nicknames resurface.

At the end of it, there was room in the company to employ one of us. Naturally, 'Brains' was the fortunate recipient. More comfortable a persona, for them, than somebody who looked more like a small-time hustler out of *Kojak* than a Master of Science. Even though I was a Master of Science.

I took my masterfulness, and new-found confidence from having spent extra time on top of my course work designing and coding a card game, to interview at Sheffield with the database giant Oracle, and at Swindon with the silicon-chip giant Intel. I remember nothing about the Oracle one. I remember that Intel paid for a nice hotel room, and that the guy interviewing me said that they worked hard and played hard.

I fantasised, very briefly, about my new life in Swindon. I would contact the glamorous Julie again, she would be swept off her feet and join me in Swindon. To start with, we would have a modest house of our own, perhaps a semi, with prices what they were. I would work hard, and we would play hard, and we could pretend to be normal well-adjusted yuppies, and perhaps even be tentatively happy, until somebody who played harder would come along, sweep Julie off her feet more thoroughly, and I would begin to play harder, more unwisely and too well. And start to wonder what I was doing at the temple of Intel...

It was deeply unfair that Denise didn't make it into the lead role of the fantasy, even though I loved her. She was quite a lot older than me, and even Julie, a little younger than me, was finding it difficult to adjust to Swindon, surrounded by my hard-drinking and hard-playing yuppie colleagues in bars and bowling alleys, raucous, with their quick brains ignorant of Van Morrison and the lesser known, more poignant tracks of the Rolling Stones in their later years. Denise gravitated to the Bluebell pub, where they got up on stage and sang jolly folk songs about brave whaling men, and she palled-up with an anarchist in a knitted jumper. They would sit up for hours talking about politics somewhere to the left of Fidel Castro, supping Martini and scoffing After Eight mints, before retiring upstairs to make passionate love.

Fortunately, the bubble of this fantasy was soon popped, somewhere near the point where tentative happiness was mentioned, and I never had to deal with the guilt of seeing my subconscious leave Denise behind in Hull with an anarchist or other suitable replacement who possessed the degree of intellectual agility that she liked. The bubble was popped, not exactly by the ever-raging river of Thatcherite structural unemployment policy, but by the economic recession of 1990. Intel was just the last staging post, a moment of hope, before a prolonged period of unemployment set in. I added to my collection of rejection letters, some hundreds thick, which was my shield against harassment from the benefits office. Such was my ingrained caution from these days, that I consigned the box of letters to the recycling bin only many years later, long after finding steady work.

One success within the doldrums was moving to a house of my own. My landlord wanted to renovate the house where the flat was, and move in himself. Goodness knows why, when he had a nice house out in Holderness away from bail hostels and petty crime zones, but que sera. There was a degree of tenancy rights then, which has in all probability been watered down since. I spoke to a solicitor, who sent him a letter. The landlord later cornered me, on one of his visits.

'What do you want?'
'About a thousand.'
'I thought six hundred.'
'Eight hundred.'
'Done.'

The dosh helped with a deposit, and I was off to the Abbey National. I had to go for an endowment mortgage, where the monthly money went to an endowment, which I think theoretically paid for the house, with you having something left over at the end when you were decrepit. Ha ha. They were all the rage; I preferred the principle of gradual repayment, but that would never work with the dole, since the initial monthly outgoings were larger. The endowment was a predictable amount, which the bureaucracy could cope with. Nevertheless, they had to be convinced that the amount would cost them the same, or less, than if they paid rent for me to live somewhere. And the Abbey National had to be convinced that the dole would come through with the monthly payment. Catch 22.

I spent a morning in Hull having discussions, shuttling from the Abbey National office to the dole office and back, waiting whilst they eventually established a dialogue on the telephone. Finally, one of them cracked, and I was able to negotiate my house purchase.

If you've got this far with the reading, you probably won't mind that I was helped by the state, but in case you're still harbouring an, as yet unexpressed, apoplectic rage at the scrounging nature of it all, please be aware that, one day in the future, I obtained a regular job and started paying my share. And did not complain about paying my share.

For a short while, waiting for the house deal to go through, I lodged with Bob. His girlfriend was pregnant at the time, and one day I helped by driving her to the maternity hospital for an appointment. This particular hospital no longer exists, but was at the time on Hedon Road, the main route out of Hull to the extreme east of Holderness, a flat land of farms, marshes, crumbling coastline, and Spurn Point. Big sky.

Denise's friend Maura used to express the view that Hedon Road, on one short stretch, possessed everything to cater for the lifespan of a typical Hull resident: a maternity hospital, a prison, and a graveyard. A mite cynical, I thought. There were also scrapyards, factories and a refinery.

I mused on all this as I sat waiting in the car, listening to the radio. People say, do you remember what you were doing when John Kennedy was shot, or when men landed on the moon? This was one of those occasions. Sitting in the maternity car park when Thatcher resigned. Joy.

My house in West Hull had been let to students previously. Probably they had worn down the landperson. At any rate, it was unoccupied. And unfurnished, apart from what I always termed 'landlord's carpet', throughout. Landlord's carpet is an extremely hardwearing form of carpet, resistant to students, swarms of locusts, and nuclear meltdown. The 'pile', if such it can be called, is less thick than the non-stick coating on the inside of a non-stick saucepan. It is made from an indeterminate material left over from an indeterminate industrial process involving nothing of ecological merit, let alone a sheep. The tiny grey strands looked like some form of glass reinforced plastic, capable, with their tiny sharpness, of doing nasty harm to any delicate part of the anatomy of anybody rash enough to indulge in an impromptu love-making session on the floor.

The second thought that I had, on moving in, was that some furniture would be a good idea. For this, I went to the locally legendary auction, Gilbert Baitson's, held weekly on a Wednesday. Or was it a Tuesday? No matter. I had, for several years, been in the occasional habit of attending this auction, as much to indulge in people-watching as to buy anything. Old Gilbert would conduct proceedings from a vivid green moveable pulpit, which was from time to time repositioned by the porters, as he clung to the rail like Captain Ahab. I remember a picture of him on the front of the Hull Daily Mail, on one occasion. There was a controversy about some old terraced houses being demolished and the go-ahead had come through. There he stood, in his role as bailiff, atop a pile of rubble, arm pointing aloft and forward, as the JCB digger next to him presumably selected a forward gear ready to advance towards the flimsy dwellings which had been homes to someone the day before.

When not doing impressions of the Duke of Wellington, he was wont to rebuke unfortunate attendees at the auction who were accompanied by rumbustious children.

'Madam, kindly remove your odious child from the premises forthwith.' You really don't get entertainment like that anymore.

At my new abode, my neighbours, either side, were very friendly. Getting by as best they could, without rolling in money. Ailsa was a matriarch who had several daughters, coming and going all the time, along with various grandchildren and extended family. Martin, on the other side, was a taxi driver. His Lada was a bit less polished than those which ran from the station, but it did the job. He was married, with, I think, some teenage daughters, of whom I saw little. From time to time there would be a blazing row heard through the walls, but mostly they were fine. Privately, I called them the Noise Family. In the back garden was a small, insubstantially built shed, home to a small Shetland type pony. It would roam from a rope, causing the back garden to be mostly muddy. They also had a white dog which was similar in appearance to, if perhaps slightly uglier than, the white dog in the Hieronymus Bosch painting which sports a cutaway diagram of people in Hell writhing in various torments within its belly. It later developed a habit, after I had installed various 'damaged repairable' cars in the back yard, of standing on the roof of one of them and barking incessantly, just when I was trying to have a doze after being out late the previous day. I would try to sneak up on it with a full bucket of water; the success rate was only about 10%, but the one time in ten that the dog ended up drenched, was incredibly satisfying.

Martin and family eventually moved, to another street nearby, so I didn't see him except in passing. Until the night out when I ordered a minicab to get home, and he turned up. Because I had started working as a driving instructor by then, he felt it appropriate to subject me to a comprehensive demonstration of bad driving technique, using last minute braking, corner cutting, and scorching away from stops, at every opportunity. As far as it is possible to 'scorch' in a Lada, of course. It was the kind of thing to which I would have subjected the infamous Sid, had I ever had him trapped in a car, so I suppose the karma of once thinking evil thoughts prevents me from complaining. Nevertheless, I thought the torture to be disproportionate, as I gripped the door handle as discretely as possible and wedged my legs against the bulkhead. Martin at least had a good time, judging by his mirth.

I forget now which application for a 'graduate level' job was the final straw with my attempts to work in a warm office, ideally getting paid well for doing not too much, but in 1994, I put it all behind me and followed up an advert offering a chance to qualify as a driving instructor. This was a course leading to the qualification of 'ADI', short for Approved Driving Instructor. Government approved to charge the paying public for your skills. Maybe, if I passed, I could make my own job.

There was some funding consisting of a small 'Enterprise Allowance' style increment to one's social security benefit payment, for a year whilst training, so I would be doing a socially responsible thing once again, by helping to keep the unemployment figures lower. The providers were an outfit from Southport called NDS.

NDS stood for National Driving School, which was perhaps indicative of unfettered ambition exceeding available resources, especially when the first phase of training consisted of 'distance learning' packages which arrived by post. For months.

Unfazed, I concentrated on the MG Midget I was restoring. Sounds great until you appreciate that the basis was a bare scrapped shell (fifty quid) plus a complete irreparable car (also about fifty quid), and although I eventually sold the completed car for over 3000 pounds, I had carefully totted up my time and other costs, which gave me a grand profit breakdown of fifty pence per hour. Not quite *Wheeler Dealers* telly programme territory.

After a few months of welding, spraying, and spannering, plus writing the occasional essay about what to do at crossroads and what a meeting situation was, I had passed the Part 1 written multi-choice test. Part 2 was a driving exam, so I expressed the opinion that some actual driving might be useful.

Eventually the cavalry arrived in the shape of a small Peugeot. It was driven by a chap who had started the course earlier than me, and, having passed the ADI driving test (the Part 2) was entitled to a 'Pink Badge', which allowed the holder to teach pupils for money. This lasted 6 months from when it was issued, enabling the new instructor to gain experience before he took, and ideally passed, the Part 3 final hurdle, the 'Test of Instructional Ability'.

The guy had a look at my driving, which he said was basically OK except that I drove everywhere ten miles per hour faster than whatever the speed limit happened to be. Then a 'real' (fully qualified 'Green Badge' instructor) turned up. Two or three trainees would spend the day with him learning how to drive to pass the Part 2 test. And by default, how to teach others to drive in this way.

One day, we were practising reversing around a corner. The side road had very high hedges. I drove forward past it, and stopped to prepare to do the reverse.

'Was there anything in the side road that might prevent you doing the reverse?'

'I don't know.'

'Why don't you know?'

'I didn't look.'

'Why didn't you look?'

'I forgot.'

'I spend every day working to teach you, coming out early, spending time, working hard. And you CAN'T EVEN BE BOTHERED TO LOOK INTO THE ROAD AS YOU DRIVE PAST!'

I began to wonder if this fellow had quite the right temperament for the job.

I did the driving test and thought I had failed within about a mile. Five 'minor' faults maximum to pass, but this was a 'major' surely? I had 'emerged' from a small crossroads and made that Metro stand on its nose.

No matter; just relax and do your best, get through it and see if it's anywhere near what they want. A baseline for when I do another test, or a measure of whether it's even worth trying.

I was staggered when Mr Birch told me I had passed. The exaggerated ticking of the test sheet when I went past Sainsbury's doing thirty-five miles per hour out of pure boredom, now made sense. That had been the fifth fault as it turned out. So perhaps that Metro had just set off and had sagging front suspension. I'll never know. Whatever. Onward.

I got as much as I could out of the tuition, which included three days at Southport with several other trainees. I only remember one instructor, and perhaps there was a woman in the office somewhere. But there is always something to be gained. The bits I recall? Anyone can be taught; and always remember to praise something good that the pupil has done.

There was a deadline on the funding for this hothouse of instructional talent. We had been told that of every 100 that began the arduous path to qualification, only two or three emerge successful after passing the Part 3. After a year time ran out and I was back in limbo.

Months went by, preoccupied now with frequent visits to Manchester during my father's final illness. He had taken great interest in the training I was doing, in particular following a TV documentary about learner drivers doing a week's intensive driving course. Footage from a car featured an instructor quizzing a woman student as they drove along. One was encouraged to ask the student 'open' questions to make them think about the driving process.

'Tell me, what do you see as we approach the roundabout?'
'Daffodils.'
'No, what else?'
'Tulips?'

I went for an interview to be a junior psychologist at the old De la Pole hospital. My father had died the week before and I was feeling somewhat detached from reality. It had been nearly a decade since I finished my university course, but you never know unless you try.

There were six or seven of us attending. All in a circle facing the enthusiastic member of staff who would make the decision. My rivals were all recent graduates aged twenty or so, four or five of them women, some of whom were very attractive. I was forty-three.

I watched with interest as the member of staff addressed one of the especially attractive young ladies, imagining a long, long reptilian tongue flickering out of his mouth, down onto the floor and along towards her, as she sat wide-eyed, semi-hypnotised in the face of his avid and undivided attention.

'So-o-o, Samantha, tell me about yourself...'

I'll get my coat.

It was time to see about getting qualified as a driving instructor.

Back on the Road

I got in touch with Pete Hodgson, who ran Ideal Driving School. He had picked up a few of the stragglers after the Hull tentacle of the omnipotent NDS had withered away. Perhaps the government funding for extensive, cheap, distance learning packages was no longer forthcoming.

Pete was very good. Recognising that I was feeling a bit fragile, he said we'd start with something straightforward, the turn in the road. There had been quite a gap, but I was armed with a promise to my father that I would see this through, no matter what. On the downside, the time since passing Part 1 was now running out, and I would only get one shot at the Part 3 before the limit expired, meaning that, should I fail, I would have to go back onto the whole merry go round again, starting afresh with Part 1.

Pete gave me two excellent tips. The first was that teaching a learner essentially involves providing a sort of safety carpet underneath them, which you gradually pull away as the process continues.

The second was that you can stop for a brief period even on a double yellow line. You are pausing, not parking. No doubt some bar-room pundits might argue with this, but I don't care, since it was to save my bacon on the test.

The examiner plays the part of a learner, for an hour-long role-play session consisting of two scenarios. They will throw in as many faults as they can, except on the mythically rare occasions where they play the part of a perfect driver. You must spot the faults and discuss them as they occur. Hence a half hour session doing a fairly well-defined exercise such as the turn in the road, might be a tad easier than an open road moving scenario where the examiner tells you where to direct them.

I had two open road driving scenarios. He briefed me at the beginning of each. The first ('I am Brian') was not a novice, but turned out to be an erratic ditherer. The second ('I am Bob') was well practised and the holder of a motorbike licence, proving to be a cocksure speeder and pain in the neck.

Pete had emphasised that I needed to 'grip him' in these situations, since if he could, he would pile one fault on top of another and I would then be toast, since he wouldn't remember the first fault of several if you hadn't discussed it at the time. Hence the usefulness of knowing that, on double yellows, you were only pausing, not parking.

'Brian', at one point, managed to get us stranded in the middle of yellow hatch markings at a crossroads, long after the lights had expired for us and the other traffic had begun to move.

'Stay where you are Brian.'
'I've got to move I can't wait here.'
'Brian, DO NOT MOVE until I tell you.'

Clearly, assertiveness was an essential tool in this arena at times. Without it, a psychology degree cut no mustard.

I'm not sure whether Pete or I was the more astonished when I passed.

'Perhaps he saw potential in you.'
Thanks Pete!

Pete knew of a local school looking for an instructor, and within days I embarked on a new phase of life, actually earning money for a change. Out of the doldrums and onto the roads, my right foot quicker to the dual brake, if needed, than Mad Max grabbing the desert snake.

I replaced a guy whose pink badge had expired. Let's call him Steve.

'This is good. Steve never took me on these roads. We just stayed on the housing estate.'

Oh. Well, perhaps I might be alright at this.

It was a baptism of fire though. The first pupil I took to an actual test was a pupil at the uni. I didn't think he was too bad, until we headed towards the test centre. The closer to it we got, the slower he went. Extrapolating from this, we would likely still be a few hundred yards away from Chamberlain Road when the universe collapsed into a black hole at the end of time. No amount of pep talk made much difference and at the end the test sheet had more marks on it than a Picasso.

Of the first ten I took to Chamberlain Road, only one finished smiling. The nadir was three candidates in one day, all of whom failed. Sorry, 'identified a need for further training'. Luckily my friends in the pub were fairly patient with the ranting and swearing. There seemed no rhyme or reason to it. The one who had passed was far from the best driver of the bunch; he'd just held it together for half an hour. Maybe there was too much 'safety rug' in use. At the end of the day you can't do it for them.

Things improved gradually, especially when one of the examiners, after a test, remarked to me that I clearly worked very hard, and 'why didn't I join a proper driving school?'

Hmm. Clearly a hint to be acted upon.

The test in question had involved a middle-aged lady who had very little chance of passing really. However, she was very keen to try and one has to earn a living. My next driving school had an instructor who operated the school's automatic car. Sometimes we would see him chatting to his pupil, usually a middle-aged lady, parked on a quiet residential road. They would still be in the same spot after we had done three turns in the road and a reverse round a corner, waving cheerily as we drove by. One instructor who turned up at the test centre told us of one of his pupils for whom the weekly lesson consisted of a drive to ASDA, half an hour's shopping, and a drive home.

Are some people just never going to make it, however conscientious and patient the instructor might be? The answer, notwithstanding the worthy ethic that nothing is impossible, would be... correct-a-mundo.

Consider the young lady to whom I explained that, having steered a little to the left to leave a roundabout, she would then need to move the wheel back towards the right in order to straighten up. This resulted, at the next roundabout, in a whirlwind of arm movement as we exited, in an attempt to apply full right lock in a millisecond. Grabbing the wheel was not an option and I had to stand on the brake. Mad Max reflexes again useful.

Or the woman who approached us wanting a 'crash course'. Never a good starting description. Mike, the owner of the 'proper driving school', was quite keen on these type of enquiries from a business point of view, but would, to his credit, try to discourage those who thought they would quickly learn to drive during a week or two when they had no commitments, having never sat behind the wheel before. Usually a recipe for disappointment.

So, if they had some experience, maybe got near test level and not followed it through for whatever reason, the routine was to take them out on an assessment drive, before discussing a course.

This particular lady was fairly insistent that she knew it all and just needed a test after brushing up. Sometimes that's code for 'I have been to every other driving school in the area and you don't know me yet.'

As we motored along the A63 on the assessment drive, I watched with growing alertness as the rump of the Ford Sierra ahead of us grew gradually larger. I say gradually but if I'm honest it was a bit quicker than gradual, and given that the Sierra was doing about fifty, that meant we were accelerating quite a lot. She gave no sign whatsoever of being aware of the Sierra's existence. Not... one... jot.

I resorted to some braking, which provoked outrage. Goodness knows what sort of a plan she had in mind should she have got any nearer to the Sierra. Driving onto its roof maybe, like in one of those Matt Damon films? The Bourne Incapability.

Mike was disappointed when I said she was untrainable. One of the few we didn't attempt to help. Usually the ones who weren't really cut out for it, would vote with their feet at some point. Like the one from the outskirts of the city who wanted to 'try again'. I think we actually managed two lessons, the second of which involved the small, winding road which led north beyond the housing estate, out into the countryside, to practise steering in particular. It's a quiet road at the time of day we were driving, and the lesson plan was good, according to a colleague. This was back at the first driving school when I was still relatively new to it all.

All went reasonably well at first. The stretch of road has no pavements and just one telegraph pole in several miles. Attempting to negotiate a sharp bend, we ended up at 90 degrees to the road, with the front wheels about an inch from the verge, before she herself stopped the car. The telegraph pole stood in front of us, in the middle of the windscreen no more than two feet from the end of the bonnet. Remembering the maxim of the NDS instructor in Southport, to 'always say something positive', I spoke cheerily.

'You found the brake. Good.'

On the whole the intensive courses worked well, if, as we said, the pupil had enough prior experience. One such was a lad called Alan, who booked ten lessons. After assessing him I said that, in all honesty, he could get away with maybe five, and save some money. He was extremely good. Nevertheless, he insisted on the ten.

He passed the test triumphantly with no faults at all. Although he didn't show me the test sheet, I had no reason to doubt his word. The course had been fun and he was the epitome of a satisfied customer.

Some months later, we had an enquiry for a similar intensive course from a woman who lived out of our area, at Driffield. She was heavily pregnant and wanted to pass if possible before the baby came, so it was a bit touch and go timewise. It was arranged that I would meet her at Hull railway station, do a two-hour lesson, and see where we stood after that.

I drove us to a quiet housing estate only a short way from the station, where we could chat and start with some three-point turns (sorry, 'turns in the road'), and drive round the block a bit to get used to the car, etcetera, etcetera.

We swapped over and did a quick cockpit drill. A young man emerged from a house nearby and approached the car. What might we be accused of now? But as he got near, I recognised him as Alan.

'Hi, Alan, nice to see you,' I said, smiling, yet hoping the chat would be brief.

After the pleasantries, he leaned in across me, addressing the woman in the driver's seat.

'This instructor is absolutely brilliant. You couldn't do better. Won't go wrong with him...'

On he went. How having the licence had changed his life. How patient and knowledgeable I was. How professional the driving school was. And on. And on, in a paean of fulsome praise about my pleasantness and skills. It felt like fifteen minutes but was perhaps more like ten.

I don't remember any more about the lesson as such. It went quite well, I said to Mike, back at the office. I do remember that the woman never rang back. Perhaps the baby came early; we'll never know.

But perhaps she just thought that it was better not to get involved with a driving instructor who was desperate enough, for whatever reason, to arrange for a paid stooge to give a ridiculously effusive testimonial at the start of the lesson, using a considerable fraction of the driving time she had purchased.

Somebody who paid for the tuition but didn't maximise his usage of the available time was my friend's son, an intelligent but at times butterfly-minded lad. On the day of his test, he was late coming downstairs, late coming out of the house, and in need of cigarettes, for which we had to go to a shop on the way.

I drove us to the newsagent, and when he came out, explained that I would drive us to the park, where he would just have time to practise an emergency stop and a turn in the road, before we would have to head for the test centre. When we got to the park, he had a question.

'Dave, you know that old woman we passed, who was walking on the pavement on Park Grove?'

There may well have been such a woman, but driving is about priorities, and although I had been aware of various pedestrians, none of them had been a potential danger and my subconscious mind had consigned them to history.

'Well, possibly, but what's your point?'

'Would that have been an opportunity, if I'd been on the test, to show the examiner my emergency stop?'

?!?!?!!

As they say nowadays, you couldn't make it up.

Another who took a long time to come out of the house, was Antonio. Whereas my friend's son was merely disorganised, the reason for Antonio's lethargy had more to do with terror. Sometimes I would have to double back to the front door to remind him that I couldn't sit in the car on the main road outside his flat for too long. There he would be, with his entirely unsuitable ankle-high heavy boots in his hand, and I would watch for agonising moments as he began the long process of lacing them to the top.

'Don't be long.'

He was a student at the university, from, I think, either Venezuela or Columbia. A place where, he told me, a driving licence could be obtained by simply meeting the examiner and giving said examiner a hundred dollars. Or was it ten? The exchange rate escapes my memory now. Either way, the purity of the corruption remained untrammelled by the untidy detail of any test of competence.

In Antonio's case, he, or more probably his parents, had invested in a ten-hour course of actual car driving. This was laudable, but it probably added up to more like seven hours by the time he'd got his boots on. And it was never going to get us anywhere near the test centre.

But I tried my best. I recall us one day driving through an entrance into a coal yard after I had asked him to take the next turning. Fatigued by such adventures, at the end of one particularly wearing lesson, I plotted a route back to his flat which featured left turns only.

We lined up to turn into Beverley High Road, where a filter lane fed the traffic out onto the main dual carriageway, separated from the large crossroads by an island on our right.

I heard a siren in the distance, getting louder. The two cars in front of us moved out onto the dual carriageway, perhaps thinking to clear the lane in case the emergency vehicle was behind us and wanted to get through. In the absence of any other information, and knowing that hobnail boot pedal control wasn't the most trustworthy resource, I told Antonio to stay where he was, whilst leaving my foot over the instructor's brake pedal.

The siren wasn't coming from behind us. It was somewhere slightly to our left, on the dual carriageway. All became clear in an instant, as a red Astra came into view, heading quickly towards us, on the wrong side of that dual carriageway. With the crossroads still clogged with traffic, the Astra, hardly slowing, turned into our slip road. The slip road wide enough for one car. I was glad we hadn't tried to move forward, and watched in fascination as the baseball-capped youth driving it flicked the wheel right, then left. This took him through a gap in the railings provided for pedestrians, and onto the pavement, where he simply drove on, parallel with the road we had come along to get to the crossroads.

The car following the Astra had the siren. It was a big blue Volvo saloon, unmarked. The driver, blue lights flashing behind the grille, in calm but fast pursuit, did the same manoeuvre. Right flick, left flick, and off down the pavement.

Before too much longer, we were back at the flat. The plan for the less stressful left turns had not really worked out too well.

'Sorry about that, Antonio. That's not normal in this country.'

'Phew! That was incredible. You said "stop", and then, wow!'

'Yes. Did you get a good look at the driver?'

'Yes. They were police. They were wearing ties.'

'Yes, but that was the blue car. I'm talking about the red car.'

'What red car?'

Later on, in the pub after work, I related the tale to a pal.

'Don't take him for a test, Dave. *Don't take him for a test!!*'

Had I been worried?

I wouldn't say so. There wasn't really time to worry. You make a decision, and live with the consequences.

There is a theory that a perfect instructor will never use the dual controls. That might work if there was such a thing as a perfect pupil, but I hope to have demonstrated in the foregoing that the theory is balderdash.

I was grateful to have a brake available. You can't hope to gradually withdraw the 'safety rug' from under the pupil without a backup plan if things go awry.

One of my pupils was a junior doctor from India. A lovely chap, great company, but an interesting driver. He apprised me of the differing attitudes.

'In your country, you drive in lanes; in my country, we drive according to the availability of the road.' And – 'In my country, if we see a gap, we rush immediately in.'

Several times I had to stop him at busy crossroads and roundabouts. Not just verbally. He was qualified in India, I should say.

'I could have gone, there.'

'I'll tell you what,' I said. 'If you bring a car (and make sure it's a very strong car), we'll try it your way.'

In the end, you have to trust your pupils and, all being well, let them go. Driving through Hull one day, I commented to my student, who was a mature woman with whom I got along very well.

'Do you think you ought to be moving across to the other lane fairly soon?'

'Who's driving this car, you or me?'

After I had finished laughing, I said with great pleasure, 'OK, you're ready for test.'

Some years after qualifying as an ADI, I was lucky to have a very modest motor racing 'career'. How did it compare with life on the streets of Hull in the driving school car?

I wouldn't say I worried. It was supposed to be fun, after all.

I made decisions, and lived with the consequences.

I made mistakes, but not as many as the pupils.

My reactions sometimes had to be quick.

There were no roundabouts, crossroads, or speed limits.

And, unless I had screwed up very badly indeed, there was nothing coming the other way.

So, really, I just went motor racing for a relaxing break.

Incoming Missile

We were in a Chevy Suburban on Highway 1, California. Living the dream, as they say these days.

I called the vehicle The White Whale, as a nod to the vast convertible in Hunter S. Thompson's *Fear and Loathing in Las Vegas*. The Suburban was hardly a convertible, more what we in the UK would call an estate car. Even though it was the size of a small bus. Thus it shared the vastness, as well as the whiteness, of Hunter's conveyance.

Perfect, then. When one of the trainees at work informed me, a few months later, that Tony Soprano drove a Chevy Suburban, it was just the icing on the cake.

'Cool,' I said.

Highway 1 qualifies as a bona fide Wonder of the World, and can be enjoyed from the well-upholstered, armchair-spec seats of your boardroom-sized sports utility vehicle, thus linking one of the most breathtakingly beautiful landscapes on earth with the acme of Detroit ironmongery in delivering an effortless heavenly experience.

The sublime sampled by the impudent.

Every few miles, we stopped, as most tourists do, to gaze at the endless Pacific below us. The sunlight reflecting up, suffusing down. Silver, dark blue waters. Infinite soft blue sky.

We even saw a pod of whales moving north. Stopping on impulse by the side of the road, we parked next to a few cars already there. Folks had congregated, looking out to sea. Someone let us look through their binoculars. There were six whales, I think, breaking the surface from time to time. The word awesome should be reserved for only this.

It had been thirty-six years since I had been this way, hitch-hiking north from Santa Barbara to Big Sur. I had the phone number of a friend of a friend who lived there, Robin. At least I had written beforehand, rather than just turning up out of the blue. Robin was an artist, the ideal occupation for a resident of Big Sur, which is rich in magnificent viewpoints, poor in supermarkets and run of the mill employment vacancies.

My lift dropped me at the nearest thing to a village hub, which was a sort of general store, possessing a phone. Robin kindly drove down and met me. We spent some time in a bar, which may or may not have been the same establishment. Either that or we drove up the mountain track to his house, met his wife, drove back down later, had a drink or two, and back up. This illustrates how memory is very selective, and can filter out non-vital details, especially over thirty-six years.

These were the days when friends of friends of friends who shared the general ethos of the hippy subculture would help like-minded travellers by putting them up for a day or two, perhaps longer if they could offer a degree of intelligent conversation and weren't mad.

Robin was an affable enough chap, an expatriate from Coventry according to our mutual friend. He did seem a little preoccupied, but warmed to me when I said that I was a writer, of sorts. It wasn't mere bullshit to oil the wheels of artistic discourse, even though forty-one years of moderately mundane existence were to elapse before I had a book published.

He explained to me, in the bar, that the source of his detached air was in a personal matter, nothing to do with my presence. Things had changed since he had replied to my letter. Now he and his wife were heading for a divorce, and the atmosphere at home, whilst civilised, wasn't the easiest. At any other time, I would have been more than welcome, but as it was... I was not to worry, though, he would find me an alternative place to stay.

The following day, Californian sun presented Big Sur in its full casual grandeur, as I stared across the valley from Robin's hillside home. He explained he had talked to a friend who had a cabin which was unoccupied at the moment. I could borrow it for as long as I wished.

A short while later, a fellow appeared at the house. He would be showing me the way to the cabin. I think he may have been a friend of the friend who actually owned the cabin. It didn't matter. He was jovial, and the only link to the next stopover in the pilgrimage of this wide-eyed, would-be Kerouac.

He asked if I'd got any proper boots, and laughed when I said that I hadn't. The suede-look, two tone brown trainers, which I had crossed the continent in, would have to do. I realised why he'd laughed after just a few yards. The route was downwards. I choose the word 'route', rather than 'path', very deliberately. Neither did the word 'valley' adequately encompass the ambience of the short expedition. 'Steep canyon, nearly vertical in places', was better.

There was little point in heading forth for a recce and retrieving my backpack later. It was a one-way trip, with my portable world acting as a potential pendulum behind me. The one thing I had in my favour was that I had spent the previous two years driving a truck for an engineering company. The manager did the servicing on it, but months would go by without him looking at it. Then he would use it for a job.

'How do you drive this?'

'Develop arms like Popeye's because you never grease the kingpins.'

He would park it in front of the welding shop and get the oxy-acetylene torch on the kingpins to get the grease softened up enough to put some fresh grease through, and we would be OK for another few months.

So the strong arms came in handy when the first part of the descent of the canyon involved a rope. It stopped short of proper mountaineering, because the rope was a permanent fixture, tied to a sturdy post a few yards away from Robin's house. This arrangement had the status of a main thoroughfare, in the context of the Big Sur universe. The section involving the rope did wonders for concentrating the mind, as I descended for perhaps twenty feet, hanging on grimly as my smoothly soled feet scrabbled for grip and I swung to and fro on the rope like a demented roly-poly man.

Mercifully, we reached the next section, which was a mere terrifying gradient, and the rope section at the top turned out to be the trickiest part of the 'trail'. Not that the rest of it was exactly an amble.

The cabin was nestled amongst the massive trees that darkened the gulley at the bottom of the canyon, and was a welcome sight. It was tiny, but adequate. Boasting a bed, a chair, and a table. And a silver, metallic bread bin on a shelf.

My new abode. I could leave the padlock key with the guy at the shop when I eventually hit the road.

I thanked the friend of the friend of the friend. We had a brief chat, during which he described to me how intelligent the local racoons were. Then off he went back up the canyon, ready to use the mountain goat skills of the typical Big Sur resident, once more.

After I settled in (not a long process), I worked my way down through the woods to the main road, and walked to the store for some provisions. I had the key to paradise for as long as I wished. But I knew that I would be on the road again before too long.

During the night there was a disturbance, close at hand. A rustling. My torch was out of reach.

I froze, trying to think what might have got in. The window had been shut, I was sure. A further bout of rustling was ended by a loud metallic clang. Then silence. I found the torch. There was no creature to be seen, nor evidence that I had been visited.

No evidence other than the catch on the bread bin having been overcome with ease. And the fact that I was no longer the owner of even a partial bread loaf.

I lingered for a couple of days in the earthly paradise before sticking my thumb out for a lift north. There were a few buildings scattered along the road in the area, when we came by in 2014, but none of them triggered a memory of where that bar had been. The cabin might as well have been in a fairy tale. I had been in a magical, beautiful realm, and my two abiding memories of Big Sur were of hanging onto a rope above a steep ravine, and being alarmed by an invisible monster in the dark, which turned out to be a dextrous racoon. Maybe that's why some people are drawn to situations which provoke a rush of adrenaline. Memory manufacture.

We were driving south this time, and could stop wherever we wanted, overlooking the ocean, to drink in the light like pilgrims. We'd come from Dallas in the White Whale, old Route 66 to LA, and were staying with Janet's uncle Harold and his wife Linda, in the Simi Valley on the north west side of LA. This was a three-day side trip, inland on 101, up by Salinas and down to Monterey, before returning via the fabled Highway 1, taking in the elephant seal beach and Hearst's grandiose castle near San Simeon. The last day was the least taxing, driving wise, from the hotel at San Simeon, and past Santa Barbara before hitting LA.

In 1978, I'd delivered a car from the east coast to LA, finishing up at Newport Beach, where I rang the owner to find out how to get to their home in a place called Fountain Valley. It took three hours to get a reply, and to finally find the address. After meeting Mrs Heiber and partaking of an orange juice, I was on my way again, technically homeless after the loss of the Pontiac station wagon in which I'd slept for the preceding week, all the way from Washington DC.

Finding a bus stop, I hailed the first bus and asked which way he was going. He simply pointed at the road in front of him, wordlessly. Ha ha. It was like the westerns I had watched as a kid.

'Which way did them thievin' varmints go?'

'They went thataway!'

I was less than amused, after half the afternoon had gone in getting the car to its owner.

'OK, what place, then?'

'Santa Ana.'

'Is that the end of the line?'

'Yep.'

'OK, I'll go there then.'

I got a Greyhound from Santa Ana to the downtown LA bus station. I'd slept in the Pontiac for the last time the night before, off a dusty side road where the interstate was still passing fields rather than buildings. It had been a good decision, because the morning leg to the lady's house turned out to be about sixty miles worth of suburban clutter either side of the freeway. I figured that the best plan would be to push on through LA altogether. You can't see everything in a city, but you can sure get a flavour of it in the Greyhound bus station.

From downtown LA, I headed north, on the bus, to Santa Barbara. I thought it might be a better jumping off point for hitch-hiking north. Given that walking to the edge of LA would presumably take at least a week...

The cheap hotel room at the Schooner Inn in Santa Barbara was entirely adequate, though I've never forgotten the remark of a guy I chatted to in a café before turning in for the night.

'It's got roaches!'

I saw a movie later, on returning from the States, one of those road-trippy, rambling stories about people on the seedier side of American life. The lead character entered his hotel room, went into the bathroom where he wetted one side of a bar of soap, then came back to the bedroom, whipped back the bedcovers, and stamped the soap down in quick succession on each cockroach that was revealed. Like Whack-a-Mole. Stick-a-Roach, with the prize being a decent night's sleep. I've always, unfairly, associated that scene with the Schooner Inn at Santa Barbara.

As an alert reader, you might be wondering at this point, bearing in mind my theory about memories being more deeply ingrained after adrenaline fuelled moments, how I happen to be able to recall piffling details like the name of the lady who owned the Pontiac, and the name of the hotel in Santa

Barbara, yet cannot provide any coherent detail about the events surrounding my arrival at Big Sur all those years ago.

The answer is a simple one. I unearthed the scribbled diary of my USA wanderings, consisting of loose pages which had dwelt at the bottom of a box for 42 years. Thus, I learnt that Robin's wife was called Kirsten, and chatted to me in the bar, before I talked to Robin again for a while, before we drove up the road to their house. Robin and I slept on the veranda under the stars after talking until late. He remarked that I was 'so mellow', compared to the local population. Rather a mind-boggling complement, considering the wider world's general perception of Californians, perhaps, although it may shed light on my later failure to build a business empire from humble beginnings using only determination and pluck.

Robin missed the rain, he said.

It may be worthy of note, also, that I met a guy of Norwegian ancestry whilst waiting for Robin and Kirsten to arrive. He told me that it was important that he should die with a sword in his hand, because of Valhalla. Consequently, he always carried a knife, which was, he thought, near enough to qualify. These sort of statements never really surprised me, during my trip. Many people seemed to be on the lookout for some sort of code to live by.

I was also reminded, reading the notes, of what the friend of a friend had said to me on seeing my face as I looked at the rope that hung over the abyss.

'Just imagine it's Piccadilly Circus.'

Thanks, mate. That's really helpful.

The guy who owned the cabin turned out to be called Alan, and I did meet him later, though I don't recall anything about it. Memory again, or not, in this case.

The notes are hardly extensive, for the most part. But useful. They reveal that "I lingered... in the earthly paradise" for four days, rather than a couple; that I saw seals; that I went to Partington Cove; that I walked five miles to Ventana for shopping, and got a lift back.

We can conclude at this point, from these findings, that if it is important to you to remember something, either do a bungee jump while you are studying it, or (easier) write it down.

One part of my progress north which didn't need the notes as an aide memoire, was the ride from San Luis Obispo to Morro Bay, in a ratty, rusty, salt-chewed little Japanese car. The driver had longish, minimally-tended hair, and his attire tended more towards casual scruff than casual chic.

I asked him what he did.

'I'm a surfer.'

'But do you have a job?' He didn't look the athletic type at all.

'No. Just a surfer.'

OK. Welcome to California.

Now here I was, near Santa Barbara once more. It was all freeway from here, an easy cruise to Harold and Linda's.

Traffic on US freeways doesn't follow the same rules as we do on UK motorways. Passing is permissible on either side. It works OK, because everyone is following the same playbook. Believe me. When you get to LA, you can have stretches seven lanes wide sometimes, so you need your wits about you when the traffic gets heavy and is moving quickly. Just go with the flow, that's the trick. Go with the flow, man. We actually used to talk like that in the seventies, in my circles. Go with the flow.

See what happens. That was another phrase we had, that covered everything. See what happens.

We were in the left lane, which is to say, the one alongside the central reservation. Don't forget they drive on the right, abroad. Did you know that traffic passing each other whilst driving on the right tends to create disadvantageous anti-clockwise vortices which translate eventually to an atmosphere more conducive to tornados and such like? I read about it many years ago in a newspaper which was reporting on some research which had been carried out. Interesting. Britain, Australia, and one or two others had got it right. Everyone else is busy ruining the world.

Surprising that the Brexit people never made use of the fact in their propaganda. I couldn't tell you the source of the research, nor the year, nor the newspaper, other than that it was a broadsheet rather than a redtop. The rest is lost to my blessedly ruined memory. I have a theory that once the memory reaches a certain level of clutterment, like a garage with too many restoration projects going on, it is necessary to periodically jettison certain items in order to accommodate any recently acquired snippets of wisdom. Certain favoured or ingrained visions always escape the cull, like the thought of humanity never being able to escape the fateful decisions all over the world, to mostly drive on the right; or, more vividly, the mind-movie about hanging off a rope at Big Sur, swaying like a gibbon on a fig tree.

The traffic built up, the nearer we came to the conurbation of Santa Barbara, and became more stop/start. Did you know that the behavioural dynamics of highway traffic follows, to a remarkable extent, the patterns seen in herds of buffalo, and is ultimately governed by chaos theory and fractal mathematics? That was in one of the Royal Institution's Christmas lectures. Again, I didn't note the year.

Suffice to say, in layman's terms, that it seems very random. You come to a stop for no apparent reason, after a while you move again, a few people skip lanes, you slow down, you speed up, you stop. Repeat. Most people who drive have experienced it.

This time, our lane had stopped, after previously making better progress than the other two lanes. We sat in our file whilst traffic in the other two lanes cruised past, moderately quickly. A slightly unusual pattern, but well within the bounds of possibility, and probably unremarkable to a fractal mathematician. Most of us just adopt the buffalo stance (wasn't that a song?) and accept that sometimes you're in the wrong part of the herd.

Then, something changed. Something that seemed to push the boundaries of even chaos theory. Simultaneously, the traffic in both of the other lanes stopped coming past. The lanes were empty, the traffic in them disappearing up the road. At the same moment, the traffic in our file had begun to move. It was my turn to follow, as the vehicle in front of me set off.

Just as he started, I heard the screeching wail of a car skidding, coming from somewhere behind us. It sounded as though it had been going pretty fast before the driver lost control.

I've had a lot of experience on the road. I even got to do some motor racing in my later years. I like the decision-making aspect. I find it quite involving. I despise the advance of 'artificial intelligence' into vehicles, even though, ultimately, they might make them safer than bad human drivers. At which point we might all be deemed to be bad human drivers, and banned from mixing with the 'intelligent' vehicles.

I marshalled the information available to me. One, there was a totally free highway ahead of our car. Two, there was an incoming missile somewhere behind us, the trajectory of which was unknown. I decided to stay where I was.

We sat there. The best thing we could do was nothing. Make sure the brake was on and bask for a few milliseconds in the knowledge that we had taken out the collision damage waiver.

The howl of the skid grew louder.

It was the kind of howl that usually precedes a sizeable crunching noise. I was quite calm because I had done all I could. The decision had been made. I supposed I hoped mostly that Janet would be OK, because her side was more vulnerable. But there wasn't a great deal of time for contemplation.

The car came past us going backwards, whilst in the process of spinning. It was a good job that I hadn't moved, since he finished up in the barrier, exactly where I would have been if I had got a car-length forward before his arrival. The spin was slewing him round as he passed us, and the back end of his car then walloped the barrier, bringing to an end his day's outing.

I later found a small black scuff on our front bumper, where his tyre, presumably, had kissed our car on its way past. As I say, always take out the collision damage waiver.

After a couple of moments, he stepped out. The traffic at this point was still frozen. They'd probably had a spectacular show. He'd perhaps been barrelling up at speed behind our stationary queue, tried to do a quick lane change, and lost it. It didn't matter anyway. Nobody was hurt.

He stood looking at the rear end of his car, in that astonished way that teenagers with Vauxhall Corsas exhibit, in Tesco's car park on a dark night, when it all goes pear-shaped and they crash into their mate's stationary Vauxhall Corsa, after their attempt to park next to it, using a handbrake turn, goes catastrophically wrong. 'Now, who can I blame for this? I'm a teenager so it must be somebody else's fault. It was, er... me. Oh.'

In California, young people are not allowed to drink until they are twenty-one, yet they are allowed loose with a potentially lethal instrument (car) from the age of just sixteen. This guy took the Sweet Sixteen persona to the limit and beyond, appearing to be about fourteen years old.

After checking that Janet was OK, I disembarked, to see if he needed any advice. A small amount of traffic had started filtering through, fairly slowly. His car was embedded diagonally, in such a way that most of the middle lane was available, tempting some drivers to use it. The only refuge which wasn't open highway was a two-foot-wide strip of concrete surface between the marked roadway and the centre barrier.

I wanted to make sure that he didn't start wandering about. He was on his mobile phone by now, engrossed in conversation, standing between our car and his. I stood next to him, hoping that he would soon finish his call to the appropriate authorities.

'Er, have you finished? Who have you called?'

'Hi. I've been calling my uncle. He's got a breakdown truck.'

'I think you should call the police and let them know. We're not in a very safe position here.'

'Oh. You think?'

'Yes. Definitely.'

'I guess so.'

It turned out that someone else had notified the police, because the next thing that occurred was the arrival of two California Highway patrol motorcyclists. Their smart fawn uniforms obviously commanded instant respect from the public at large, because, once more, the southbound lanes were rendered quiescent, all traffic waiting behind one of the riders, who stood imposingly next to his machine in the centre of the carriageway, whilst his colleague rode up to us at the scene of the accident.

After brief conversations with myself and with the missile pilot, and after ascertaining that the wrecked car was physically drivable, the officer directed us to follow him. We moved our cars across the empty lanes and on to the hard shoulder a little further along. Here, in relative safety, we were able to give our details and brief statements.

A third witness was a woman in a saloon, who had pulled over on the hard shoulder near where we were, presumably shortly after the crash. It turned out that she was the one who had reported the incident. Much better than phoning an uncle.

She reckoned she had changed lane a bit abruptly just before the kid lost control, and might have had a hand in precipitating the incident. I don't think I would have been quite so ready to queue up for any blame after the other driver had left evidence of his speed, in the form of more skid marks than on a Jackson Pollock, across several hundred yards of Highway 1, but there you go. It's a free country. She was a nice lady.

She was the last to be interviewed, after the cop had taken details from the baby driver and myself. By this time, the uncle had shown up. His pick-up truck was surprisingly modest in size for an American one. Smaller than an intercontinental locomotive. If he did own a tow truck, he had left it at his garage.

The kid's car was something called a Saturn, a make I hadn't heard of. It's an offshoot of General Motors. The car had been a small saloon, styled in the school of unprepossessing jellymould. It must have been worth only a few hundred dollars even before the whack into the barrier introduced some wild origami jaggedness into the bland curves of its rear quarters. The lad had earlier been muttering about whether it would repair; but I felt sure that the Saturn had completed its final orbit.

We watched for a while from the car as the uncle chatted to him. It was a case of waiting until the Highway Patrol guy dismissed us all, so we just studied the body language to entertain ourselves. It looked like a tow truck from the police's list would be required, presumably for legal reasons. The uncle must have explained the situation and told the kid to see if there was anything in the car which he needed to take with him.

I became excited and spoke to Janet.

'Get your tablet. Take a picture with it! He's coming to the back.'

The youngster had finished his quick inspection of the interior, and now approached the boot to see if he could get the lid open and salvage the most important item of luggage. The thing that meant most to him in the whole world.

In a few minutes we would be back on the road. Back to uncle Harold's. Harold, who had left the UK as a young man, and built a life in this earthly paradise. The land of everlasting sun, of private castles, of Disney characters, of tech entrepreneurs ruling the world from space, knowing what their billions of social network customers had for breakfast. Knowing the intricacies of your preoccupations.

The land of farmers drilling ever deeper for sources of underground water, the land of forest fires consuming entire settlements, the land of trophy wives killed horribly by cult members or deranged public figures from the entertainment industry.

I loved California.

Janet's photography skills were rewarded as she pressed the virtual button on the screen of her device, just as the boy pulled the vital item from the storage compartment of his wrecked Saturn module. The one thing above all, that he needed to save. The item which was the very quintessence of life as an adolescent in the Golden State.

His skateboard.

I wonder what he will be when he grows up?

Passion

I had a conversation with a woman from somewhere in the world, the other day. It was a computerised conversation, so, at the cost of a bit of typing, you could avoid face contact and have time to think what you wanted to say.

I thought the woman was in California, because she hoped that I was having a wonderful day. In fact, I remarked as such, together with the observation that, in the UK, we tended to be pretty happy if we were having a reasonable day, and that a wonderful one wasn't necessarily required.

After a lengthy pause for considering whether I was a nutter, she replied, calmly noting that she was in Columbia. The text seemed calm anyway, although civil unrest and gun battles with a drug cartel might have been taking place outside her window, for all I knew.

'Crikey,' I said, to indicate British-flavoured friendliness and sympathise with her position on the great Ludo board of planet Earth. I was able to say that I hoped things were alright where she was, due to the world wide Covid epidemic of the time, rather than have her think that a blinkered perspective of South American life led me to believe that civil unrest and feral drug gangs were a constant feature of her environment.

In the end, after the pleasantries, Karen was unable to resolve my query, providing instead a phone number which promised contact with another person somewhere else in the world, via the double-edged medium of actual speech, possibly even within the UK. I needn't have worried, though, because after progressing through the automated menu, I was spat out through the other end with advice to find a subsection of the user-unfriendly menu in front of me on the computer screen.

This got me in touch with Assakhana, who could have been a bewitchingly named exotic beauty in India, Baku or Milton Keynes, or a robot. There was no way of knowing. I typed in my query, was spat out for using more than 255 characters, and shortened my query. Then I was able to properly begin my relationship with the mysterious Assakhana.

Back in the late eighties, a computer-savvy friend had told me how good Norton was, for protecting your PC against malicious hacking. I had presumed Norton was some clever guy in a well-appointed garden shed, obviously in the UK, licensing his clever software and moving to a proper office in due course of time, wearing a shirt and tie.

I'm now more worldly-wise, and know that all software, unless Chinese, belongs to Californian billionaires who wear T-shirts. I also presume that Norton must be the same, though their website is hard enough to negotiate, without wasting time to examine the small print to find out whether their HQ is in Palo Alto. It doesn't matter anyway, as the tentacles of these companies now reach across the globe.

I was attempting to renew my Norton anti-virus software, after paying for a small piece of cardboard with a code number on it, in a shop. The whole process involved agreeing to automatic renewal, then paying with my code number, then later disagreeing with automatic renewal if I still had any mental strength after the stress of engaging with the Norton website.

Assakhana, with her gentle and seductive text responses, guided me through the labyrinth. It wasn't impossible, and saved me hacking at random through their various menu headings too much. Still a lot of work to save a tenner, I thought. But her air of cool competence helped; I had nearly been driven to distraction by the difficulty of understanding an Asian woman's accent on the phone, when I had cancelled my McAfee automatic renewal a couple of months earlier.

Assakhana soothed me, with her hypnotic little flowing dots saying she was typing, giving me time to compose myself and resolve not to completely flip at the unreasonable need to undergo this whole process. I imagined her at the court of Tamburlaine the Great, serving him entrancingly perfumed tea as she shuttled back and forth in her intricately patterned silk robe.

Or she could have been a robot. Was it loving concern that she showed when I took rather a long time following her prescription of how to navigate the website? It was simply that I had come to a point where I was forced to choose automatic renewal, or abandon the quest.

'Are you all right David? You are taking rather a long time to respond. Is there anything I can do to help you?'

In the end, she promised to help me to cancel the automatic renewal after I had paid with my cardboard code. She never did.

By then, I had become vaguely familiar with the stupid website, and could see how to do the cancellation. Later, when I had recovered from the encounter. So I wasn't worried.

It still hurt, though. Not re-engaging to fulfil her promise.

'Your session has timed out.'

There was a limit? How naïve I had been, chasing disembodied women all across the world, from California to

Columbia, and on to Xanadu and who knows where, if it had continued?

It was like a Dear John letter. 'David, while you were away fighting the Skynet menace in a distant theatre of war, I have met someone else who can give me the responses that I need. I'm sorry it had to end this way, but you just spent too long hacking around the menu and moaning about its inadequate design. I don't know why you had to be like that. Everyone else in the world seems to manage successfully.'

Yeah, right. When they weren't closing down the computer in disgust.

I thought I'd done well to keep it together. I was about an hour late having lunch, all to save a tenner. I'd not thrown anything across the room in a blind rage. When I was younger, I probably would have done.

I was explaining all this to a girlfriend many years ago. The awful temper, just like my father's. I never worked out whether it was temperament, or learnt. The former, I think. If anything, it was worse than his, but my tendency to smash inanimate objects to pieces was a release, I found.

She was probably being diplomatic when she replied.

'It's good to be passionate.' Meaning, at least react, to show you're alive.

Karen had been passionate. Wishing me a wonderful day rather than a merely average one. Yet Assakhana, from the same company, had turned out to be, if I dare say it, a tease. All nice and friendly at first, concerned about me when I was offline for a while, then nagging, nagging, 'Where are you?' before the final bitter heartbreak. It just goes to show how people who seem similar at first can turn out to be totally different.

What is constant, though, is that Norton, as a company, isn't passionate. It exists only to take money off you, and do it in the way that suits Norton best. To this end, its website is designed to deal with you automatically. All these tech companies hate to have to talk to you. They will tell you that they are passionate about this, that, and the other, but it's only skin deep.

Everybody seems to be passionate about almost anything these days. It's no longer enough to merely say you're keen on something. No, you've got to be 'passionate'. Everything is amazing, everything is awesome. The vast panoply of available language reduced to a fig leaf after mass culling of dictionaries, with only casual superlatives now available.

'Awesome' must now be used as an adjective meaning 'very slightly better than average'; 'amazing' for something that engages the interest of a modern person with the attention span of a gnat, for more than a couple of seconds. And 'passion' has been coerced, handcuffed, and frogmarched into service as a marketing tool.

Consider the car marques Jaguar, Aston Martin and, lately to the party, Bentley. All now 'brands' rather than mere manufacturers. All owned by corporate giants or a mega-rich consortium, all 'passionate about their heritage'. All having made or announced the making of 'continuation cars' to exploit that heritage. These are cars which look like their famous cars of the sixties – or in Bentley's case the thirties – built with modern facilities, no doubt better than the originals in build quality. But unuseable in the sense of being completely unable to meet modern regulations for car manufacture, because they replicate the original technology. Driveable sculptures, in effect, for the private roads of your estate. Where, perchance, you can use the Bond-inspired machine guns on the Aston to eliminate hoi-polloi who may stray onto the property.

For sure, these companies are passionate. Passionate about milking the coin from those of their billionaire clientele stupid enough to buy these white elephants. Sorry, British Racing Green elephants. A celebration of their heritage, they say. No it's not, it's a bastardization of it.

Passion should be reserved for your wife or equivalent, or used for smashing up poorly designed components which don't do what they are supposed to do.

And maybe for hating wealth-burdened self-satisfied pricks who over-use the word 'passion', with a passion.

Tribal

I asked one of the lads at work what his tattoo meant.

'Tribal,' he said.

Oh. OK. It looked a bit like that dazzle camouflage on some of the First World War battleships. Lots of zigs and a few zags.

Or maybe copied from a Mauri. Mauris and Fijians didn't have to explain what their tattoos meant. They had fierceness and could do what they wanted to do, for thousands of years, until the white man came and identified that they were only armed with clubs, and could be relatively easily spotted in their peaceful idyllic settlements, despite their attempts at optical camouflage.

It was less obvious why the lads at work wanted tattoos. Maybe to seem too fierce for employment at a fast-food outlet. They had probably looked through catalogues at tattoo parlours and been told that 'tribal' was popular. The tattooists would perhaps have opened their books of designs at the 'random fierceness' pages, and gently guided the aspirants to designs with great swathes of zig-zaggy blue ink, for which they could charge a fair bit more. I presume this because the designs tended to be ink-rich.

The other benefit for the tattooist would be that the recipient would be pretty much stuck with it, as it would never be easy to disguise the design with one featuring more blue ink. Because of the pre-existing ink-heavy nature of it.

So the recipient would generally go, 'Oh well, I might as well have another design somewhere else on my body, now I've started. Now I'm no longer an unsullied inkless virgin, so to speak.' They would have used, in their mind, vocabulary just like that, I'm sure.

They will have also said to their mates, 'Tribal,' when asked about it. And their mates will have thought, 'Hmm. Tribal.' And the word will have spread throughout the land, and will have felt good to those who had heard the word.

Those who had not heard the word were fated to wander aimlessly through the land, un-inked and ill at ease, trying to cope with the ambiguities of the modern world without a clear belief system. Poor bewildered souls.

Clearly, there is a deep need in most humans to have some sort of tribal identity. A sense of belonging, kinship, and willingness to snarl at someone a bit different. Civilisation has advanced to such a degree nowadays that there is a myriad of tribes available. Something for everyone, so that we can all feel happy and secure and never have to pick on a weaker group to bolster our pathetically insecure self-image.

I must have been in need of something tribal in 1966, because I joined the football tribe. I think the underlying reasons were: enjoying kicking a ball around; being fourteen; and liking to peruse league tables. Plus the deep-seated psychological imperative to be tribal, obviously.

Many people then would have been transfixed in front of black and white tellies listening to Kenneth Wolstenholme saying, "They think it's all over. It is now!" during the World Cup final, and you would be forgiven for thinking that this momentous event had triggered my interest. Far from it, though. On holiday in North Wales at the time, I was forced to engage with the climactic extra-time epic in front of a neighbour's TV, with their two much older boys cheering everything that West Germany did. I've never been much of a nationalist but it was nevertheless slightly traumatic.

No, my interest in top-flight football had been sparked off by the FA Cup final, a few weeks earlier. Sheffield Wednesday were playing Everton, and since I had been born in Sheffield, I decided to join the 'Sheffield Wednesday supporters who lived in south Manchester' tribe. It was a small tribe, but I felt it was worth it when Wednesday took the lead, then extended it. Two-nil, this was superb. One of the goals scored by the mellifluous McCalliog. What could be more poetic?

Everton's slow, remorseless comeback, to take the match three-two, became engraved on my young, impressionable mind for years to come. Nobody in the family was football oriented, and thus nobody fully understood my glum mood during our excursion to the cinema later that evening.

The high, and massive low, had left me addicted, though, and hope remained for many years. The mellifluous McCalliog scored one of the goals that sunk England at Wembley in 1967, their first defeat since becoming world champions. In Scottish minds, this meant that their team were now world kings, but nobody bothered telling the rest of the world to change the record books. No matter, a Wednesday player had been a key figure. Tremendous.

As the seasons ticked by, I was able to watch Wednesday losing to both Manchester United and Manchester City, and even went to Wednesday's famous Hillsborough ground once with my cousin Margaret and her family. A lovely, joyous person, Margaret died a few years ago after fighting cancer. I remember her helping me get my cufflinks sorted on the day of my wedding. She had the illness by then, but had chosen to tell nobody.

The vicar at the funeral was a Sheffield United fan. Highly amused, he told of how Margaret was first given a season ticket at the age of eight, by her father Albert.

"That's *sixty years* of watching Sheffield Wednesday!!!"

No finer exposition of any individual's inner fortitude could, surely, ever be expressed in tribute.

By then, though, the Wednesday thing was effectively far behind me. The last straw had come in 1993, when they lost two finals in the same year. Both to Arsenal, who had more than sufficient trophies to their name already, and both by the same score, two-one.

It was beyond enough. No more the fool, no more the very part-time but ardent Wednesdayite. No more listening to the chant of 'Monday, Tuesday, who the hell are Wednesday?' on the Man City terraces or from Peter John Addison in the school classroom (neither of which I had heard for over half a lifetime). It just wasn't rational, and I absolved myself from guilt and forgot all about the wretched club. Coincidentally I also stopped smoking that year, but I'm sure there was no connection.

There simply weren't enough lifetimes to see Wednesday finally ascend to the summit of European football where they belonged. Or even get to the FA Cup final again. Their effort last time I saw them on TV, in 2019, ended against the billionaire Arabian owned squad of Manchester City. Home at Hillsborough, one-nil down, I watched on telly as they seemed drilled not to wander across the halfway line. When one-nil down with less than fifteen minutes left. How spineless can you get? Pah! At least go down fighting.

The lads at work would usually support one of the top six teams, with the odd Everton straggler. That way, they had a chance of cheering something. Man U. was the most popular choice among non-Mancunians. I didn't approve of it of course, but liked to tell them about how I saw George Best leave Tony Book standing on the halfway line before scoring in the first few minutes of a Manchester derby match, or how the supposedly affable Busby, at United, always tried to ship out rejected players to lower league clubs so that they didn't return as an opposition threat.

I liked the history of it all, highlighted in Eamon Dunphy's book *A Strange Kind of Glory* (Dunphy, 1991), and Colin Schindler's study of the social background to footballers' existences, in *George Best and 21 Others* (Schindler, 2004). They have academies for young players nowadays, and the fans choose teams as if selecting a fashion item. Owners, managers and players migrate from afar to bountiful England, whilst the shop doorways of perfidious Albion seem to be home to more people than ever before.

And only the stubborn die-hards support teams like Sheffield Wednesday, knowing that it will teach them resilience. Like the biblical Job, they cling to their faith, however threadbare its promise.

In the wider world, thankfully, the more sophisticated members of the population are free to purchase Man U. shirts, where they can advertise the Chevrolet tribe, or whoever are the sponsors that year. The global village, pick your tribe! Just the other day, I saw the football stars MESSI of Barcelona, with MANE and FIRMINO of Liverpool, entertaining a crowd of four or five, on a beach near Great Yarmouth. Great of them to give their time. Surprising how small they are in the flesh, though, they only looked about nine years old.

We can see from all this, that there is absolutely no excuse for not having a tribe these days. The choice is vast, though, and don't forget you will be paying well over the odds to have the tribal name on the shirt you eventually choose. So take your time and enjoy the decision making process, you need to feel happy with what you've chosen, it's an important statement.

As a first step, it's a great idea to get the generic dazzle camo zig zag tattoo before you get more specific. That shows your devotion to tribalism without the final commitment. An influencer will help you choose it, using tweet or blog. Good luck going TRIBAL.

Olympian

I've just seen a car go by, outside the window. A very small boy, say, six years old, was running after it. We recently saw a lot of another car going up and down the road, almost daily, accompanying a teenage girl in her running outfit.

Logically, I've got to assume that they're training for an Olympics. The very small boy will be training for an Olympics eight years later than the Olympics the teenage girl is training for. Therefore he will be even better prepared.

The Olympics will probably be held in a very hot country, where running is especially hard work with a risk of people passing out. A very gigantic stadium will be built for the main part of the Olympics, even though there might be some football stadia that they could borrow. This will be to provide some of the host country's slum-dwellers with employment for a while; however, not all the slum-dwellers will want to fall off high scaffolding whilst pouring concrete, so they will be augmented with slave labour from countries where people normally earn a living by making gravel from a rock using a small chipping hammer.

Athletes will come from all corners of the world to compete, which means a very high standard of competition, where events are usually won by a wiry African, certainly in the case of long distance running races. This means, for Europeans from suburbia, that they must start training now in order to stand a chance. Meanwhile, Ethiopians will have to run across a mountain range, dodging war zones, every morning, just to get a pint of milk from the Co-op.

There are various techniques that the wily, rather than necessarily wiry, Europeans can use to level the playing field, though. Saying you've got asthma at the start of training is a good idea. As well as gaining sympathy for your effort against the odds, you can later use a special inhaler if you come to a particularly tough mountain route in the Olympic host country.

If the apparently privileged European is involved in a more technical sport such as gymnastics, which amounts to more than just putting one foot in front of the other rapidly, other sophisticated methods can be brought in to the preparation. The main sophisticated method in use, is to be shouted at constantly by highly-paid coaches, whilst attempting to perform perfect manoeuvres, whilst injured. This is called endurance and will be rewarded with aspirin. The coaches follow strict behavioural science principles, which can be summarised as follows: the more lottery money the coach is paid, the louder and longer he or she will shout.

We need to note here that, although the Europeans from Britain may seem privileged relative to, say, naturally talented Africans or Jamaicans, there is still an ample supply of underprivileged UK citizens from the back streets of Leeds, Middlesborough and Liverpool, for example. So these can receive lottery money to help them succeed and can be boasted about to the world at large. Notice, on most events, that the commentator talks mostly about the British competitors, proving that there is a larger reservoir of poor people being helped. Most rival European countries, you will see, tend to have just a single competitor struggling somewhere at the back, whose name you will never remember.

After the Olympics are over, the television money and the corruption money will be carefully shared out, and things will gradually revert to normal. The population of the host country will be inspired to get more exercise, which they could have done before if they were bothered, and they will think their country has prestige in the eyes of the world. This will make them feel a tiny bit better for a while, unless they are slum-dwellers who have access to a small rock and a Zen chipping hammer, and are able to empty their minds of all political thought whilst making gravel.

Sport itself, can of course be a source of spiritual satisfaction; the modern equivalent of the Buddhist monk's journey toward enlightenment, enabled by Nike. To endure the endless practice needed to succeed, the aspiring athlete must have either a: the fortitude and patience of a Zen master; or b: a massively high boredom threshold. Just think, what must that six-year-old boy have been contemplating as he plonked past my window, behind his mother's car?

'Crikey, this is boring. I wonder if we're going past the duck pond today? Maybe when this is over, I'll win a medal, participate in a modest advertising campaign for a lesser supermarket, and fade back into obscurity, wondering what to do with my life. Or, if I work hard at school and become well-spoken, I could use my kudos as an Olympian to become high in the ranks of corrupt sports officials, and be a Lord or even a Sir. There is about one chance in half-a-million of that happening, so I will have to work hard.

'In the meantime, crack on with this. Wonder what's for lunch? Will she let me have a biscuit instead of a banana today? If I've been good?

'Left foot. Right foot. Mind the loose drain cover. Left foot. Only another sixteen years to go, till I'm at my peak.'

PEACE AND LOVE AND FIGHTING

A friend of mine became married when we were all still fairly young. There was no pregnancy involved, they were just in love. How sweet. This would have been the early seventies, when you would dress for a wedding in green trousers, fawn jacket, blue shirt and yellow tie, and look quite normal in the crowd.

Because of British tribal ritual, a stag night had to precede the wedding. This would involve trying to withstand the effects of excessive consumption of the fairly unappetising beers of the day, such as Watney's Red Barrel. The other requirement was to wear a tie, so that you could get into a club later on.

This was supremely ironic in view of what happened to us on this occasion. Why doormen think a tie is a symbol of respectability and potential for decorous behaviour, is unaccountable. I suppose it's fair to say, in their defence, that the more appropriate attire of tank-top vest and boxing gloves wouldn't bode too well either.

The club chosen was called the Lonsdale Club. Even I knew that the name came from the boxing world, where an impossibly large belt is given to a person in a gym who is the best at battering all the other people in the gym. Boxing is usually, though not exclusively, practised by males, which gives a clue about it being fairly violent.

But this meant little to us, beyond laughter at the ridiculous name, as we descended the narrow stairs into the cellar. Lucifer's helpless brainwashed neophytes, lost souls into the depths of Hades. Or Manchester, at least.

The lost souls had been tempted, not by the prospect of pugilism, but by the lure of pulchritudinous women divesting themselves of raiment. Strippers, in short. It all went well to start with. A large crowd of men in varying degrees of inebriation crammed into a tiny room trying to get the best view of a woman with hardly any clothes on. There were two or three tables with chairs around them, but sitting down was not a realistic option. It was possible to manoeuvre oneself within a personal space of about two inches either side of one's body, and I had a reasonable view of the stage.

It seemed, around the time that the third young lady came on, that somebody behind hadn't got such a good view. Served them right for being latecomers, not everybody could be at the front. One particular fellow wasn't prepared to accept that simple formula, and began to burrow forward through the ranks, like a determined mole.

He didn't resemble a determined mole, physically. He resembled the largest, most stoutly built man in the crowd, with a mass index lower than that of a collapsing sun, yet larger than a concrete bomb shelter.

I felt this degree of solidity when it began to press against my shoulder. Feeling that 'might is right' was a generally unfair principle for organising the world, I defended my viewpoint (of the stripper rather than of my occupation of the moral high ground) and dug my heels in. The next thing that happened was that the solid man pushed harder, and with fierceness.

I flew through the air, knocking over one of the small tables and a chair, landing on my back. If there had been a script for what would happen after digging my heels in, this wasn't in it. I wasn't having it!

There followed, for the second and probably last time in my life, an experience of accessing supernatural powers. Instead of merely propelling a slice of egg across the room, as in my childhood, I now moved my whole body without discernible muscular effort. Normally, getting up from a supine position involves some manoeuvring of the legs and arms in preparation for the levering of the body. Not this time. I would say I sprang upwards, but springing involves pushing against some sort of solid base. This was more like a rocket launch, but Werner von Braun would have struggled to describe the physics involved.

I shot upwards, semi-sideways, towards an eventual standing position, simultaneously extending my right arm, which curved around so that, just in the instant that I arrived at the full standing position, the arm completed its arc and my balled fist connected with the chin of the solid bully.

The consequences of this were twofold. Firstly, if it may be termed a consequence, my adversary simply stood there, with his face registering incredulity. He had taken my best shot and I had returned to human form.

The second consequence was that the entire assemblage of men in various degrees of inebriation erupted into a seething mass of movement, a shoal of ocean life spooked by a shark. One of my friends later said that it was like an Andy Capp cartoon where a pub brawl is depicted as a grey cloud with various fists and feet poking out of it. I presume that, by this point, the lady on the stage had decided that she need not go to the trouble of unclipping any more apparel.

Nearer to the door than most, I was propelled upwards through the narrow stairwell like a cork, reaching the street quite quickly, where I gulped air as if I'd popped to the surface after my boat went down.

My friends, at this juncture, were still battling upwards, fighting for survival in the thin venturi of the tight, steep stairwell, accompanied by the soothing soundtrack of a bouncer shouting, 'Get me a stick, get me a stick!' Civilised.

Before they emerged, the solid bully popped out of the top doorway, accompanied by his two mates. I had lost interest by this time, maybe due to the energy-sapping metamorphosis as I regained human form, maybe due to the dim realisation that, if I hit him again, he would not fall down.

He confronted me again. His mates were telling him to leave me alone. He settled for headbutting me. Fair enough, I suppose. One-all in hitting one another. I was a bit surprised by the head butt, but I realised it must have made him feel better. Someone must live a fairly aggressive lifestyle to think that the head is a good choice of weapon, given that it's quite a vital part of the body, best protected from harm. But that's just my opinion; what do I know of pugilism?

My friends came to the surface and, after a quick inquest, we made our way home, away from the wreckage of the Lonsdale Club, before the bouncer found his stick.

Totting it all up, I didn't consider I'd lost any dignity by being headbutted, but did regret the loss of my spectacles at some point during the fracas. They cost sixteen quid to replace, which doesn't sound a lot now, but was quite a substantial wedge in those days.

Which was a good incentive not to access my superpowers ever again.

Looking for a peaceful solution to things has a lot of advantages, but is not necessarily the default position in human life. For a brief time in the sixties, the idea, of peace and love being a starting point, appeared to be gaining a foothold.

The counterculture in the USA had moved from the beatnik generation to the psychedelic generation. From the booze of Kerouac to the LSD of Timothy Leary and Ken Kesey, the blissed-out trippers who offered a new vision. If a drug that provided a glimpse of heaven, a shortcut to ecstasy, didn't change the world, nothing could.

That leads us to the conclusion that nothing could. From the summer of love of 1967 to the seedy, seamy, casual violence of Altamont, the dream had the stamina of petals in a storm. I left school in 1970. Missed it. Behind the curve. In 1968 we listened to Jumping Jack Flash, born in a crossfire hurricane, in between news flashes on the car radio about Bobby Kennedy being shot and Russian tanks rolling into Prague. All this punctuating the normality of a family holiday in North Wales. Seeing the pictures of the Prague events in the paper made me go upstairs and cry. This was the last time I cried in such a fashion over a political event.

So that was politics sorted. Life conducted under a carapace of cynicism ever since. The peace and love part took a little longer. A period of experimentation with what they now call substances, swanning about the country talking about magic and philosophy whilst young men of my own age were having petrol bombs thrown at them in Belfast or Derry.

The best refuge is normal life, as most well-adjusted people instinctively know. And along the way find your own peace and love if you can.

Recently I saw a film of Arthur Lee performing at Glastonbury. He was the leader of the group Love, who produced one of the masterpiece albums of the sixties, *Forever Changes*. His set at Glastonbury pretty much reproduced that entire album, and at the end of it he exhorted the audience to love each other. Where had he been for over thirty years? It doesn't matter. The sentiments were still the same, still relevant, and if all you do in your life is produce an album like that, you've done more than your bit, more than most artists will achieve.

What did the audience make of it? Was it just a lucky dip in a smorgasbord of music they'd mostly never heard of?

Most young people I meet nowadays seem to be mostly interested in just getting by, and having the odd holiday if they can. Glastonbury, though it still hosts gems like Mr Lee, looks like one more leisure outing option amongst many, to be considered on the family budget balance sheet. And very expensive as far as I know.

I remember going there in, I think, 1984. I first motored down to Stonehenge, where there was a free festival opposite the protected monument, in a 1957 Austin A35 which I had resurrected. Hawkwind were on, and the Welsh psychedelic band Man. Hypnotic acid guitar music for half the night. In the morning, I set off for Glastonbury, picking up a Dutch hitchhiker from amongst the hordes near the exit track. Who I then had to ask if he wouldn't mind looking for another lift, after I spotted Bruce and Graham from the university, further along. There wasn't room for three passengers and all their luggage in the tiny car. The Dutchman graciously thanked me for the shortest lift ever.

Bruce and Graham had enjoyed some substances. Bruce in particular looked as though a couple of matchsticks, to hold his eyelids up, might have been helpful. As we bowled along, I enjoyed the brisk drive, fifty-five to sixty miles per hour plenty enough with the weight of three of us and all the camping kit.

'How fast are we going?' said Bruce, from inside his cloud. To him, it was obviously spaceship velocity.

I liked Bruce. He had once declared that he intended to write a novel. The first words would be, 'Somewhere, a dog barked.' Superb. Bruce, did you ever do it?

The festival was great. I can't remember if we had tickets, or managed to blag our way in. I think there were still a couple of loopholes in those days, or maybe I am romanticising.

I had provided the lift, and they had plenty of substances, so we teamed up. Fela Kuti was on, with a giant orchestra and many lady dancers shaking vibrant hips in feathery costumes. You could properly swing and sway and forget yourself, which is surely what these things are all about. Fela Kuti was a powerfully talented musician and politician, who stood up against the corrupt regime in Nigeria. A man who left this life having done much more than most to try and improve it. At great cost too. Can you imagine a thousand troops ransacking, say, the mansion of Simon Cowell, and throwing his elderly mother out of a window, because of him criticising the Conservative government?

The last Glastonbury I went to was, I'm pretty sure, 1987. I went with a friend in her car, and she had to get back to London in good time, so I missed Van Morrison at the end. An anti-climax really. The world ends not with a whimper, but with failing to access your Van Morrison.

Van Morrison sang about the hippies taking the eyeballs out of your head in *The Great Deception*, which makes him even more cynical than me, quite an achievement.

I came across 'hippies' in Brewer's Dictionary of Phrase and Fable (Room, 1995), whilst writing this. Funnily enough, during a search for 'Hell'. Acid, sometimes known as the Heaven and Hell drug. You could pay your dues for the Heaven bit, believe me.

The book said that hippies drove around in ramshackle vehicles and depended to some extent on "begging, scrounging and the Department of Social Security"!! Oh dear!!

Some of my old workmates aren't going to like that one. It would seem, if you believe social media, that they've retired to their turrets to spend their days seething about immigrant, homeless, scrounging beggars, and most Europeans, though it's OK to have a holiday in Europe if pandemics allow.

According to Brewer's, hippies have now been replaced by New Age Travellers. Still in ramshackle vehicles, presumably. They have, specifically, replaced hippies as "the venerators of Stonehenge."

Is that all? One would hope that the truth is a little wider. If the Department of Social Security helps them free up time from scrounging to sit in trees in a desperate effort to stem state-sponsored vandalism upon our environment, I would say good luck to them with my bit of taxpayer money.

Spiritual Quest

My grandfather, the minister of religion, was an erudite man who wrote several books. We found copies of them when clearing out my aunt's house after her death. I thumbed through a few of them on that day, but time and earthly matters intervened, and in the spare bedroom there were numerous pristine empty jam jars and hundreds of Sunday supplements to recycle. I did however retain a useful memory of one striking quotation, which I was able to bring into play during everyday life later. Its flavour will give you a clue as to why I still feel the need to explore more of his writing.

Every so often, in my later working life, I would walk into the office, and someone would ask a very open-ended question, by way of routine greeting. You know the kind of thing.

'Whadd'ya know, Dave? What's going on?'

'Well, you could ask, "Are we special beings in the eyes of God, or are we just maggots on the cheese of the Earth?"'

The main issue with religion, of course, is the God thing. It might not be too bad otherwise. I don't blame grandfather. It was probably all he had to work with in those days. My father became a scientist as a reaction to it. A humanist, as the minister at his funeral termed it. It was a Methodist funeral, at my mother's instigation. She had been very fond of my grandfather, and was still something of a believer, I suppose, even after years of being married to my dad. It does show how people can get along, which is a heartening thing that I say without irony.

We had the odd religious education lesson at school. A sop to society's framework more than anything: the school was far more interested in exam results and in getting clever Manchester lads into Oxford or Cambridge, than any dalliance with theological matters. I remember only one particular lesson. Without recalling whether the guy taking the lesson had any significant religious background, his thesis pretty much negated any strong faith in religion which he might have harboured.

It was that God had been suggested as being a 'God of the gaps'. In other words, at the dawn of thought, humans had little knowledge of the mechanics of the world, other than that the sun rose every day. Whereas now, so much is known of how the world, and even the universe, works, there are fewer 'gaps' in knowledge. Therefore, less room for god, small 'g' by now. To put it another way: caveman, 99% is done by God; modern man, 99% is done by science. You could say religion is struggling, taking a back seat, were it not for the colossal amount of atrocities perpetrated, by humans, in its various names.

Why do they do that? The main tenet of Christianity seems to be, put other people before yourself. Great. So why go 'crusading' in the Middle East, with the excuse that you know more than the rival religion, whose disciples need to learn your righteous ways? At swordpoint. Something went quickly wrong there, didn't it?

Let's look a little deeper. See if we can figure out why Christianity doesn't follow its own principles. Although my school wasn't steeped in religion, we still tended to hear a biblical parable as part of morning assembly. Perhaps they were a guide to Christianity in its pure form, before people with swords kept borrowing it.

These parables were a bit like Aesop's fables, or Brer Rabbit stories. The main difference being that God kept cropping up in them, sometimes disguised as a wealthy farmer, but it was clear that you were meant to realise that the wealthy farmer, or suchlike, was obviously God. If we can isolate God's influence in these parables, that's the essence of Christianity, right?

Here are a couple of examples. The first is about a man with three sons. There were always two or three sons in these parables. This is my memory of it, which we will follow up with the actual parable, so don't fly off the handle if the first version is wrong, stick with it.

The wealthy farmer gives some money, known as talents, to each son. Two of them are careful with it, save it, bury it, whatever. The third son goes off and uses the money to grow more money, and is praised to high heaven. We would be waiting there, in assembly, thinking, the first two sons were good and careful, the third one's going to come home and get a right bollocking. But no. He's taken a risk, gambled it, got away with it, and is now the big star! So, it's a *capitalist* fable. Wow. So much for gentle, obedient, junior farmers with their careful husbandry. Damned as losers! A big shock.

A little research reveals this to be the Parable of the Talents, which shows how memory can warp things. Nonetheless, it's on the same lines, and in the end even more stunning. In this version, the three men in question are not sons, but servants of the landowner, who goes off and leaves them in charge of varying amounts of talents. Five, two and one, to be precise. The playing field is tilted already. He comes back to find the first two have invested the talents in the money markets in town; they are duly congratulated.

The last servant, who only got one talent to look after, is terrified, naturally, of what the master will say if he loses it. The poor, cowering sod admits his fear to his master. He has buried the talent, knowing his master to be a man who "reaps where thou hast not sown". A heartless asset stripper, in other words.

His reward? A complete lambasting from the outraged landowner, who says that he was expecting to "have received mine own with usury". No thought that the guy with one talent only had to make one wrong move to screw things up, and that at least he was careful. Hilariously, the landowner then twists the knife, instructing that the single, presumably soil encrusted, talent be given to the faithful guy who turned five talents into ten. From "him that hath not shall be taken away even that which he hath. And cast ye the unprofitable servant into outer darkness. There shall be weeping and gnashing of teeth." This section of text is probably enshrined in the secret version of the Conservative Party manifesto, not for public consumption. Those who have shall be rewarded, those who start with almost nothing shall end up doing the wailing. And shall be deemed to be "wicked and slothful" servants. All the better, of course, if you can convince them that it's all their own fault. How dare they be unprofitable!

Next up is the old standby, the prodigal son, this author's version. Again, rich father, two sons this time. Boring son keeps working hard, nose to the grindstone, day in day out, ploughing, propagating, sifting gravel. Prodigal son? No, too tedious for him. Goes off on his travels. Wine. Women. Even a bit of song. Leaves the other guy slaving away. Then, later, exhausted from song, not to mention the amount of wine and women, he decides he's had enough of all that, mainly due to becoming destitute having blown all his money. He sees the light, that working in a pigsty isn't the way forward, and slinks home to his dad's gaff.

Monumental bollocking for putting his old man through anguish and despair? Not a bit of it. The big star treatment. For he was lost, and is found again. Etcetera, etcetera, etcetera. No matter that the other brother kept the ranch running. Prodigal guy was lost, and is found again. Licence to party! Like an Eton schoolboy. Born to rule, dad's favourite, different rules apply. He's somehow worth more for being a bastard! Another shocker from God, sorry, the wealthy farmer. The steady puritans, His natural constituency, taken advantage of, taken for granted, shafted again.

Thus far, we've seen the reckless capitalist and the feckless rich kid, feted at the expense of the plodding but loyal worker. Now the clincher. It is harder for a rich man to enter the realm of heaven than it is for a camel to pass through the eye of a needle. Really? The two winners in the parables, the five-talent hedge fund manager and the Old Etonian party animal rich kid, look at this statement and think.

'OK, we've got two chances to achieve eternal salvation. Number one, invent a shrinking ray to use on a camel. Number two, er, well there isn't a number two is there? Zilch, nada, nothing. So we might as well just crack on with the donations to the tory party and enjoy earthly life at everyone else's expense.

And that's Christianity in a nutshell. Capitalist ideology, rewarding of anti-social behaviour, and ultimately, no guarantee of eternal bliss for its punters even though they've paid their premiums by hoeing fields and chipping rocks into gravel, or, at the other end of the scale, spent their time in non-stop partying, gambling and womanising. Who's the mug?

No wonder the tory party gets recruits.

Horses versus Fishes

A short history of the role of livestock in a modern technological society.

From our curator of species.

In the beginning came the motor car. Before, there were horses. "Which" magazine once did a survey, applying their consumerist principles to pet choice. Horses won easily, being by far the most satisfying creature to own, yet the most demanding to look after.

So, unless you consider a whale, which would be a nightmare to look after without having your own personal ocean and tracking system, we can say that horses are top of the realistic pops both in pleasure and in maintenance.

Fish, on the other hand, small fish possibly brightly coloured, are at the other end of the scale. It was reckoned by "Which" that they were easy to look after, yet this undoubted perk was counterbalanced by their inability to provide much pleasure.

You're talking about maybe going downstairs in the morning, saying to yourself, 'Don't my brightly coloured fish look great? I hope there's not a dead one floating on top today,' then getting your breakfast and heading out to work. And that's it really. Not a thought about them for the rest of the day, other than, 'I hope there isn't another one floating on top when I get home,' in between your work tasks if you've got time.

This leads to a thought. Do they bring even a slight bit of pleasure? If you're worrying about them even whilst you're at work? I suppose some people could just turn off from it, but surely that's rather a heartless, hard-as-nails attitude. Phew. Who knew we could get into such a moral dilemma so quickly?

The trouble probably stems from the fact that the "Which" research took place many, many years ago, when life was much simpler. It's likely that "Which" were thinking of the traditional cartoon fish from the fairground. You would win one in a game of throwing rings over a box, bring it home in a transparent plastic bag, put it in a bowl that you had quickly bought as an afterthought, and then the poor thing would die a day or two later. Of boredom, probably.

Simple. Get fish, put in water, fish dies, pour down toilet. Funfair man has your money and you have empty plain glass bowl in cartoon shape that will never make it on to Antiques Road Show. You have learnt. So even at this level, it's a worthwhile experience, but maybe not thrill-a-minute. You could, if you wished, easily draw the shape of the bowl, and a simple fish inside the bowl, like the ones that Christians draw, pin the drawing to the wall, and dream of next year owning another fish after the fair comes round.

But most people don't.

And so you would go on to live your life, in the nineteen-sixties, unperturbed by thoughts of fish other than once a week in the context of being accompanied by chips.

And the goldfish would make it into the "Which" Hall of Fame, under the heading, Pets: Low involvement, Low maintenance.

Not these days, though. Nowadays fish are many-coloured, not just orange. And lots of different shapes, not just the standard Christian fish. And they are kept in proper tanks, with squareness and oxygen bubbles and temperature control. They come from the pet emporium, not the fairground man or woman. They have to be attended to and given names, which makes it all the more tragic when they don't survive.

I knew it would end in tears when the grandkids decided that coloured fish were a good idea. The upside is that when you go round to their house, you can stare at the fish if you remember to, and be soothed as if you are in a waiting room anticipating medical treatment or a job interview.

But otherwise it's a complex web of emotion. They are a modern family, so have a labour-saving artificial lawn. That means, every so often, a cortege of parent(s) plus kid(s) turns up at our house to use the burial facility under the tree at the bottom of the garden. We provide memorial ice lolly sticks, engraved if required, and refreshments. But not embalming.

Both parents happen to have a black car, which lends appropriate formality to the final procession bearing the deceased in his or her jam jar. You might have noticed that a high proportion of new cars today come in black or silver. This is so that children can more realistically experience the trappings of a funeral ceremony, in case they wish to gravitate towards a career in undertaking, when they grow to adulthood.

In our family's case, the kids have already progressed to the stage where they bring a dignified professionalism to the proceedings, to properly and solemnly celebrate the life and achievements of whatever Harry Potter character the latest dead fish is named after. When they are not laughing.

The sad thing is that, of late, they have stopped naming the fish, knowing that it will later be easier to bear the trauma of loss. Yet is it not the case that, with this trend, we are losing some of that individuality which we so prize in the context of a post-modern post-industrial society? That the fish have become a metaphor for a monocultural system, subjugated drones deprived of will in an Orwellian nightmare, serving only the imperatives of an all-powerful state apparatus?

Or should we merely say, life's a bitch and then you die?

You can see from all this, that in the era in which we now live, things can suddenly get very complicated indeed. Our poor fish, once so simple, and easily drawn by a child, are now multicoloured and multifarious, reflecting a society nowadays so complex that their human counterparts, like the fish, know not whether they are coming or going.

If things are this bad in the supposedly simple fish world, in terms of philosophical conundrums, how are we going to cope with analysing the lives of their opposite numbers on the "Which" scale, the horses?

Fortunately, it's not half as difficult as we might fear. Despite the massive amount of hay procurement, shovelling of stable, and rubbing fondly that a horse requires, and despite the cocktail of intense emotions that give horse people such a buzz, the situation is in fact far simpler.

We said at the start of this, that life began with the motor car. It replaced the horse. So we needn't worry about horses!

They are an evolutionary triumph, and a creature of wonder. But obsolete in terms of work, since the early years of the twentieth century. We replaced city streets covered in horse shit, with city streets harbouring unhealthy fumes from vehicles. So now you just have horses for riding (leisure), sitting on (being photographed by tourists or keeping out of reach of football fans), racing (being spectacular or falling off and breaking collarbone), betting on (insidious and potentially life-ruining activity though not quite as pernicious as the on-line gambling industry), and being wild. If wild, horses are good for looking at and going, 'Wow, they are amazing.' But, more importantly, for telling someone that 'they wouldn't drag me away.' Even though you might go away later if the going got tough. Because you are male, a psychopath, or a politician. Or possibly all three of these at once.

Horses still have all sorts of uses, then, but we don't use them for transport any more. The times when horses were used for transport crop up in the category of historical drama, or period drama, in TV and film. To be honest, these productions have to have a really involving plot to interest me, because, generally by definition, it's pre-car era, so there aren't going to be any Bullitt-style chases going on. Don't get me started about the implausible car chases of recent years. And, secondly, the women's costumes are much too voluminous and fussy to hold any interest for a modern man. Remember, we said the universe began with the motor car. Anything before that was just an evolutionary path to get to where we are today. 34,000 years ago, people were hunting mammoths to survive. Anybody good at mammoth killing was like the Harry Kane of the era, lauded as a hero and role model. You could, at that time, get to Europe without needing the Channel Ferry or Eurotunnel. But you had to walk. Life was grindingly tough.

Leap forward to the Victorian era and life was still tough, although they had Darwin and steam engines. For most people, slaving in a satanic mill had replaced mammoth-cornering as an activity to feed the un-birth-controlled family. Had they really come much further than the mammoth hunters, in terms of available leisure time and disposable income?

With the Times predicting, in 1894, that the streets of London would be nine feet deep in horse manure by 1950, it was time for a change of tack. Thank goodness, then, for Mr Benz and his mate's daughter with a nice sounding name. Just think if she'd been called Shania or Gertrude or anything like that. And with the small detail of Mr Benz's motorised carriage to add to the mellifluous Mercedes name, the twentieth century was ready for lift off. Speaking of which, the Wright brothers soon chipped in with the outrageous idea of powered flight. There was an earlier attempt in 1853 by a man called Sir George Cayley, at the village of Brompton-by-Sawdon near us in Yorkshire, to fly, by jumping off a hill. In fact, it was Sir George's coachman piloting the full-scale glider, Sir George only having done the inventing. To be fair, George was seventy-nine at this point, but he might have taken a minute to jot down the hapless coachman's name for posterity. Nevertheless, this hardly counted as powered flight. Sorry, Yorkshire, but just for once you weren't pre-eminent. Hard to believe, I know.

By the middle of the twentieth century, a sort of Goldilocks moment had arrived, where the level of technology usage was just right. In the first half, the rapid strides made were spoilt by humanity's unfortunate tendency to use technology to slaughter large swathes of other humankind. Not mosquitoes or wasps. Humankind.

Even our old friends the horses were caught up in it. Hard to credit that they were still being flogged to death, literally, during the much mechanised First World War. This was about the last straw for them. After this crass mismatch, they more or less went, 'That's it now. We're off, at least in the Western world, to be creatures of leisure. No more beast of burden shite.' The exception to this was of course the fictional horse from Orwell's *Animal Farm*, who just said 'I will work harder,' every time the totalitarian government cocked things up.

After the fifties and sixties, we were treated to the digital revolution, which eventually enabled the Big Bang in the London Stock Exchange, which in turn enabled most ordinary people to have no idea how money moved around the world, but also to appreciate how a bewildering variety of clothing, electronic devices and video games would now enrich their lives.

In summary, we have moved from a world where people were skilled in winding wet clothes through wooden mangles and sheltering from Nazi bombs (too dark), to a world where people can have anything and want everything, and are skilled at turning their electronic device off and then on again, if it goes wrong (too easy). What's interesting about the latter case, is that children are now taught that switching something off, and then on again, is a thing to be revered and respected, as it represents advice of great wisdom, coming directly from their parents. Of course, it also represents their parents' sum total of knowledge on the subject of electronic devices.

As a child of the early fifties, I came into a world where everything was 'just right', as Goldilocks would have put it. We didn't have world-wide conflict, genocide, and the threat of totalitarian rule (pre 1945), or world-wide conflict subcontracted out, genocide, and a lot of actual totalitarian rule (let's say post 1962 for the sake of argument). All we had to worry about was the threat of nuclear annihilation.

Which we didn't worry about. After all, what was the point? Unless you were a Vulcan bomber pilot, who was told, 'If it all kicks off, just carry on flying, there won't be anything left here to come back to. Try and land on the Steppes somewhere, and find a nice Russian or Mongolian woman to settle down with.'

Yeah, right.

'Do you fancy a night out? Have you got any good restaurants here on the Steppes? What's that? I've got to ride a horse, you say? I thought the world had got past that stage. What? What's the plane for? You don't hear from Moscow

on the radio anymore? Hmm, well. Can we gloss over that? Your brothers are on their way back, on their horses?
 'Oh shit...'

Evolution

BY JACK MITTY, OUR
GENETICS/RELIGION/HISTORY/MUSIC/LITERATURE
CORRESPONDENT.

Written from lockdown, summer 2020.

On the day after we were told the distancing situation will last a whole lot longer, we are going to take some time out and do some contemplation, as it looks like contemplation skills will be needed for some while before we are allowed to get back to dashing around like blue-arsed flies and rubbing up against one another in bars. Regarding dashing around, it is OK if you've got a sporty model of Audi, as even in the current time of nearly empty roads, you are allowed to try it out on the A63 at three-figure speeds.

A good contemplator was Buddha. We will be having a look at his contemplating and seeing how it relates to religion, the Theory of Evolution, and modern entrepreneurship and workers' rights in an era of steadily diminishing planets to exploit.

Buddha was a pretty cool guy from the olden days; you can find lots of references to him in books and even Cleaning Windows by Van Morrison where he (Van not Buddha) reads Christmas Humphreys' book on Zen. Did you know that Christmas Humphreys was also a judge at the Old Bailey? Put it in your book of facts for the next pub quiz on Zoom.

What Buddha did a lot of, and we can all learn from this, was finding a forest or even just a tree if you're stuck in a city situation, and conducting research into whether it made a sound when he wasn't there. We are hearing quite a lot of light hammering sounds from one of the trees behind our house at the moment, and are contemplating whether it might be a woodpecker even when we're not there. Except we are there a lot at the moment 'cos of lockdown.

But I must emphasise that it's not the tree that's making the noise, it's the woodpecker. So that doesn't count in proving the tree noise theory of Buddha.

It was things like this that Buddha had to mentally wrestle with. They were difficult, so he probably took some downtime and spent time contemplating what the Theory of Evolution would look like when Darwin showed up. There would have been plenty of birds to look at while he formulated his take on how it happened. Buddha, that is, remember Darwin hadn't put his oar in at this stage.

We have seen here, for example, our birdhouse that was completely filled with fluff and stuff, which we had to clear out recently. It was worse than if students had been living there! This proves that the birds have evolved to keep stuffing moss and feathers into a hole and will keep on doing it until nobody will live there and it has to go on Flight Move or Homes Under the Hammer for a really knockdown price 'cos of the neglect. How does that fit with natural selection? Those birds are just like student birds who fly off and don't leave behind anything to further their species – how can that work as an evolutionary strategy?

If you contemplate about it a bit more, there must have been an original bird at the start, who showed up in front of a female bird with a twig in his beak.

'What are you doing with that stupid great big twig?'

'I think it makes me look cool.'

'It makes you look a dork. Put it down and get some moss off that shed roof over there.'

'I was going to use it to put between some branches in the tree, as a basis for supporting further construction involving lighter materials, as I am the first genius bird and have invented engineering.'

'Huh! Well you'd better get some more of them, one's not going to support me and the eggs. And when you've done that, I want some pink fluff in it, I'm not just sitting on those hard twigs.'

'I know where there's some blue fluff.'

'You can think about that later, don't get ahead of yourself. We can do that when everything else is sorted, but the blue fluff that you're talking about won't be right, it will need to be pink fluff painted blue.'

So it will have gone on like that, and Buddha will have gazed in wonderment, thinking that in many centuries time there will be loads and loads of shades of blue available in the home décor market, due to Darwinism and Capitalism replacing a large part of organised religion as the dominant economic model. For further reference on the philosophical debate behind this, see the Scopes Trial of 1925 in Dayton, Tennessee, USA, which was in part motivated by a prominent local businessman's desire to raise Dayton's profile. Marketing genius!

Another marketing genius of the modern age is the electric car mogul, Elon Musk. He has a space company as well, working on giving flights to space if you are a millionaire. The other one doing this is Richard Branston, the UK pickle magnate, but at the moment he is juggling with channelling some government tax revenue into his airplane company so that he won't have to use the government tax money that he got through his railroad. And all the time he is doing this, he won't have time to fly his balloons, let alone his spaceship. What a loser!

Musk on the other hand, has put forward plans to fly spaceships in fifty years' time, to Mars! He will be old by then, but fifty years is plenty of time to use cybernetics to become an android and live forever so that's no problem. They will be tremendous spaceships of great size, so they will have to be parked in orbit and people will fly up to them, and each one will have a crew of 100 or it might be 500 I can't remember. So there will be a multi-storey orbiting space ark park up there, waiting to go to Mars.

It will be also egalitarian, not just for millionaires. If somebody can't afford it, Musk will give them a loan! It can be paid back from work on Mars, as mostly what they expect to find on Mars is lots of exotic metals for batteries and no water. So the workers will pay for water from their loans and if they kick off and want to come back to Earth 'cos of the conditions, they can't! 'Cos Musk owns the spaceships! Marketing genius! This is what evolution has led to, which is called progress.

Meanwhile back on Earth, there will be just a few people left, contemplating like Buddha. They will realise that the logical conclusion of his contemplations was to accept that there is no noise when trees are being cut down in the once beautiful Chilterns, unless protestors have been camping there to bleat against progress.

Progress has to continue, because construction companies that still exist because of not siphoning off too much money to build the mansions of their board members, will need to keep their workers occupied ready to build more mansions. This is because Russians and Arabians will own all of London by that time, and the owners of the construction companies will have plotted to build their own mansions near Birmingham in the

Midlands which is cheaper than London. Then they can hop on the railway they have had built to get to London and look important in the House of Parliament, which it will be called because the old House of Lords will have gone because of voting against the other House of Parliament once too often. But the actual Lords will still get their money for being lords, they just won't have to come to London and negotiate the homeless people on the pavement.

The new railway will be built right up to the door of the House of Parliament for this reason, and because only people going to the City of London to recline on the benches of the House of Parliament and visit their bank and advisers to get more money for their construction companies and mansions in the Midlands will be using this high speed railway. All of the more ordinary people will have to use Teslas which will not have anywhere to park in the central exclusion zone, except Tesla charging points, where the ordinary people will be able to have their credit cards siphoned by Starbucks, as well as Tesla, while they wait. Marketing genius!

I think you can see from all this, that evolution has served humanity well so far and they needn't worry about whether a tree will fall soundlessly on their house in the future because the only trees will be ones near mansions that will be watched by security anyway at all times.

That's all for now. Maybe next time we will look at how mansions in forests have evolved since Buddha's time.

The History of Exploration

BULLETIN FROM THE FUTURE CONTAINING ALL YOU NEED TO KNOW ABOUT THE PAST.

By our history of the world correspondent Remi Nissan.

Here I am sitting in the big house, in my room. I've got all of my memorabilia here, which came in the Transit van.

Today I'm looking at a picture of me at Blenheim Palace posing to show what an explorer like, say, Columbus, would have looked like on the prow of his ship, when he said, "Land ahoy, probably India but it could be America," to his men. Columbus was, I think, Italian, but sailed from Spain, so it could have been more like, 'Ola, sono cappo di tutti cappi d'America,' or something of that actual drift.

Blenheim was the birthplace of Lord High Winston Churchill, who was a great war leader, but not as great as Tony Blair, who had the cleverness to go out and find wars against weaker countries, instead of just defending our country against a powerful aggressor.

The thing I've always envied about Tony Blair, is that he identified when the time was right to sell his soul, and was able to do it quickly through Beelzebub, acting as Satan's broker, for an excellent price. I inquired about selling my own soul way back in the eighties, but was told by Beelzebub that I hadn't got one of the really sought-after models of soul, and that the best he could do, was take it away if I paid him!! Obviously as a Yorkshireman, I was never going to entertain that, but it has been a source of bitterness from time to time.

Moving on, I'm inspired to discuss the history of exploring, which begins with people like Columbus, Magellan and Vasco da Gama. Or vast coast of llama as he was known when he mistook South America for China in his first little known circumnavigation. Columbus had told him, get out of Lisbon, down a few miles, and turn left. He turned right! What a bozo.

In those days, they were said to have wooden ships and iron men. This lasted until about the days of whaling, when ships from Hull went out to catch whales. The species of whale they hunted was the slowest one that they could catch up easily. They named the species the Right Whale, because it was the right whale to catch. True fact! For goodness sake, though. All the imagination of minds in Hull, from Andrew Marvell to Philip Larkin, and that was the best they could come up with? Typical Hull.

The era changed to one of iron ships and wooden men, although they were still pretty tough until after the Cod War, when it changed to very big iron ships crewed by men and even women, from all over the globe not just Hull, and the giant ship is steered by a tiny little joystick, like an absolute apology for phallic-ness, and carries people spending their children's inheritance (Cruise), or lots of massive containers containing plastic toys from China (Freight).

But we need to go back to the dawn of time, or specifically medieval-ness, to see why they thought of ships in the first place. In medieval days, people lived in squalor next to a pigsty, except kings and lords who had velvet and ermine cloaks. Other people who got a bit of velvet when it was available were Catholic Church rulers, unless they were rank and file monks, who just got always brown robes, with a hoody for bad weather, and a stick to defend themselves with if they walked too close to the council pigsty and the people who lived there were in the mood to be ruffians. Meanwhile, over in America, the native inhabitants were living on sunlit magical prairies amongst plentiful buffalo, in comfortable leather clothing with jewellery. This will become relevant to our story later on.

You can see why people got fed up, just living next to pigs all day and gathering the odd vegetable. So somebody came along, whose name is unrecorded, who remembered what the Vikings had done, and said, 'Why don't we find some countries abroad that we can go to and annoy them? Better still, I have invented a new verb, plunder. If we make some ships, we can sail from probably Plymouth, and go and make some money.'

The people next to pigsties thought this was a great idea, and started chopping forests down. Meanwhile in Spain, they were doing the same thing, so much so that there are still no trees in the middle of Spain. True fact! We were more ecologically minded, and left a couple of trees standing in the Chiltern Forest, which is now being rectified by some HS2 people, who were transferred from fracking when it was found that fracking wouldn't be an economic way to convert the green bits of the country to a wasteland.

So, we now had people building proper ships, not just rafts in the Pacific or Roman galley things full of slaves heaving on oars. It is no use having loads of slaves heaving on oars if you've no room left to carry the plunder. See, incidentally, how plunder can be used as either a verb or a noun? That's why it was such a key, versatile invention and a massive breakthrough in the plotting of the think tanks of the Elizabethan Age. People do plotting and come up with plots. Verb, noun. See a pattern beginning to emerge here? But the word plunder, in its elegance, topped the lot. A seismic invention equivalent to the steam engine or the digital computer, for the people of the day.

So, the new ships had room for cargo, and guns. Job's a good 'un. As an afterthought, there was room below decks for press-ganged crew and scurvy, so they had every element needed to boldly go. They were propelled by sails, so goodness knows how they got them to go the right way. Probably the civilisations waiting to be plundered were at the end of powerful winds and currents, which was unlucky for them.

Navigation was by simple 'Bloke in a Crow's Nest going Ahoy!', a primitive form of sat nav. As back up, the captain would have some parchment maps in his cabin. These would run out of world half way through the voyage, and would be inscribed that 'Here be Dragons' or some such. How did the map makers know that the Welsh had been that far? It was blatant surmising, and fake news really. What was certainly true, and yet to be proved otherwise, was that if you went too far, you would fall off a massive edge into infinity. Nobody knows where you would end up except perhaps going down a massive helter-skelter that would turn into a sort of giant Mobius Strip that would bring you back to the present time, but warped round so that everything was very slightly different and weird.

With the fear of that sort of thing, it's no surprise that all these ships stopped well before the edge, somewhere like China, India or far Cathay. Then they would just set up companies and start trading. The things they got were exotic spices, jewels, tea and silk, or in the case of Cortes in South America, lots of gold, which was a bit more easily bankable. In all examples, it is not recorded in detail what the inhabitants of the civilisations at the end of the 'trade currents' got in return, except usually a civil service and accounting system. These accounting systems were very detailed and complicated, and had to be administered by trained administrators brought from the 'old countries' (even though the 'new countries' had often had a civilisation before the 'old countries').

The really clever part of the accounting systems, which perplexed the inhabitants of the, let's call them 'exotic countries' to avoid confusion, was that everything that was taken out of the exotic countries was filed under the same column. Have you guessed it yet?

Yes, that's it. Plunder! Brilliant! This was such a good idea that it persists in the same underlying form even to this day. It is just couched in different terms. For example, every five years or so the group of people that usually rule Britain have to tell the people of Britain what they are going to do. Because they don't want to disturb or worry the people of Britain, they say a lot of things, all mainly on the lines of 'You won't have to live next to a pigsty,' and 'Big ships will bring you lots of things from China.' That sort of thing. On and on. What they would really like to do is send a leaflet out with just one word on it, to save printing costs. Have you guessed it yet?

Roughly the same thing happened everywhere. The countries that had lived for centuries, just keeping to themselves and enjoying life, except for the victims of human sacrifice under the Aztecs, had to wake up quickly as progress came. As well as accountancy, progress included things like opium addiction and an early appreciation of the military/industrial complex. There was a lot to get their heads around and they found it hard to keep up.

In America, they even got to the stage where the people who had lived forever on magical plains in comfortable leather clothing and jewellery, had to watch on as the Spanish, French and British battled each other because they wanted all of the plunder (noun). Eventually, they said 'OK, if you give us the rusty 1949 Buick you promised, when it gets to about 1963 and before everybody thinks rusty 1949 Buicks are valuable, we'll accept some tumbledown shacks in the Badlands and just watch you fight amongst yourselves because we are just sick to the back teeth of the way you behave. And you'd better lump some opioids into the deal because we'll have to sell the rusty Buick before it becomes 'cool', just to get by.'

And that's roughly how 'The Right to Plunder' (verb) became enshrined in the constitution of the United States. A country that wasn't even an 'old country' in the first place. Remarkable, and makes you think.

But I must pause now; the nurse has just arrived with my Van Morrison.

An Economist Speaks

I'm writing this from 2022, in the hope, and barely justified belief, that humanity will continue to struggle on through 2023 and beyond. If it doesn't, the planet will be OK for another five billion years or so. The planet doesn't need to be saved. It will still be here after we are gone, populated mainly by geese, cockroaches and pink flamingos on the bits of it that have super-alkaline or hypersaline boiling shallow lakes.

We count our span in tens of years rather than billions, and sometimes pause the treadmill to wonder where several decades went. First, we try to survive. When we see that we've got that sorted, barring accidents and disasters, we try to have some fun.

Survival for me, in 1987, had to do with driving taxis and claiming benefits. I can't remember if they overlapped. At one point I claimed on a government scheme called Enterprise Allowance, which gave you a tenner a week more on your benefit, as long as you were trying to start a business. I think you had to also rustle up a thousand pounds in a bank account, to show the seriousness of your intent and your ability, as an entrepreneur, to beg, borrow or steal a thousand pounds.

I think I declared that I would be repairing cars. The memory is hazy from this distance. They didn't seem to ask enough questions to find out, or care about finding out, that my premises consisted of three rickety lock-up garages behind my first floor flat, from which I would run a power lead down the garden, through the back door of the main garage where the welding and swearing would take place.

This would tend to happen in mid-morning, after I had been sitting up in the early hours writing pieces about Carlos Castaneda's view on the power of snails, or about somebody stealing a bus from Hull town centre in the depths of the night and roaring along the roads near the flat pursued by a posse of blue lights. This did actually happen, although when I was woken by it, I thought initially that it was possibly an alien spacecraft intruding on my earthly stupor, with its loudness and weird lights. The following day's paper put me straight.

These written pieces I would send to Alan Coren, the editor of Punch magazine, who obviously thought I was too mad to be a feasible contributor. I can't now recall whether he indicated this by means of polite rejection, or simple absence of reply.

At any rate, I was able, during the period of Enterprise Allowance receipt, to continue driving taxis as a sideline to car repairing and unappreciated writing genius, without illegally claiming benefit whilst working.

Taxi driving was an activity that would nowadays be referred to as being part of the gig economy. You were self-employed, although the work came through a company; no pension rights, minimum wage conditions, nothing like that. Regarding building my car repair business up, well, I pottered about, there was no pressure, but I wasn't exactly going to be some sort of business tycoon by the end of the year.

Leaving aside the handy side effect of keeping the unemployment figures down a little bit, the Enterprise Allowance scheme was a study into how a dose of hard toryism might transform the fortunes of those members of Joe Public who wanted to sample the delights of entrepreneurship, with its potential to solve all ills.

Imagine your dream is to have a cake shop. To turn your baking skills into a profitable business. You sink all your savings and your mortgaged home into a shop in the middle of town, which luckily has enough footfall to provide at least the minimum amount of cake eaters you need in order to keep going.

The fame of your excellent cakes grows. People come from out of town to sample the delights. You open another shop, you patent your recipes and train underlings in the application of these recipes. An investor from the City of London pops in one day for a slice of your cake. He has more money than he knows what to do with, so he lets you use some of it.

You move to a factory, your recipes become productionised. You advertise your cakes in a clever campaign which makes it seem as if every cake is lovingly baked by a wise little white-haired grandmother using natural ingredients from the guy who runs the windmill just along the babbling small river from the grandmother's tiny thatched cottage. As well as the natural flour, the cakes incorporate jam produced from berries picked from the wild hedges nearby in the rustic landscape, and the jam is prepared with a healthy portion of care and love.

Almost none of your cake buying clientele believe that this is a true reflection of your production methods, but they continue to snap up your offerings. They don't have the time or the inclination to bake for themselves, and you provide their cakes at a competitive price from a supermarket within range of their front door. You also offer a premium range, with a bit of extra sugar and in different boxes, for which the middle classes are prepared to fork out.

During your rise to industrial prominence, several other cake shops in your town started out, but their owners didn't share your perspicacity in obtaining a shop on a suitably busy corner, or your willingness to work sixteen-hour days over a hot oven when you first started. Some of these less savvy and less industrious cake shop owners went to the wall; some of them bimble on at the level of scraping a living, proudly-independent but nearer the breadline than the cakeline; some of them were bought out by yourself after you undercut their prices using the economies of scale that you had so cleverly engineered.

Now that production is almost self-governing, you spend some of your sixteen-hour days scrutinising the accounts to make sure that no resources are being wasted and that nobody is being overpaid for the work that they put in. You also have to spend part of the day looking over the shoulders of middle-management, but this still leaves quite a lot of time to play golf and conduct extra-marital dalliances, should you so wish.

You survey your domain from your mansion, and realise that you sit at the top of a pyramid of cake eaters, so to speak. You own and organise, through your cleverness and willpower, the means to produce the cake.

Below you are your senior management, let's say four of them, looking after accounting, resources, production and distribution. Then we go down the chain, through the foremen, lorry drivers, shop floor factory workers and so on. More people have a role nearer the base of the pyramid of society, because of the simple premise that it is not possible for every member of the population to own a cake making factory.

As you rose, you were too busy to think much about politics, but now you are free to shoot the breeze with your cronies at the golf club, who explain that the elite people at the top of the pyramid of society should always vote for the Conservative Party, commonly known as the tories, for the simple reason that they act to *conserve* the status quo, within which your cake factory is prospering.

This is fine, of course, but what is puzzling is that the people in the cake factory who work for you, who donate their *labour* in return for a wage, don't all vote for the Labour Party, whose purpose is to act in various ways to nag you to give these workers higher wages.

Remember, there are far more people at the base of the pyramid! Not everybody can own the cake factory! So it is lucky that some people at the base of the pyramid of people vote for the Conservative Party who *conserve* your interests. They give you their *labour* but do not vote Labour.

Laughingly, you raise this point with your cronies over a single malt whisky after a round of golf. It's certainly lucky, but shouldn't we be worried that if the people at the labouring level all voted Labour, this could result in disruption, unrest and even potential loss of control of the cake factory? They might press for more money, which you need for your mansion and racehorses.

One of your friends chuckles and explains that yes, life is far easier if the Conservatives *conserve* our interests, but to enable this, some of the votes of the numerous paid *labourers* must, by definition, be captured. There are simply not enough voters occupying the zone of pure and rarefied air which we breathe at the top.

The project of capturing the votes of these labouring people is achieved by making them worry that they could be made worse off if they vote for their own party. They could be collectivised, made to work in party-run communes. What little they have scraped together to have a stake in the world could be taken from them. Foreigners could be let in to take their jobs. Their taxes to government could be increased to fund charity, and even though some of them believe charity is a good thing, the country can't always afford it. Especially if it goes to poor people abroad.

Frowning, you remark that this sounds a little far-fetched, except maybe the tax bit. You say that, in reality, they should be worrying more about the new biscuit-sorting machines you have ordered, which will enable you to introduce some redundancies instead of improving working conditions or distributing more profit within the workforce.

In conclusion, both your crony and yourself agree that the whole thing is quite a mystery, whilst simultaneously giving thanks that nebulous concepts such as personal freedom and the ability to follow and achieve your dreams still somehow weather the onslaught of grim reality, as far as the hapless wage-slave masses are concerned.

And don't forget, adds your friend, the Marxism card. For some reason, they have thought for years that the tory party are the only ones who can save them from this ever-present threat.

'Thank god for Marxism,' you say, after you have finished laughing, before you beckon the bartender and order another whisky.

The Ragged Yellow-Jacketed Philanthropist

My friend Bob is a staunch socialist. He attended Ruskin College, as did John Prescott, the former deputy leader of the Labour Party. Both were helped to do this by a scheme whereby the National Union of Seamen sponsored a promising candidate, who might later rise through the political ranks and be able to help the National Union of Seamen.

Prescott became famous for owning two Jaguars, punching a heckler, and giving rise to speculation about whether, when conducting an extra-marital affair during working hours at the Houses of Parliament, any physical machinations involved in the liaison had taken place upon the burnished antique furniture, thereby constituting a misuse of government property.

Bob only became famous as a charismatic working class hero among the younger, almost exclusively middle class, students on the Sociology and Politics course he later did at the University of Hull. But that's the way the cookie crumbles sometimes.

We catch up roughly every six months, when the whim arises and I can prevail on my wife's kindness to collect me from our rendezvous haunt and drive me back out to leafy suburbia at eleven p.m. I have offered, on occasion, to drive to the usual pub, but Bob's view is that I would therefore remain sober, and a proper meeting of minds cannot take place if one of said minds has not reached at least an approximation of the level of inebriation of the other. Fair one, I suppose.

In the early to mid-nineties, Bob owned a van and a small truck. He was in the haulage business, for which you need vehicles rather than a sociology degree.

At the time, I was using my psychology degree mainly to laze about and daydream, for which you need daydreaming skill. I impinged upon the real world only by welding and generally repairing various old vehicles either for sale or to give their owners another year or two on the road without having to reach into their threadbare pockets too deeply. The money coming in to me would be passed on to the local purveyors of food, beer and petrol. Traders in new clothes, new curtains and new furniture were less prominent, in fact non-existent, in my budgetary plans.

I look back and recall that I was reasonably happy during this era. As long as I could travel about without relying on bus or train, getting out of town on a whim to some place where Denise could sunbathe on a beach, life seemed good. I was a king of the Western World, eating the miles in an old Rover or MG, just enjoying existence.

Karl Marx is said to have looked forward to a day when everyone would have time "to hunt in the morning, fish in the afternoon, raise cattle in the evening, criticize after dinner... without ever becoming hunter, fisherman, herdsman or critic." (Marx, 1846).

That's the same Marx that tends to be held up by the tory press as the brooding, malignant mastermind whose philosophy has led to the creation of societies where individual freedoms have been crushed in a world of grey conformity and thwarted ambitions.

On reading this, I felt that I had always chimed with it, albeit not necessarily the hunting, farming and fishing part. Criticizing, in the pub after dinner, maybe.

What I did do, some years later, was some motor racing, enabled in the first instance by a windfall. But I never wished that I could go motor racing when I couldn't. It never entered my mind that I was missing it in my life.

I was, then, lucky when I couldn't and lucky when I could. Existential philosophy at its best.

Bob's efforts in the transport industry caused some ripples in my peaceful universe of contemplation, in which I enjoyed the Zen of welding rust to thin air with a gas torch, and criticizing after dinner *a la* Marx. Sometimes he would ask me to cover a driving job when he couldn't get away from his routine work. I would return exhausted from Scotland or Devon in the early hours, to plonk myself in front of the downstairs gas fire and doze off, only to be woken up again far too soon by next door's dog.

This was by now Butch, who had replaced their previous 'Hieronymus Bosch vision of Hell painting' dog in the duty of climbing onto the roof of one of the shabby cars in my back garden and barking incessantly to announce the new day. Thanks, Butch, we already knew that the sun was out. Once, I did stir myself and manage to sneak near enough to Butch to drench him with water from a full bucket, but I was a little too weary to fully savour the triumph.

As time went on, Bob became involved in what I termed the parcel wars. Michael Heseltine, the political assassin of Thatcher (good), had been invited back into cabinet by Major, her successor, and tasked with looking into how the Post Office could be decimated, privatised and asset stripped, or some combination of these three options (bad).

Various things were tried, with the side effect of making working conditions at the Post Office so intolerable that the system of deliveries began to degenerate, with workers simply losing the will to care. At the same time, globalisation was a growing phenomenon, and delivery franchise corporations from the US, Australia, Germany, and various international outposts began to wage cut-throat competition for a slice of the UK parcel pie.

Bob was doing a lot of work for a haulage company operated by a chap called Ted, who drove a white Jaguar and was a workaholic. I met him only once or twice and visualise him now as a white-suited thin lipped chain smoker, but I could be way off beam there. I know that when drivers spoke of him, it was always with amazement that he was still at the reins of his empire, sitting in his Portakabin hut pulling the strings of multiple haggard wagon drivers. He's probably still there at the age of 126, allocating jobs to a small remaining zombie-eyed retinue of veteran drivers who would be susceptible to crumbling into dust if they found themselves anywhere further than a few yards away from the UK road network for more than six hours in any one day.

Ted got involved in the parcels delivery mayhem for a while, which meant that Bob's vehicles were roped in to the daily effort. The franchise they were part of was a large organisation called Hellmanns, nothing to do with mayonnaise. After a while Ted took his company out of the franchise, presumably unimpressed with the prospects.

Into the breach stepped another outfit, with whom Bob now threw in his lot. I began to be called upon to fill in, doing odd days of deliveries around York, or north of Scarborough. The latter area was particularly picturesque. Small parcels went to small places on small roads. The days were long but I enjoyed them, as long as they were not too regular. After all, I had, as my regular pastime, project cars to lie underneath with my head in a puddle. One day I delivered a parcel to a guy in a remote workshop who was in the process of restoring a vintage Riley racing car. Magic.

All the small parcels were an obligation, though, for the franchise to cover the geographical area. The actual income came from the consignments which were *collected* from customers during the round. I found this out when I was too late to collect an important pallet at the end of the working day somewhere near Bridlington. Bob and the two guys with whom he was now in partnership were wailing, and there was gnashing of teeth. If only someone had told me about this, I could have sacrificed some drops further north and got back earlier. But nobody thought to do that.

Every day was a crisis. A lot of the delivery stuff consisted of one book in a small parcel. A pile of undelivered ones accumulated at the back of the warehouse.

Bob's partners were younger guys in their thirties, whereas he and I had begun to enter the phase of life known as 'grizzled'. This was ironic, as they were pretty much office based, whilst he and I were galloping about frantically handballing packages from the truck around York city centre. This was an activity which had to be accomplished within the restricted time windows at the beginning and end of each day when vans were allowed within the hallowed historic streets. Don't get me wrong, I don't mind a bit of hallowing, just not as a timed sport.

One day Bob found himself in Grimsby in the firm's small Ford Escort van. This actually had the firm's name and details in neat graphics on the side panels, unusual within their motley fleet. What it didn't have was a properly working starter motor, and Bob had been warned not to turn the vehicle off after it left the operation's headquarters at the start of the working day.

This is why he emerged from a shop having delivered a parcel, to find the van had been stolen by a miscreant. Not to worry, though, because the street was a one-way street, only two lanes wide, one of which was occupied by parked vehicles. And there was a traffic jam in the other lane.

Bob set off on foot towards the van, which he could see a little further along. He planned to remonstrate with the scoundrel in the driving seat. Coming level with the door and looking down, he noticed that insult had been added to injury due to the perpetrator now calmly smoking a cigarette from Bob's packet which he had found in the cabin.

This added considerably to the level of force now applied by Bob, in dragging the vile wretch out of the driver's seat prior to advising said wretch to become scarce.

Just another day at the office, as they say. At least he had regained control of his office.

One didn't set out to come into conflict with all and sundry, but the stress levels did tend to be quite high at times. I had an interesting experience one day when setting off on what should have been an uneventful trip to York. Two pallets had to be dropped off at a local company first. It was no use having them occupying the truck all day, especially as I would never be back by the time the company had shut up shop.

I was in Bob's truck, which coincidentally was another vehicle without a dependable starter motor. The instructions were to park it somewhere with a slope, if necessary, in order to jump start it if you turned it off. This fell down, however, when the handbrake became unreliable, so the technique in somewhere like York would be to deliver to a flat place, but also turn the front wheels against the kerb for a bit of security, whilst leaving it running, delivering quickly, and hoping no miscreants appeared who might like this kind of truck. To be fair, miscreants were probably more partial to Escort-sized types of vehicle, but it remained a worry.

I had consulted Bob for instructions on what to do if I became stranded with the engine off and not on a slope. He showed me where a long stout rope was stowed, under the passenger seat.

'Just find another truck and see if he will give you a tow start.'

OK, so that would be something like, 'Hello, good sir, I see you are from a well-established and less desperate haulier, I wonder if you could find time in your busy schedule to help me. You don't have to mess about looking for a rope, for I have in my possession just such a device.'

In fairness, a reasonable proportion of the population are kind and helpful, and like to help, on a basis of 'there but for the grace of god go I.' I simply don't like having to rely on it. Miserable of me, I know.

What it all boiled down to was time. Repairs weren't impossible, by any means. There was just never any time...

The truck had what is called a 'tilt' body. Fundamentally a flatbed with a framework supporting a roof and canvas or tarpaulin removeable sides. I've always thought the terminology to be rather odd, associating the word with a wobbly pinball table or a gambler in Las Vegas losing the plot and starting to chase their losses in an irrational frenzy, whereupon the word rapidly spreads amongst the professional gambling fraternity, who home in on the hapless innocent like sharks.

'Punter on tilt! Punter on tilt!'

On this particular day, I was to give the term a slightly new variation. The company was some sort of cash and carry warehouse catering to smaller retailers. I pulled in to a massive, almost empty, car park. Most of these places got going at about 8.30. It was about 8.15, but I could see that the main door was open.

I wandered in and found a lad that was approachable.

'Sorry to bother you. Is there any chance of getting a couple of pallets off as soon as you start? I've got to get to York but these need to come off first.'

'Yeah, sure, but I've got to wait until the manager opens the loading bay.'

'OK. Where's the manager?'

'He'll be in that car out there.'

'OK. I'll see if I can have a word.'

By now there was a red Fiesta sitting on its own in the middle of the car park. I walked up to it and peered through the window, where the driver sat impassively.

'Excuse me.' Impassive.

'Excuse me.' Impassive.

'Sorry to bother you. Are you the manager?' Impassive.

'I was wondering if you could help me. I know it's a bit early but...'

I gave up. He exhibited less reaction than a statue in Trafalgar Square shows when a pigeon lands on it.

I drove the truck round to the side of the building where the loading bay was, and passed the time by having a bit of a fume.

If he'd have wound the window down and said, 'Sorry, mate, we don't start till half past,' or, 'Sorry, I can't help you yet because the insurance doesn't cover us 'till working hours start,' I could have accepted it. Fair enough, if a tad frustrating.

The bay eventually opened and the lad got the stacker truck going, then unloaded the pallets from the truck.

'You're OK, you are. Thanks for helping. You're OK, but your boss is a complete tw*t.' It wasn't twit, I can reveal.

'Your boss is a complete tw*t and if I see him on the way out I'll tell him so.'

The lad laughed.

I did see him on the way out and I did tell him so. Memory is hazy now, but I think it involved getting out of the truck and walking back into the building to tell him. This was of course counterproductive to my early arrival in York, but I was on tilt now and the lit fuse could not be stopped. There was a lot of finger jabbing.

'You're an absolute f*ck*ng complete tw*t. Didn't your wife f*ck you lately, is that why you're so far up your f*ck*ng arse?' And words to that effect.

I thought the reference to sexual congress belonged in the realms of pop psychology rather than proven academic research, but that it was nonetheless pithy. My partner Denise was very enamoured of the idea that a sexually satisfied person was a relaxed and well-adjusted person, and it had rubbed off on me. Her conviction was possibly influenced by having had an affair with her therapist in her younger days. Was that unprofessional, or merely cutting to the chase? He was a follower of Wilhelm Reich.

I digress.

When the complaint finally came through a couple of days later, Bob said to them that he was shocked because I was a completely mild-mannered man, and that he couldn't quite believe it. He could, but had conveniently omitted to remember the several occasions where he had seen me throw spanners at the garage wall.

It turned out that the cash and carry place wasn't a very frequent customer and I didn't lose my job that wasn't really a job.

Sometimes I would be prevailed upon to drive the overnight trunk lorry when they couldn't find another free driver with an LGV licence. Bob would be on the phone, the bid going up as I protested.

'I don't really want to do it, Bob.'

'It's worth thirty quid.'

'But I don't really want to go tonight.'

'Forty quid.'

'I've told you before. Can't you get anyone else at all?'

He could be heard in the background talking to his partners.

'Fifty quid.'

'Oh, all right then. At the warehouse at six?'

It wasn't even anything to do with the money. They just sounded so desperate.

A lot of the players in this whirlwind of shuttling parcels had 'hubs' in the English Midlands, from which lorries would ply to the multifarious regional centres of their operations. Ours was near Tamworth, a massive yard of manoeuvring lorries around a huge warehouse shed. Fork lift stacker trucks whizzed around the yard from all directions, threatening life and limb if you were at all unwary walking from the truck to the warehouse to find out where they wanted you to be.

On one or two occasions, there was a run to a lesser hub somewhere in the Stoke-on-Trent area. On the way down, I had to collect a loaded pallet from Mansfield Woodhouse. This was at the premises of some sort of general engineering company who dealt with parcel collection as a sideline to their main business.

Of course, anybody working there had long since gone home for their tea by the time I arrived, and the open, roughly surfaced, bit of waste ground which served as a yard would be in darkness.

I would have to dance around near the building, where somewhere there was a sensor which triggered a bright outside light. Then I would be able to find a key under a brick. This was the ignition key for the stacker vehicle. The stacker vehicle was a very well-worn multi-purpose thing with a sort of bucket at one end which had forks attached as an afterthought. I would open a dangerous alligator-style engine cover and hold it open with one hand whilst spraying Easy Start into the air intake, from a can which had kindly been left near the driving seat.

Then I would go back over to the building to dance and trigger the bright lamp which had just gone out. After this I would go back to the ancient tractor/digger/dumper truck/stacker truck and see if it would start this time. Once it had started I would go to my lorry and move it to throw some illumination from the headlights onto the old lorry parked in the corner near the perimeter fence, from which I would extract the pallet by manoeuvring the fork lift contraption, making allowance for its unusual arc of movement due to its alternative role as a digger.

Next I would load the pallet onto my truck. Then I would dance near the building to trigger the light again, and drive the dumper/stacker back to where I had found it, then shut the back door of the old lorry from which I had extracted the pallet, and finally dance once more at the building for the light to illuminate the brick so that I could return the key to its hiding place.

After all this choreography, I was able to enjoy a leisurely drive to the Stoke-on-Trent area to find the lesser sub-Tamworth hub to pick up my main cargo for the night.

Here, on the first time I did this run, I found the mechanic who worked for Bob's partners. He had brought another truck down to assist with the run, which he had, however, had to abandon on a country road near the hub after getting lost trying to find the hub. Turning round to reverse course, he ended up with the rear wheels in a grassy off-road area where there was no traction.

I had to wait to get loaded anyway, so it was no big hardship to take him to find his truck and attach a rope to it for a rescue. As this was the first time I had done the Stoke run, I had no idea if this was a typical iteration of it.

I sensed that the end of the parcel pandemonium era might be nigh when I turned up at the warehouse one evening to find six men gathered around a loaded pallet which they proceeded to struggle to lift onto the trunk lorry I would be driving.

The fork lift truck had been repossessed.

This followed a period during which men in suits had been engaged to chase all the money owed to the firm, for a commensurate fee. The men in suits company called this 'factoring', but it could probably have been called 'feeding like hyenas over the last throes of a stricken wildebeest on the plains of Africa' if you wanted something more colourful.

It was beyond sad when the days of doing deals to exchange ownership of vehicles over drinks in the pub after a stressful sixteen-hour day drew to a close, but it may possibly have saved Bob's life, I thought. You can't run on adrenaline and Guinness for ever.

The turnover of money was colossal, but turnover isn't necessarily profit, of course.

Was it worth all the effort and anguish?

Bob's view was that he had to try, because this was almost certainly the only chance he would have in his life to become a millionaire. Some people did, no doubt, after the dust had settled on this Wild West period.

Do you see any conflict here between the desire to be prosperous, and a moral outlook as a committed socialist? I don't see any issue with it. The world is as it is, and you operate within it. Being able to earn a living by merely talking and writing about politics and philosophy is, for most, a luxury. Bob ended up with a modest motor cycle repair business. We blinked one day, and fourteen years had gone by.

Coming up towards retirement age, he found himself working part-time for a company which imported those three-wheeler Piaggio things. I can only describe them as a cross between a scooter and a pick-up truck. Think tuk tuk, as they're known in India, and the picture might become clearer.

They're very crude devices, some of them with feeble, low capacity, oily two-stroke engines. But they propel a sizeable part of the third world economy. How they pass an emissions test in the UK I have no idea.

Bob was there because he held an MOT tester's ticket. He'd obtained this from government sponsorship to do a training course after having to fold the motorcycle business. We were by now heavily into the Duncan Smith world of pressure on any dreadful scroungers who dared to enter a state of unemployment, to immediately get on their bikes, if they owned a bike, and pedal into the world of opportunity that was the Cameron/Osborne austerity universe at the end of the tory rainbow. The screws had even been turned up a few notches since Thatcher's day, quite an achievement really. Thus, agreeing to do any training that might improve the scrounger's chances of not scrounging would be a way of taking the pressure off for a while, whatever the training might or might not lead to.

Lots of resources were flung at this, civil servants to organise the claimants, trainers to train the claimants, management consultants and training experts to train the trainers, premises in which to train the trainers who trained the claimants, and so on. All the effort had a blanket title, something like Jobsearch. People, sorry, scroungers, would have to gather together in soulless rooms and learn how to improve their CVs to apply for jobs which might or might not exist. The gathering together in soulless rooms was a subsection of Jobsearch and was called Passport to Employment. Bob made the young civil service woman laugh one day when he called it the Passport to Disappointment.

The job at the Piaggio importing company, although only part-time, saved Bob having to claim the scrounging money and its accompanying surveillance of the scrounger's life.

The owners of the Piaggio importing company ran about in Porsches, but they couldn't find enough money to buy tools for Bob to use. This was OK because he could sometimes scrounge them from the engineering firm in the adjacent works.

Part of Bob's role was to inspect the new Piaggios and get them ready for their roadworthiness test. He would often have to do some of this in the open air, which was fine because he had scrounged a thick yellow hi-vis coat from somewhere on his travels. It no longer gleamed, but was warm.

He was outside because the main workshop was reserved for fitting the all-important coffee-making machines to the Piaggio chassis, after which excited would-be capitalists would pay well north of twenty grand for these devices, so that they could park them in the city centre to sell cups of coffee to yuppies and other capitalists, who could then be seen wandering through town clutching cardboard cups full of coffee, thus demonstrating to all the world that they were very busy and very successful yuppies and capitalists.

Some of these mobile coffee entrepreneurs would look forward to selling coffee at festivals and the like. They might well find that they had to pay for a large truck or trailer to transport their Piaggio to the site, because otherwise it might take several days to get to the site under the Piaggio's own power. It was also quite feasible that if the festival's coffee dispensing zone featured a dip in the terrain, the Piaggio, with its heavy coffee machine on the back and puny single-cylinder engine, might become stranded in the hollow until a powerful tow vehicle turned up.

This was all accepted without qualm, because the tuk tuk three-wheeler was cute. The coffee capitalists could have invested in a vehicle which was able to get to and from Glastonbury in a reasonable time, but it would not have been so cute.

All the while, Bob laboured outdoors in all weathers, solving arcane ignition problems necessitating access to the engine flywheel, coming indoors occasionally to phone the manufacturers in Italy, perhaps warming himself up as a by-product.

Bob is much enamoured of a book from the early twentieth century, *The Ragged Trousered Philanthropists*, (Tressell, 1914) by a man called Noonan, who used the pen-name Tressell. It is a famous socialist tract and none the worse for that, very readable for its day albeit far too long.

It tells the tale of a gang of house decorators who are exploited to the hilt by their employer, laid off when work is scarce, barely able to afford clothes to work in, one financial hiccup away from the dreaded workhouse.

Bob seemed to have become a Ragged Yellow-Jacketed Philanthropist. The philanthropy part of the equation consists of letting your employer have your labour and expertise for the bare minimum they can get away with, in other words taking pity on them and working for a low rate so that they might more easily be able to afford the payments on their Porsches.

Eventually Bob got through to pensionable age, and the part-time wages became a bonus rather than a shield against benefit office harassment. The inevitable day dawned when one request too many for a cheapskate fix to an engineering problem proved the final straw. This time it was at the potential cost of safety on a Chinese-made airstream-style trailer.

'Can't you just weld it?' Bob's employers' talents lay in entrepreneurship and delegation, rather than welding or in fact any form of engineering whatsoever. In fact, Bob spoke very lowly of them in the latter respects, and now felt the moral imperative to withdraw his philanthropy once and for all.

Not to mention rest his weary bones from crawling under tuk tuks in puddles.

The cutting of corners in work featured heavily in both the ragged trousered book and the ragged yellow-jacketed tuk tuk inspector's story. It had the effect of depriving the protagonists of any pride in a job well done, on top of the wage exploitation. Bob was always being asked to find a cheap way of doing things, even if it was a bodge that might well come back to haunt the purchaser of the coffee conveyance further down the line. Or even have to be re-done before the vehicle could be viable, the archetypal false economy.

Bob's years of practical experience, in ships' engine rooms and with motorbikes, cars and vans, counted for nothing in the face of the directors' instinctive mechanical wizardry.

After a few drinks, Bob had shown a keen interest in us collaborating on an original book-length work about *The Ragged Trousered Philanthropists*. Its wisdom should be propagated widely, he thought. When I told my wife, the next morning, about this idea, she suggested that Bob probably wanted me to write the book for him. Despite his university education.

The next time we caught up, after a few pints, Bob admitted that he did indeed want me to write the whole book for him. The statement was refreshingly honest, I thought. What collaboration there would be, would take place in the pub. Then I would remember the enthusiasm later, and convey it to paper form at my leisure.

OK, Bob. In the end I did do that. But it's not book-length, and in fact you've just read it.

Journey to the End of the World

'Would you be capable of springing out of the car and running across to any checkpoints to get our card stamped, if need be?' asked Phil.

I assured him that there would be no springing, no agility, and definitely no running. Knowing my escape plan in kit car racing had been 'I'll get out quicker if I'm on fire', he was happy with this approach, which concluded our strategy meeting.

We were planning for the forthcoming Guild of Motor Endurance event, over four days in the Pyrenees, starting from St Jean de Luz. We had done two of these events before, in 2002 and 2007, so we knew what to expect. They were not competitive events; however, the Guild organised some fairly tricky routes with various checkpoints to find along the way, so neither were they a gentle scenic amble. Spirited motoring of an absorbing intensity, might be the best description.

As well as a robust and reliable sports car, a good degree of teamwork was needed. As the event instructions said, "crew failure is not uncommon." The ultimate target was to finish, solving any vehicle related and/or navigational issues that might crop up along the way.

Our baptism in 2002 involved three days of incessant heavy rain (or snow) within a five-day event from Spa to Florence.

In a Sylva Phoenix without a roof. The assemblage of kit cars, obscure classics, and unique home brewed specials that took part had to be seen to be believed. In more recent times the entry had evolved from kits and low volume sports cars, to a preponderance of mainstream production sports cars.

This time we were to be in the relative luxury of Phil's Caterham 7. He had meticulously assembled this over the previous few years, acquiring a kit which had never been fully built up, and achieving a properly specified 1600 K Series de Dion-axle pukka car. This satisfied a long-time ambition of his; kit cars are all very well, but a 'factory-spec' descendant of the original Lotus 7, designed by Colin Chapman, is undeniably a benchmark, whatever the pros and cons of alternative offerings. Possibly the best-known exemplar of this car is the one driven by Patrick McGoohan which appears in the opening sequence of The Prisoner, a cult TV series of the sixties. I was looking forward to trying it.

Yes, luxury. It even had a 'Half-hood' in Caterham-speak, which is a sort of canopy without a back window. Given that the car had a proper windscreen and hinged side screens, and that you are hopefully moving in a forward direction, it was a pretty effective arrangement.

Phil had spent most of the previous weekend grappling with the installation of a Brantz tripmeter. This device gives a precise readout of distance and time, to aid rally competitors with navigation. On an older car with a rotating cable speedometer operation, a sensor arrangement has to be spliced into the cable, necessitating some careful cutting of the outer sheath. I knew Phil to be a fastidious mechanic, and he had previous successful form installing a Brantz in the Phoenix of 2002 with its similar Ford Type 9 gearbox mechanicals. Nonetheless, this time was more troublesome, the speedo downing tools after a few kilometres on two test runs.

In the end, the third iteration of Brantz-plugging had survived a fairly lengthy test run, before the faffing time expired, and we were committed to hitting the road, with fingers crossed.

Once in the Caterham, it was snug and comfortable. Once in. Never mind. There were only four days of careful body folding to manage, during the event itself.

The Brantz connection lasted a relatively impressive twelve kilometres or so before packing up, never to be heard from again. Of course, the trouble with the fault was that it took out the ordinary speedo reading with it, so even the option of using the standard trip meter and employing maths to convert to tenths of kilometres, whilst being flung around mountain roads, would be denied us.

Our fatalistic mindset and beers on the boat served us well. After a stopover in Santander, I was finally able to try the car as we drove to St Jean. The gearshift I found a bit notchy, and the clutch needed a long push, but it was more a case of acclimatising to it than any inherent fault.

Pre-event scrutineering preceded food and a sensible amount of beer, then at eight a.m. the following day we queued at the hotel gate ready to be waved away at one-minute intervals. The weather was pretty crummy, but Spa-Florence 2002 had inured us to anything it could throw. On that event I had done the morning stint, and Phil the afternoon. So we started the same way, me in the relatively unfamiliar car that wasn't mine, in the drizzle. Lovely. Phil had kindly said, though, that the little '7' was to be regarded as 'our' car for the event, to reflect our team effort. Whether he felt quite the same when I shot out of the first junction just in front of a looming Renault as I finally found the clutch bite, I'm not sure. I did see it coming. Just.

Soon we were on a serpentine B-road with the surface of a draining board, and I'm not talking about the moisture. As the rain worsened, I focused on the twisty road through the forested gloom, via windscreen and side screen alternately.

The rattling misery ceased with a pitstop on a gravelly knoll to have a headscratch. The impossible dream of achieving a mistake free event was already slipping away, with about 3.95 days of the four-day event still to go. Firmly mired now in the alternative reality of Guild-world, we retraced our steps to the junction we had missed.

Of course, had we had a working Brantz, the ambiguous junction could have been pinpointed as occurring at the 8.53 kilometre mark or whatever it was, and we would have known to turn left.

Phil was remarkably sanguine about it all. He was distracting himself from the debacle by exploring the capabilities of an app which he had downloaded onto his phone the evening before. Another Guild member, James, had kindly tipped him off about this app, which mimicked a rally tripmeter using GPS. It was called Tripsmart, or Tripwise or Tripdemon, or something. I can't remember exactly, except that it was about £1.79 from Amazon. Often in this life, you get what you pay for. But what did we have to lose?

Eons later, we reached the lunch rendezvous, after descending from a foggy summit. But the actual lunch stop, in a temporal rather than geographical sense, had long since passed into the mountain mists of history, given that we were scheduled to be there at about 12.30 and it was now something like 2.45.

Hmm. I actually can't tell you what happened to get that far adrift. It's not censored or anything, I simply have no recollection of anything other than driving doggedly along through mist, fog, thick rain, cloud, thicker mist, and more cloud.

We cut our losses with the route book, and navigated the most direct way to the overnight hotel.

Before the treadmill resumed at eight a.m. the following day, further research into the intricacies of the Triplabyrinth app had revealed the technique of swiping the screen, to turn the red bit orange, then tapping the orange box to turn it green, then tapping it to start. Or something. Naturally you were a few hundred yards down the road by the time you had done this, but what the heck. Technology is technology, and we had some.

Phil had further refined it by gaffer-taping his mobile to the dashboard; I just had to remember not to knock the charging lead off from underneath it whilst posting myself into the car. And become accustomed to rebooting it when the screen timed out just as you were approaching an important decision point. Probably. If the distance measurement was accurate.

Road testers in magazines get sniffy about expanses of black plastic in Japanese car cockpits. All I can say is that we were pretty chuffed with the way the black gaffer tape blended in with the finish on the Caterham dashboard, as we lined up for the off, just outside the hotel.

Opening the road book, I realised that there was a roundabout marked after fifteen metres. Decisively, I replaced complacency with panic and suggested we had better turn at it. This had the effect of sending us on a round trip of Luchon after I realised that we should have just gone ahead. The arrow, on the 'tulip diagram' in the road book supplied by the organisers, had been a pretty good clue.

Consequently, this resulted in us approaching the roundabout, which had been just in front of us when we started, about ten minutes behind schedule. This in turn resulted in Phil deciding to press on a bit. This is always interesting, with his experience of serious competitive rallying in his youth coming to the fore. I call it Nuvolari mode, although he stops short of slapping the side of the vehicle to urge it on, as the Italian maestro sometimes did. Obviously it is more relaxing for the co-driver to see both the driver's hands on the wheel, so that's quite good.

At mid-morning, we came to a GOME checkpoint, where the marshals advised us that the Spanish border ahead would be shut due to a protest movement. We were advised to turn round and make our way, via whatever route we could, to the lunch rendezvous, if possible, and on from there... A couple of crews decided to push on ahead, but we joined the great majority in a convoy of ten or eleven cars, retracing our steps down the mountain in glorious sunshine as we looked down from above at the cotton wool cloud mass covering the valley.

Reaching a town, we noticed two cars had stopped, but our faith remained with the convoy, saving us a bit of thought. Until we reached a roundabout a few miles later. Some went ahead. More turned right. Some turned right and stopped. Two did a couple of circuits of the roundabout and then went ahead. The strategy of not thinking had failed us completely.

For a while we travelled in company with another Caterham, a Nissan 370Z and a Lotus. We paused with them at an unmanned fuel station. As the others planned, I wondered if Phil felt like following them.

"Nah. They haven't got a clue have they?"

It was peaceful when they had gone. Out came the maps. Of course, we didn't have a clue either. Finding out where you're going, in life as in Guild, is somewhat easier if you know where you are in the first place.

Phil motored on as I worked out a main road route which skirted Andorra. Eventually we reached a small town called

Ur, after which we were stopped by a crew of gendarmes near the border.

They advised us that the border would be shut until at least five p.m., but that there may be 'small roads' elsewhere. We retraced our steps (no biggie for Guild veterans) through the Babylonian-sounding village, and turned down some narrow lanes behind the main road. After a mile or two of deserted single-track road, we came to a T-junction with a main route. Triumph! We must now be in Spain.

As we progressed, it gradually became apparent that the tiny earlier road was not the only one with a Marie Celeste vibe, for we had not seen a single vehicle going either way. This is what the end of civilization will feel like, when you go for that ride with your very last gallon of petrol. Ur...

An intersection finally appeared, where we came across Nick and Charlie in the Lotus, parked up for a headscratch. At least Guild-world was an improvement on Apocalypse-world. Bravely, the two cars proceeded forwards, until we reached... a border post. Plainly, being already in Spain would cut no mustard...

After spinning round and driving to a completely different border post, we resigned ourselves to the five p.m. close of play, and occupied ourselves chatting to some of the affable Catalan demonstrators.

Eventually we followed the Lotus to the night's rendezvous at Olot, a sizeable town where we only took several wrong turnings before finding the hotel, which was a sumptuous establishment.

The third day started with me doing the first stint until lunch. At one point in the morning we shared a disintegrating concrete mountain road with various cows and goats for a wincing few miles, but otherwise the route north was excellent flowing fun. I began to warm to the sturdy-feeling little 7, which was obviously capable of handling quite a lot more than I was pushing it to.

Finally, we made the day's scheduled lunch stop after two and a half days of trying. I even found time to scoff a sandwich whilst we tidied the cockpit. Luxury!

After I folded myself into the navigator's seat again, a solicitous Peter, the main organiser, leaned over to ask how we were getting on, advising Phil to 'keep taking the tablets.'

'He doesn't need tablets,' I smiled.

Peter glanced at the Tripkenstein app thing taped to the dash, as I waited for its display to realign itself from its tendency to be 90 degrees at odds with the rest of the world. His tolerantly bemused expression spoke volumes.

'It has the virtue,' I explained, 'of being slightly better than nothing.'

The rest of the event was most pleasurable, with me happy to let Phil have the remainder of the driving in the car he had gradually assembled whilst negotiating various house moves and hurdles. It never missed a beat. The standard 1600 K Series engine seems, touch wood, to manage quite reliably in a car as light as the 7. It may only have 115 brake horse power, but do you actually need much more in a road spec 7-esque machine? Not from what I witnessed on the twisty and challenging GOME routes.

Despite, or because of, the intensity of the experience, people would come back for more, time after time, to accept the mental pummelling. Moments like the time we arrived at the auberge in the mountains in glorious sunshine, for the lunch rendezvous on the fourth day, were magic. We only realised as we stopped that it was the same building that had loomed out of the first day's fog, so long, long ago.

You were left with the feeling that you'd passed through some magnificent scenery, without a moment to properly savour it. Yet the concentration required put a completely different complexion on things. Doing one of these events would always burn a wealth of vivid memories into the consciousness. You may not have known exactly where you'd been, other than the name of various countries, but that never seemed to matter.

So, superb event, highly competent car, excellent company.

After I got the Caterham off my hips, we discussed whether we would ever do it again, maybe in something like a Mazda MX5. I was feeling my age.

It turned out to be a hypothetical question. Peter and his team of volunteers had been working hard, organising and reconnoitring these mad expeditions on an ad hoc basis for many years. The time had come to hang up the Brantz, or at least unplug it.

We were able to retire on our laurels. The organisers were very kind in presenting us with a small gift for representing the Spirit of the Event, at the end of proceedings. I think this had to do with Phil's dogged and precise driving on the third and fourth days, the determination to get a good result on these days despite the first day debacle, and overcoming the limitations of the TripwiseTripmeisterWhatsit App. I worked out by the last day that the further we went, the more inaccurate it became, so that a distance of 12 kilometres in the road book, for example, was about 8.7 kilometres on the display when we got there. Useful knowledge for next time. Not.

They may also have had a smidgeon of sympathy for a certain crew member, more often from the navigator's seat, heaving himself upward and backward, inch by inch, towards getting out of the car. And sometimes, with a gasp of exhaustion amid the dramatic tension of a cliffhanging scene in a movie, sinking back down to where he started from, in the tight clutches of the bucket seat. Thence to start the agonising process all over again.

All I can say is, it wasn't an act.

Bibliography

1. Asbrink, E., 2018. *1947: When Now Begins.* London: Scribe.

2. Baden-Powell, R., 1908. *Scouting for Boys.* London: C. Arthur Pearson.

3. Camus, A., 1942. *L'Etranger.* 1st ed. Paris: Gallimard.

4. Dunphy, E., 1991. *A Strange Kind of Glory.* 1st ed. s.l.:Cornerstone.

5. Huff, D., 1954. *How to Lie with Statistics.* New York: Norton.

6. Leary, T., 1970. *The Politics of Ecstasy.* Paperback ed. s.l.:Paladin.

7. Marks, H., 1996. *Mr Nice.* s.l.:Secker & Warburg.

8. Marks, H., 2015. *Mr Smiley my last pill and testament.* s.l.:Pan Macmillan.

9. Marx, K., 1846. *The German Ideology.* s.l.:s.n.

10. Ronson, J., 2011. *The Psychopath Test: A Journey through the Madness Industry.* s.l.:Picador.

11. Room, A., 1995. *Brewer's Dictionary of Phrase and Fable.* 15th ed. London: Cassell.

12. Schindler, C., 2004. *George Best and 21 Others.* 1st ed. s.l.:Headline Book Publishing.

13. Thompson, H. S., 1971. *Fear and Loathing in Las Vegas: A savage Journey to the Heart of the American Dream.* s.l.:Rolling Stone magazine.

14. Tressell, R., 1914. *The Ragged Trousered Philanthropists.* 1st ed. s.l.:Grant Richards.

Music

1. Darkness on the Edge of Town. 1978. Bruce Springsteen. Columbia Records.

2. Love is Like Oxygen. 1978. Sweet. Polydor.

3. Baker Street. 1978. Gerry Rafferty. United Artists.

4. 24 Hours from Tulsa. 1963. Gene Pitney. Written by Burt Bacharach and Hal David. Musicor.

5. Tommy. 1969. The Who. Mostly composed by Pete Townshend. Track Records.

6. Universal Soldier. 1965. Donovan. Written by Buffy Sainte-Marie. Pye.

7. Quadrophenia. 1973. The Who. Composed by Pete Townshend. Track Records.

8. The Great Deception. 1973. Van Morrison. Warner Bros. Records.

9. Forever Changes. 1967. Love. Elektra.

10. Cleaning Windows. 1982. Van Morrison. Mercury.

Filmic

1. Easy Rider. 1969. Directed by Dennis Hopper. Written by Peter Fonda, Dennis Hopper, Terry Southern. Columbia Pictures.

2. Pulp Fiction. 1994. Written and directed by Quentin Tarantino. Miramax Films.

3. Metropolis. 1927. Directed by Fritz Lang. Written by Thea von Harbou and Fritz Lang. Production by UFA. Distributed by Parufamet.

4. Watership Down. 1978. Directed by Martin Rosen. Based on the 1972 novel by Richard Adams. Cinema International Corporation. Nepenthe Films.

5. Camberwick Green. 1966. Created and written by Gordon Murray. BBC1.

6. Trumpton. 1967. Created by Gordon Murray. Written by Alison Prince. BBC1.

7. Cloppa Castle. 1978-1979. Produced by John Read and Mary Turner. String puppet series.

8. Starsky and Hutch. 1975-1979. Action TV series. Columbia Pictures Television.

9. The Blob. 1958. Directed by Irvin Yeaworth. Written by Kay Linaker and Theodore Simonson. Paramount Pictures.

10. Star Trek. Created by Gene Roddenberry. A sci-fi media franchise. Paramount.

11. Supercar. 1961-1962. Thunderbirds. 1965-1966. 'Supermarionation' puppet series. Created by Gerry Anderson and Sylvia Anderson. Various production companies. Shown on Lew Grade's ATV.

12. Wheeler Dealers. Reality TV car restoration series. Attaboy TV (First 12 seasons); Discovery Channel in UK (since season 13); Motor Trend in USA.

13. Mad Max. 1979. Directed by George Miller. Produced by Byron Kennedy. Written by James McCausland. Production by Kennedy Miller Productions. Distributed by Roadshow Film Distributors.

14. The Prisoner. 1967-1968. Created by Patrick McGoohan. Directed by Patrick McGoohan; Pat Jackson; Don Chaffey; David Tomblin. Written by Patrick McGoohan; David Tomblin; Anthony Skene; Terence Feeley; Vincent Tilsley; George Markstein. Production by Everyman Films for ITV. Original network ITV.

About the Author

Dave Roberts grew up mostly in the Midlands and Manchester, where he received a privileged education which he mostly squandered, except for being grateful to be able to write English.

After a year in an office counting bricks and building materials, he rejected quantity surveying as a career and gained a place at Trent Polytechnic art college, from which he was able to drop out of mainstream society with more of a flourish.

He made a living driving various vans, trucks and taxis, finding time to get a degree in psychology and a masters in information technology, before a period scratching around repairing various jalopies in unheated premises convinced him that a future life sitting in heated vehicles teaching people to drive would be a more comfortable environment.

In 2002 he built a sports car from a kit, which he then took motor racing. His experiences in the following years formed the basis of his book *The Blunt End of the Grid*, first published in 2019, and in a second edition in 2023.

He has travelled the world in his quest for gradual enlightenment, getting as far away as Mexico, San Francisco and Hull. He failed to throw a double six to get out of Hull, for many years, but he didn't mind.

Dave now lives an idyllic existence in a leafy suburb in the north of England.

www.ingramcontent.com/pod-product-compliance
Lightning Source LLC
Chambersburg PA
CBHW020135130526
44590CB00039B/181